FROM
CHILDHOOD TO
ADOLESCENCE

ADVANCES IN ADOLESCENT DEVELOPMENT:

AN ANNUAL BOOK SERIES

Series Editors:
Gerald R. Adams, *Utah State University*
Raymond Montemayor, *Ohio State University*
Thomas P. Gullotta, *Child and Family Agency, Connecticut*

Advances in Adolescent Development is an annual book series designed to analyze, integrate, and critique an abundance of new research and literature in the field of adolescent development. Contributors are selected from numerous disciplines based on their creative, analytical, and influential scholarship in order to provide information pertinent to professionals as well as upper-division and graduate students. The Series Editors' goals are to evaluate the current empirical and theoretical knowledge about adolescence, and to encourage the formulation (or expansion) of new directions in research and theory development.

Volumes in This Series

Volume 1: **Biology of Adolescent Behavior and Development**, edited by Gerald R. Adams, Raymond Montemayor, and Thomas P. Gullotta

Volume 2: **From Childhood to Adolescence: A Transitional Period?** edited by Raymond Montemayor, Gerald R. Adams, and Thomas P. Gullotta

Volume 3: **Social Competence in Adolescence**, edited by Thomas P. Gullotta, Raymond Montemayor, and Gerald R. Adams

FROM CHILDHOOD TO ADOLESCENCE

A Transitional Period?

Edited by
RAYMOND MONTEMAYOR
GERALD R. ADAMS
THOMAS P. GULLOTTA

ADVANCES IN ADOLESCENT DEVELOPMENT
An Annual Book Series Volume 2

SAGE PUBLICATIONS
The International Professional Publishers
Newbury Park London New Delhi

For information address:

 SAGE Publications, Inc.
2111 West Hillcrest Drive
Newbury Park, California 91320

SAGE Publications Ltd.
28 Banner Street
London EC1Y 8QE
England

SAGE Publications India Pvt. Ltd.
M-32 Market
Greater Kailash I
New Delhi 110 048 India

Printed in the United States of America

Library of Congress Cataloging-in-Publication Data

Main entry under title:
From childhood to adolescence : a transitional period? / edited by
    Raymond Montemayor, Gerald R. Adams, Thomas P. Gullotta.
        p.   cm. -- (Advances in adolescent development ; v. 2)
    Includes bibliographical references.
    ISBN 0-8039-3725-3. -- ISBN 0-8039-3726-1 (pbk.)
    1. Adolescence.   2. Puberty.   3. Adolescent psychology.
I. Montemayor, Raymond.   II. Adams, Gerald R., 1946- .
II. Gullotta, Thomas, 1948- . IV. Series.
HQ796.F786   1990
305.23'5--dc20   89-28707
                                                            CIP

FIRST PRINTING, 1990

Contents

Preface

Advances in Adolescent Development is a serial publication designed to bring together original summaries of important new developments in research on adolescents. Each chapter is written by experts who have substantially contributed to knowledge in their area or who are especially well qualified to review a topic because of their background or interests. The chapters in each volume are state-of-the-art reviews of advances in adolescent studies. Some authors also present new data from their own research. The theme of each volume is selected by the senior editor of each volume and is based on reading of the latest published empirical work, discussions with the other editors, suggestions from editorial board members, and ideas provided by colleagues. Chapter topics and authors are selected in a similar way. Readers with ideas for future themes should contact any of the editors.

Many people contributed to the completion of this volume. Our editors at Sage have been enormously important in this enterprise. Terry Hendrix helped conceive and give birth to the series and C. Deborah Laughton cheerfully and effectively nurtures it along. Of course we happily express our gratitude to the authors who wrote and revised these chapters.

Acknowledgments

Editing a book like this is a sizable task which was made easier by the help we received from others. We would like to thank the following peer reviewers for their many thoughtful comments on early drafts of chapter manuscripts.

Dale A. Blyth
B. Bradford Brown
Christy M. Buchanan
William M. Bukowski
Cindy Carlson
Steve Carlton-Ford
Lora D. Dorn
Jerome B. Dusek
Robert Enright
S. Shirley Feldman

Richard D. Gordin
William M. Gray
Megan R. Gunnar
Daniel Hart
Scott W. Henggeler
Grayson M. Holmbeck
Judith G. Smetana
Douglas Teti
Patrick Tolan

I want to thank the graduate students in my seminar on adolescence who read and wrote comments on most of the manuscripts. We spent many stimulating Wednesday afternoons together in the Autumn of 1988 discussing and arguing about the transition from childhood to adolescence.

Keith Abrams
Karen Beal
Mary Eberly
Daniel Flannery
M. Elizabeth Fohl
Janice Fulmer
Lisa Green

Dale Grubb
Michele Kent
Christina Nyirati
Barbara Schaffner
Deborah Serling
Marion Whiteford

—Raymond Montemayor
Senior Series Editor

Introduction

The purpose of this book is to examine development between childhood and adolescence. Specifically, authors of this volume examine two questions: first, in what areas are children and adolescents different and in what areas are they similar?; and second, is the onset of early adolescence a transitional period for those characteristics that are different in childhood and adolescence? Adolescence is often portrayed as a period when many new behaviors and abilities emerge. The transition from childhood to adolescence has long been regarded as developmentally unique because during no other period of life except infancy do as many biological changes occur in as short a period of time. Many theorists and clinicians believe that puberty profoundly alters childrens' self-concepts, psychological functioning, and interpersonal relations. These widely accepted ideas have not been thoroughly and critically evaluated, however, and this book is the first comprehensive review of the literature on change and stability between childhood and adolescence. Topics for review were selected to broadly cover normal development. Unfortunately, two chapters on cognitive development, originally scheduled for the volume, are not included because authors had to withdraw from participation. In the 11 content chapters that follow, the issue of change and constancy between childhood and adolescence is examined, and in the final chapter an attempt is made to integrate these reviews and assess the current state of knowledge about this issue.

Before examining developmental change between childhood and adolescence it is necessary to define the boundary between these two periods. At least five criteria have been used to delineate the end of childhood and the beginning of adolescence (Montemayor, 1986). In everyday speech, many people distinguish the two by chronological age, considering childhood to end and adolescence to begin at age 13. Among social scientists the onset of puberty is the most widely used single marker for the beginning of adolescence. In America in the 1980s pubertal changes become noticeable in males and females at about 12.5 and 11.5 years respectively. Recent evidence indicates, however, that hormonal actions and biological change may occur as early as three years before they become manifest in observable physical change. Adolescence also has been defined in terms of the appearance of new cognitive abilities and psychological characteristics,

9

such as formal operational thought, postconventional moral judgment, a differentiated and integrated self-concept, and concern about
one's identity, to name a few of the most frequently discussed characteristics. Legal scholars are also concerned about defining adolescence. Its beginning is defined by age, which is viewed by jurists as a
proxy measure for competence (Zimring, 1982). Although ages vary
from state to state, in most states adolescence begins at 16 years of age
and ends at age 21. The onset of adolescence can be defined by social
experiences and life events, generally considered by members of a
society to signify the end of childhood. For example, finishing elementary school, starting to date, getting a part-time job, and learning to
drive indicate a change of status from childhood to adolescence. All
these criteria have been used by researchers to define this transition,
and each is evident in this volume.

What kind of evidence indicates that: (1) adolescents are different
from children; and (2) the onset of adolescence is a transitional period
between childhood and adolescence? Clearly, the similarity of a characteristic in childhood and adolescence is evidence for continuity
between the two periods, and indicates that the onset of adolescence
is not a transitional period. In contrast to stability, developmental
change is indicated by a difference between children and adolescents.
This difference can be either quantitative or qualitative. One cannot
assume that such a difference first emerges during the transition from
childhood to early adolescence, however, as change may occur during
any period of life or may be gradual and unaffected by the onset of
adolescence. Establishing the onset of adolescence as a transitional
period for a characteristic means demonstrating a relationship between some early adolescent event, either biological, psychological,
or social, and alteration of the characteristic. Another kind of evidence
indicating that adolescence is distinctively different from childhood
is when an underlying process controlling a characteristic or behavior
is different in the two periods. Although the characteristic may or may
not change, if the processes controlling it are different in childhood
and adolescence, then transition has occurred.

It is not a simple task to determine if adolescence is distinctively
different from childhood or if the onset of adolescence is a transitional
period. Various approaches can be used to examine continuity and
discontinuity, to define the onset of adolescence, and to determine and
examine the impact of early adolescent events on psychological and
behavioral development. This diversity reflects the current state of
conceptualization and methodology in research on adolescents.

CHAPTER SUMMARIES

The first three chapters of this volume focus on the impact of puberty and physical change on behavior during childhood and early adolescence. In the first chapter, Montemayor investigates continuity and change in the behavior of nonhuman primates during the transition to adolescence. He examines the physical development and behavior of pre- and postpubescent nonhuman primates living in their natural environments. In particular, he explores the social development and social relations of developing animals with their mothers, adult males, peers, and individuals in other troops. Evidence for a nonhuman primate adolescent period, distinct from juvenilehood and adulthood, emerges from this review, but the existence of this period is clearer for males than females. Puberty and the onset of sexual maturation profoundly alter the behavior and social relations of nonhuman primates. Montemayor concludes this chapter by examining the possible adaptive value to a species of an adolescent period and speculates on why this period might be more characteristic of males than females.

Malina focuses on the timing and tempo of the early adolescent growth spurt and on sexual maturation in humans. In addition, he examines the impact of these maturational advances on male and female physical performance. He also considers biological development from an anthropological perspective and, where available, provides cross-cultural data on physical maturation during adolescence. According to Malina, many gender differences in physical performance first appear during early adolescence. Biological factors emerging during puberty lay the foundation for these differences, but social factors also influence motivation, level of physical activity, and interest in performance, all of which lead to greater improvements in the physical performance of males relative to females.

In the third chapter, Paikoff and Brooks-Gunn examine several process models by which biological change during early adolescence might effect social-emotional development. They explore the relationship between pubertally induced hormonal change and adolescent aggression, sexuality, depression, and moodiness. Both direct and mediated effects on models of the relationship between endocrine change and behavior in early adolescence are examined. Current research suggests that variation in hormonal concentrations during early adolescence contribute to interindividual variation in aggression and sexual behavior, especially in boys, and possibly in depressive affect and mood lability as well. Paikoff and Brooks-Gunn conclude that because of pubescent biological change, adolescence is distinct from childhood, and the onset of early adolescence is a transitional period.

Context refers to the social and physical environment. The need to examine development in context is an important idea present in every chapter in this book, but is the building framework in each of the next four chapters. In chapter four Collins examines development between childhood and adolescence in a family context. Specifically, he reviews research on developmental changes in parent-child interactions, affect, and expectations. He then examines the impact of expectancies on parent and adolescent behavior. In his conclusion, Collins argues that some aspects of parent-child relations are altered when a child goes through puberty, but these alterations are gradual rather than discontinuous. Furthermore, not everything changes and the parent-adolescent relationship is similar in many ways to the earlier parent-child relationship.

In the next chapter Patterson, Bank, and Stoolmiller examine the family as a social context in which children learn to act aggressively. They describe results from their ongoing longitudinal study of the development of aggression in childhood. Aggression is highly stable between childhood and early adolescence and both parent and child contribute to the long-term maintenance of child deviant behavior. Specifically, parenting practices are significant determinants of child antisocial and coercive behavior which, in turn, disrupt future parenting. Patterson and his colleagues examine the impact of multiple child transitions (pubertal maturation, changes in school, residence, and family structure) on parenting practices and adolescent deviant behavior. They show that these transition stressors disrupt social interaction between parent and child and lead to increases in irritable exchanges and child aggressive behavior.

In Chapter 6, Eccles and Midgley examine developmental changes in academic motivation and school achievement. These academic qualities decline between childhood and early adolescence, especially when students make the transition between elementary school and junior high school. Drawing upon "Person-Environment Fit" theory, they propose that one reason for these declines is that a mismatch exists between the developing needs of early adolescents and typical junior high school environments. Eccles and Midgley suggest several factors that are different between elementary school and junior high school, which might lead to differences in academic performance, such as teacher expectancies about student performance, curriculum demands, standards of student evaluations, and school organization and structure.

Huston and Alvarez examine the impact of families, peers, schools, and television on gender-role development in middle childhood and early adolescence. They investigate several hypotheses about adolescent sex-role development, but mainly evaluate the idea of gender intensification (i.e., that gender roles become increasingly differentiated during early adolescence). They conclude that early adolescence is a period of consolidation and intensification of gender-related behaviors and attitudes. According to Huston and Alvarez, peers and television become increasingly important socializing influences during early adolescence. Young adolescents are intolerant of deviations from traditional sex-role norms, especially in regard to dating where a high value is placed on conformity to cultural ideals of masculinity and femininity. They also suggest that increases in cognitive abilities make adolescents more sensitive to the subtle gender stereotypes that predominate on television programs and commercials.

The authors of Chapters 8 through 11 examine social cognitive development, especially changes in thinking about oneself, motives for helping, and friends. Lapsley uses cognitive-developmental theory as a framework for examining adolescent egocentrism, skeptical doubt, interpersonal understanding, and moral judgment. Lapsley contends that while there are alterations in social cognition between childhood and adolescence, the onset of early adolescence is not a transitional period. Instead, the evidence indicates that social cognition is continually changing, and that most changes are gradual rather than sudden.

In Chapter 9, Harter examines self-concept development and describes several differences between children and adolescents in the content of self-descriptions. The most well-documented shift in development between childhood and adolescence is from self descriptions that primarily focus on external characteristics and behavior to descriptions that emphasize the psychological interior—emotions, beliefs, and motives. She also reports data from her own work that reveal developmental increases in self-concept inconsistencies. Concern about inconsistency peaks in middle adolescence. Harter links these age differences in self-descriptions to developmental change in underlying cognitive abilities. According to Harter, changes in self-conceptions represent qualitative alterations in how children and adolescents conceive of themselves, which reflect underlying discontinuous cognitive development. Harter believes that besides cognitive change, other biological, psychological, and social alterations occur during the onset of early adolescence that make adolescence largely discontinuous with childhood.

In the next chapter, Eisenberg examines developmental change in prosocial behavior and reasoning. In the behavior area, she summarizes research on age changes in helping, donating and sharing, and comforting. Most of the chapter is a review of the literature on the development of moral attributions and prosocial reasoning. Specifically, she discusses changes in the inferences children and adolescents draw about the causes of their own and others' prosocial actions. Eisenberg concludes that while the frequency of most prosocial behaviors does not change between childhood and adolescence, thinking about prosocial behavior undergoes a qualitative shift. For example, adolescents are not any more helpful than younger children, but their motives for helping are more other-oriented, while children are more focused on themselves. Eisenberg ties the development of moral thought to underlying cognitive development. Virtually no research has been done investigating aspects of the onset of adolescence on moral thought or behavior.

In Chapter 11, Berndt and Perry review current knowledge about friendships in childhood and early adolescence. The chapter focuses on conceptions about friendships, but several aspects of friendship behavior are also discussed. They examine developmental differences in attitude and value similarity between friends, the impact of friends on the individual's behavior, and the relationship between friendship choice and peer status. Both developmental discontinuity and continuity is present in the literature on friendship. Current research suggests that, in contrast to children, adolescents value intimacy, place more emphasis on loyalty, and are more cooperative with their friends. Many aspects of friendship are also continuous, however, such as the importance of frequent interaction, mutual liking, and giving assistance. Little research exists on the impact of specific early adolescent events on the transition of friendships.

In the final chapter, Montemayor and Flannery use the empirical evidence presented in this volume to draw general conclusions about differences between children and adolescents, the degree to which developmental change is gradual or discontinuous, and whether the onset of early adolescence is a transitional period. They also discuss several issues that emerge from the reviews in this volume, such as the difficulty of defining the transition from childhood to adolescence, the need to examine the process of change, and the importance of examining development in context.

REFERENCES

Montemayor, R. (1986). Boys as fathers: Coping with the dilemmas of adolescence. In A. B. Elster & M. E. Lamb (Eds.), *Adolescent fatherhood* (pp. 1-14). Hillsdale, NJ: Lawrence Erlbaum.

Zimring. F. E. (1982). *The changing legal world of adolescence.* New York: The Free Press.

PART I

PHYSICAL MATURATION AND GROWTH

1. Continuity and Change in the Behavior of Nonhuman Primates During the Transition to Adolescence

Raymond Montemayor
Ohio State University

In this chapter, two issues about adolescence are examined: (1) Does an adolescent period of life exist between childhood and adulthood among nonhuman primates? (2) What changes and what remains the same during the transformation to adolescence? The focus is on the physical development and behavior of pre- and postpubescent non-human primates living in their natural environments. Specifically, the author examines the social relations of developing animals with their mothers, peers, others in their troop, and individuals in other troops.

The value of investigating adolescence in species other than our own has been demonstrated in several recent examinations of the behavior of pubescent nonhuman primates (Altmann, 1986; Coe, Kayashi & Levine, 1988; Lancaster, 1986; MacDonald, 1987; Savin-Williams & Weisfeld 1989; Steinberg, 1989; Weisfeld & Berger, 1983). In these reviews the adaptive value of various adolescent behaviors are identified, along with environmental pressures that might account for the diversity of these behaviors. By examining the period of adolescence in nonhuman primates, one gains an understanding of its evolutionary significance and, consequently, approaches the study of human adolescence with a deepened appreciation of its importance for human growth and development.

In this chapter continuity and change between childhood and adolescence among nonhuman primates is examined in order to identify characteristics of this transition typical of most primate species. There is not one primate pattern; behavior varies with such environmental factors as ecological niche, population composition and density, and recent group experiences and history, as well as with taxonomic position (Dolhinow, 1972). Thus, in the following review of primates ranging from lemur to chimpanzee, the search is not so much for one definitive pattern as for common themes from which variations are derived.

THE PERIOD OF ADOLESCENCE

The first task in examining primate adolescence is to define its onset, duration, and termination. The juvenile period of life among nonhuman primates, corresponding to childhood in humans, ends with the onset of puberty (Pereira & Altmann, 1985). The start of adulthood among nonhuman primates is more difficult to define than the end of childhood because adulthood is not only the end of physical growth and development but also includes behavioral and social components, as it does in humans. What does it mean to be a primate adult? The clearest answer to this question is that adults reproduce: males impregnate and females become pregnant. Most primatologists, therefore, consider a primate to be an adult when she becomes pregnant or when he has sexual access on a regular basis to cycling females. A secondary criterion of adulthood in males is entry into the troop dominance hierarchy, which determines sexual access to adult females.

Some primatologists have found it useful to subdivide the period of life between juvenilehood and adulthood into two stages: *adolescence*, from puberty until the onset of reproductive capability, and *subadulthood*, between the onset of reproductive capacity and the attainment of adulthood, that is, the beginning of regular reproductive activity and the completion of physical growth. There are two reasons for this distinction. First, as one moves up the primate phylogenetic scale—from prosimians to New World monkeys to Old World monkeys to apes to humans—a period of life between a juvenile and adult stage, yet distinct from them both, becomes more evident. This period first emerges as an adolescent stage among lower-order primates such as New World monkeys. Among lower-order primates, sexual maturity equals adulthood and a stage of subadulthood does not exist. It is only among the higher primates, apes and humans, that one finds a true subadult stage. A second reason for distinguishing between adolescence and subadulthood is that subadulthood is more characteristic of males than females, as will become evident in what follows.

CHANGES IN PHYSICAL CHARACTERISTICS

Several changes in observable physical characteristics occur at puberty. A pubescent growth spurt takes place for most primates

(Baldwin, 1969; DuMond, 1968), starting earlier but ending sooner for females than for males (Chandler, 1975; Glick, 1980). In most primate species males add muscle and develop a more angular and muscular body in comparison to females, resulting in a clear sexual dimorphism (Gingerich, 1972; Schaller, 1963). Dramatic changes in body hair composition and coloration are also common after puberty (Kummer, 1968; MacKinnon, 1979). For example, the black hair of prepubescent gorillas turns silver after puberty (Schaller, 1963). Among female primates, changes in sexual swellings and the beginning of menstruation occur during puberty. For example, juvenile chimpanzees exhibit a sexual preswelling-swelling cycle that, during puberty, becomes regular, reaches the adult cycle, and culminates in menstruation (Tutin & McGinnis, 1981).

For most primate species, considerable regularity exists in the sequence of pubescent events, which is different for males and females. Among primate males, including humans, pubertal development starts with an increase in the size of the testes and penis, and the growth of body hair or changes in hair color or texture. Then comes increases in growth, height, and finally, the onset of reproductive capability (Tanner, 1978). In female primates physical changes are first observed in the enlargement of nipples, followed by estrus and accelerated growth (Tanner, 1978). Consistent primate sex differences in the rate of physical development have also been observed. Generally, females reach physical and sexual maturity at an earlier age than do males.

CHANGES IN MOTHER-OFFSPRING RELATIONS

During the early months of life, primate infants spend most of their time in close proximity to their mothers (McGinnis & McGinnis, 1978). With time, this attachment bond gradually weakens and the infant is weaned from its mother. Weaning does not complete the separation process but, rather, initiates it. Juveniles remain highly dependent on their mothers and spend more time with them than with any other individual.

It is not until puberty that another major step toward separation occurs. Offspring begin spending more time with unrelated peers and adults than with their mothers as they start to assume their adult roles in their troop. For example, a juvenile bonnet macaque will doze next to its mother and be groomed by her, although more and more time is spent with same-age playmates (Simonds, 1965). Studies by Nishida (1979) and Pusey (1978a) show that between birth and four years of age infant chimpanzees are 100% dependent on their mothers, a figure that decreases to 85% for juveniles, 50% for adolescents, and 20% for subadults.

Attraction to others appears to be a stronger force for leaving the mother-offspring orbit than a maternal push toward separation. Peers exert a strong pull on both sexes, while postpubescent females are also attracted to adult males. Most postpubescent primates associate more with same-age peers than with their mothers. Mother-offspring aggression and conflict decrease as offspring, especially sons, grow older and stronger (Bernstein & Ehardt, 1986). Aggression between mothers and offspring of all ages is infrequent and consists of pushing or nipping rather than severe attacks (Dixson, 1983).

The timing and patterning of mother-offspring separation differ for males and females. For example, among chimpanzees, as in most other primates, males leave their mothers and travel without them earlier than do females. Attraction to peers is probably the main reason males separate (Goodall, 1986; Hayaki, 1988; Pusey, 1978a). After puberty a female gradually establishes social relationships with adults in the troop, especially males, and interactions with her mother decline in frequency (Sugiyama, 1981). In particular, interactions with her mother drop sharply when a daughter starts her first full estrous cycle. Attraction to adult males may be the primary factor in causing her to leave (Goodall, 1986; Nishida, 1979).

After puberty, relations between mothers and their subadult and adult offspring are different from those between unrelated individuals (Koford, 1965; Kurland, 1977; Rosenblum, 1971; Simonds, 1965). For example, prepubescent chimpanzee males frequently copulate with their mothers (Goodall, 1968; Pusey, 1978b). After puberty, however, copulation is not observed even though sons are with their mothers during estrus. Furthermore, even after subadult males establish dominance over all other adult females, they continue to defer to their mothers and allow them to eat first (Goodall, 1968). Also, many subadult Old World monkeys groom their mothers more than they groom other adult females (Struhsaker & Leland, 1979).

Bonds between mothers and their female offspring are stronger and longer lasting than mother-son bonds in most primate species. Adult females maintain a loose association with their mothers, often until the birth of their own offspring, and sometimes after that (Klopfer &

Boskoff, 1979; Tattersall, 1982). Among Japanese macaques, this sex difference appears to be a function of the mother and the offspring: Both mothers and daughters seek and maintain physical contact with each other, whereas neither mothers nor sons initiate contact with each other. Although postpubescent daughters continue to associate with their mothers they are not on an equal footing with them, and subadult and adult females remain subordinate to their mothers (Kurland, 1977).

There are many reasons mothers maintain a longer relationship with their daughters than with their sons. First, mothers may have a like-sex preference based upon physical and behavioral similarities. Second, the mother-son relationship is more aversive for mothers than the mother-daughter relationship. Males are more aggressive than are females, which could lead to more mother-son fights, shortening their relationships. Lastly, the longer mother-daughter relationship may result from the fact that young females show more fear of strangers and therefore remain attached longer, while males are less fearful and detach sooner (Fedigan, 1982).

Another advantage of a continuing mother-daughter association is that it allows the daughter to practice handling infants. "Aunting" behavior, first identified by Rowell, Hinde, and Spencer-Booth (1964), includes affectionate, maternal, protective, and playful behavior toward an infant by a female who is not its mother. For most primate species, including squirrel monkeys (Baldwin, 1969; DuMond, 1968), baboons (Kawai, 1979; Ransom & Rowell, 1972), chimpanzees (Goodall, 1968), and gorillas (Fossey, 1979) the individual other than the mother most likely to carry, groom, and fondle an infant is a late juvenile or adolescent female sibling. Although subadult and adult males have been observed engaging in aunting-like behavior, frequently this behavior is actually a male protecting an infant from attack or using an infant to defend himself against a threat (DuMond, 1968; Fedigan, 1982).

Aunting may be an important preparatory experience for mothering among adolescent females. This "learning to mother" theory is the most widely accepted explanation of aunting (Hrdy, 1976) and has some experimental evidence to support it. In one study of captive marmosets, it was found that females removed from their natal family before they had a chance to help care for younger siblings almost always neglected and often killed their own infants (Epple & Katz, 1983).

CHANGES IN SEXUAL BEHAVIOR

Primate sexual behavior does not suddenly appear after puberty; most of the basic mechanics of copulatory behavior are present in infancy. Puberty does, however, affect the frequency and form of copulation. After puberty some new sexual behaviors appear and some prepubescent behaviors are altered. In addition, important changes occur in male-female interactions preceding and following copulation. Mature sexual behavior is not reached until early adulthood.

Prepubescent primate males are capable of erection, mounting, insertion and thrusting. Erections and occasional masturbation have been observed among infant males in most species (Albrecht & Dunnett, 1971; Neville, 1972; Trollope & Blurton-Jones, 1975). Opportunistic mounting of adult females by prepubescent males occurs, although adult males attempt to prevent it and chase off young males they observe copulating (Hasegawa & Hiraiwa-Hasegawa, 1983). Therefore, mounting by prepubescent males usually takes place secretively, during play, or when adult males are preoccupied (Hayaki, 1985).

Many changes occur in the copulatory behavior of males after puberty. The most important new component of postpubescent sexuality is ejaculation. The capacity to inseminate a female is a critical qualitative difference between pre- and postpubescent males, but its appearance does not signal an end to sexual development. For example, mounting after puberty becomes more patterned and coordinated. Prepubescent chimpanzees mount and thrust, but their pattern is different from the copulation pattern and position of subadult and adult males, which includes an inverted quadruped stance, thrusting with the entire body (Goodall, 1968).

Several factors may account for the rapid learning of copulatory behavior after puberty. Some aspects of copulation may be learned through imitation. Immature primates often observe adults mating (Harcourt, Stewart, & Fossey, 1981), so the opportunity for direct observation of adult copulatory behavior is frequent. Prepubescent practice mounting may be another preparatory experience, but it does not appear necessary for normal sexual development. A study of captive macaques revealed that males with limited access to females before puberty were almost as quick to reach an adultlike sexual behavioral form as those with many juvenile mounting and thrusting practices (Michael & Wilson, 1973). These findings suggest that some components of copulatory behavior may be biologically "wired into" the organism.

During adulthood the copulatory pattern of males and females becomes more clearly tied to specific partners and certain situations (Mitani, 1985). Although pubescent and adult male macaques are equally likely to mount females in the swollen stage of the estrous cycle, older males are apt to mate with older females, who are the most "attractive" and able to bear young (Loy, 1971; Simonds, 1965). In addition, timing of mounting changes after puberty. Prepubescent male baboons seldom mount during the swollen phase of the female cycle, when fertilization is most likely. Pubescent males sometimes mount swollen females, while adult males mount almost entirely during the swollen phase (Cheney, 1978). Furthermore, adult females in estrus present rarely to juveniles, sometime to pubescent males, and usually to adult males.

Prepubescent female sexual behavior is rare. In most primate species sexual behaviors such as presenting and embracing are rarely seen before first estrus (Hanby, 1976; Harcourt, Stewart, & Fossey, 1981; Kummer, 1968; Trollope & Blurton-Jones, 1975). When mounting does occur it is likely to be by other prepubescent males (Lindburg, 1971), accompanied by shrieking and wrestling from the unwilling female (Baldwin, 1969). Adult females often tolerate the sexual behavior of juveniles but only present to adult males (Albrecht & Dunnett, 1971).

Although pubescent females copulate with adult males, they show little interest in subadult males. After puberty the choice of a sexual partner remains very much a female prerogative. Despite all this sexual activity pubescent females rarely become pregnant, and it appears that they go through an "adolescent sterility period" (Galdikas, 1981).

Postpubescent females are generally sexually responsive and interested in sex. Galdikas (1981) observed that on a number of occasions subadult female orangutans initiated contact with adult males by approaching and indicating sexual interest. Moreover, subadult females generally responded favorably to attempts by males to initiate copulation. Galdikas also reported that males initiated sexual activity with adult females, but copulations with subadult females invariably followed female proceptive behavior.

In general, there is a stronger relationship between the occurrence of puberty and adult sexual behavior in female nonhuman primates than in males. After the onset of regular menstrual cycles, females will receive mounts by males, present to males, and use sexually related vocalizations and gestures (Hanby, 1976). After puberty the full female copulatory repertoire appears.

CHANGES IN AGGRESSION AND DOMINANCE

For males of most primate species, a dramatic increase in the frequency and intensity of shoves, slaps, hits, and bites occurs after puberty. Adolescent males are often involved in intense antagonistic episodes with adult males both as the initiator and recipient of aggression. The underlying cause of this violence appears to be the initiation of the adolescent male into a troop's male dominance hierarchy, as well as competition among males for sexual access to females. In general adolescent males are subordinate to adult males but dominant over younger males and all females. Female aggressiveness is low and largely unaffected by puberty.

Adolescent males start out very low in the male dominance hierarchy (Budnitz & Dainis, 1975). For this reason, adolescent males rarely challenge adult males directly, especially high-status dominant ones. When attacks do occur they tend to be hit-and-run and harassment. For example, adolescent male patas monkeys sometimes taunt and harass adult males during copulations (Loy & Loy, 1977) and feeding (Zucker & Kaplan, 1981). Such behavior indicates a growing boldness coupled with caution.

Adolescent males are more frequently the recipient of aggression than the aggressor (Richard & Heimbuch, 1975). Adult male squirrel monkey generally pay little attention to juvenile males until they reach adolescence, at which time the number of interactions, primarily antagonistic, increase dramatically. In dominance interactions with adult males, adolescents do not fare well; they often suffer major scars, torn ears, and missing fingers (Baldwin, 1968).

By early subadulthood, a male primate begins to prevail in dominance interactions, first defeating adult females and low-status males. When he establishes a semipermanent position, he is treated like an adult. Rank does not equal breeding power, but it does establish access to females, leadership position, travel arrangements, and feeding arrangements (Johnson, 1987). In chimpanzees, males enter into dominance interactions on a consistent and sustained level in late subadulthood (Goodall, 1968). They first threaten low-ranking chimpanzees, signifying that the subadult apprenticeship is over, as is maternal protection and adult male tolerance of insubordination.

The initiation of adolescent males into male dominance hierarchies may not be the only reason for the increase in aggressive encounters with adult males. Another factor that may be important is pubescent hormonal changes. The observed increase in aggressive interactions among adolescent males correlates with increased output of androgens by the enlarging testes (Dixson, 1980). The adolescent's newly emerging sexuality is also an important cause of increased aggression. Among Old World monkeys and chimpanzees, the more sexually advanced an adolescent male is, the more apt he is to receive adult male aggression, especially during the breeding season (Albrecht & Dunnett, 1971). The clarity of a troop's dominance hierarchy may also affect the level of male-male aggression. In langur troops with one clear dominant male, social relations between adults and adolescents are relaxed. When there is no dominant leader, relations are often tense and aggressive (Boggess, 1982).

Pubescent female primates are rarely involved in aggressive interactions, both because they flee from potentially aggressive encounters and because they exist outside male dominance hierarchies. This is similar to their juvenile and adult patterns. For example, pubescent female chimpanzees rarely engage in dominance interactions, despite the fact that they are in a precarious position in the group: likely to be threatened by adult males and females and by juvenile and adolescent males (Goodall, 1968).

MALE PERIPHERALIZATION AND GROUP LEAVING

Spatial positioning in a troop, where an individual spends most of his or her time, especially during travel, is not random but a function of age, sex, and social status. The center of most primate troops is occupied by mothers and their prepubescent offspring. About the time of puberty, many male primates move out of the center away from their mothers and form all-male groups that occupy the periphery of the troop. When male gelada baboons reach puberty, they often leave their troops for several days and travel alone, after which they enter into all-male groups composed of adolescents and subadults (Kawai, 1979). These groups are found on the periphery of the larger herd, and a strained relationship exists between the individuals in them and the herd leaders. Members of the all-male groups constantly fight with the leaders in an effort to take over their dominant positions. Relations among all-male groups are primarily agonistic. Friendly interactions between members of different groups are rare.

The peripheralization of adolescent males and the formation of all-male groups is, in many cases, a step toward the emigration of males out of their natal troop and into another troop. Emigration is widespread throughout the primate order and has been reported for lemurs (Jones, 1983), tamarins (Epple & Katz, 1983), orangutans (Galdikas, 1981), gorillas (Fossey, 1982; Harcourt, Stewart, & Fossey, 1976), and chimpanzees (Kano, 1982; Nishida, 1979; Sugiyama, 1981).

Usually adolescent males leave their group, although female transfer has been observed in a few species such as red colobus monkeys (Starin, 1981), baboons (Dunbar & Dunbar, 1975; Kummer, 1968), and chimpanzees (Pusey, 1978b). In addition to this sex difference in frequency of emigration, males and females who leave their natal group do so in different ways. Male red colobus monkeys, for example, generally are forced to emigrate by adult males and may not be allowed entry into a new troop, while females transfer voluntarily and are welcomed into their new group (Starin, 1981).

Males who occupy peripheral positions remain at some distance from the center of their troops, occasionally spending long periods out of sight without interacting with troop members. During such independent forays, subadult males occasionally come into contact with other troops. Such behavior, with a marked increase in frequency, heralds the beginning of the transfer process. It appears, then, that the peripheral and independent behavior of subadult males is symptomatic of social pressures within the group and is instrumental in providing the social contact with other troops necessary for the eventual transfer to a new troop.

Several factors influence group transfer. Social forces exist that push males out. When subadult males reach sexual maturity, they receive hostile repercussions for sexual or competitive acts by adult males, who eventually drive them away (Koyama, 1967). Adolescent male langurs are often evicted from their natal troops, usually by their fathers but sometimes by other adult males. They then join with other males in nomadic all-male bands (Hrdy, 1977). In addition, internal, pubertally induced biological alterations may also be implicated in troop leaving. Hormonal changes during puberty may result in increases in restless behavior, which results in males leaving their natal troops in order to explore the larger physical and social environment

(Hausfater, 1972). These two forces are not mutually exclusive. Wanderlust may have a genetic biological basis. Prepubertal males may wander, but such behavior is more likely to occur during adolescence than at any other time in development because of the added social pressure of antagonism from adult males. Peripheralization, solitarization, and relocation may have a biological substrate, activated by external, social provocation.

A third possibility is that the pubescent male is drawn out of his troop by attractive aspects of other troops. Perhaps unfamiliar females are more attractive than familiar ones. Other rewards associated with non-ñatal troops also might exert a strong pull on pubescent males. For example, the destination of the emigrating animal seems to be influenced by the presence of relatives who have themselves previously emigrated. A case of nepotism was reported by Meikle and Vessey (1981) who observed that subadult male rhesus monkeys were most likely to transfer into groups with older brothers. Once in the new group, brothers often approached each other, formed coalitions during agonistic encounters, and avoided disrupting each other's sexual interactions. Thus, recognition of brothers and the possibility of living with them may be a strong enough attraction to pull subadult males away from their parents and into another troop.

Leaving one's natal troop has several important advantages for male subadults. They escape some adult male aggression and perhaps serious injury or death. The wanderlust drive is satisfied, frustration is eased, and sexual drives are more apt to be fulfilled through the acquisition of sexual partners. Also, subadult males form all-male bachelor groups, establishing a bond among themselves that may last when they rejoin their troop at a later age. This male bonding benefits the group by having males "committed" to other group members, thus ensuring a cohesive social group.

CHANGES IN PLAY AND PEER SOCIAL RELATIONS

Pre- and postpubescent peer relations are different, at least for males. Adolescent males often move to the periphery of their troop, frequently drop out of normal interactions, sit and sleep alone, and sulk. What changes occur in female social relations are not as dramatic.

One important change in peer relations during adolescence involves play. Males move from a late juvenile noncontact, chasing type of play to an adolescent rough and aggressive play. Play becomes almost indistinguishable from dominance fighting. During subadulthood the level of play decreases until it reaches a low adult level. For example, play among macaque males decreases between adolescence and adulthood. An increasing amount of the remaining play is rough and tumble, often forcing younger playmates to flee in pain and fear. Play between juveniles primarily involves chasing, while male adolescents, like male adults, are more apt to wrestle (Simonds, 1965).

The amount of time spent in play declines sharply after puberty for male and females. In one study of chimpanzees, juveniles were seen playing in 70 out of every 100 observational periods, but by adolescence this number had dropped to 30 for females and 15 for males, which was similar to the adult male average of 5 per 100 observation periods. The quality of play also changed during adolescence, and play became increasingly boisterous, usually ending in fighting and screaming (Goodall, 1968; Pusey, 1978b).

While males become more playfully aggressive and active during adolescence, female aggressive play remains low (Meaney, Stewart, & Beatty, 1985). Baldwin and Baldwin (1977) believe that these differences are attributable in part to hormonal differences between the sexes: higher levels of testosterone in males produce more assertiveness and activity. And too, males are larger and stronger, especially during pubescence, which is conducive to exploring and playing. Females are more apt to withdraw from aversive interactions, protecting their genetic potential. In addition, females quit rough-and-tumble play at an earlier age than do males perhaps because they reach social-sexual maturity earlier. Besides, females have to contend with male aggression.

Baldwin and Baldwin (1977) have examined why both the quality and quantity of play is altered during pubescence. The physical changes of puberty produce an increase in activity and agility as well as the obvious increases in size and physical strength. Previously harmless play now has the potential for becoming destructive and painful. Short, playful bites may become sharp nips as jaws strengthen and canines erupt. Other factors also may contribute to the decline of play during subadulthood: Being more familiar with the social environment, sensory stimulation during play is less rewarding, and individuals can benefit more by conserving energies for other activities, such as feeding, sex, and caring for their young (Baldwin & Baldwin, 1977). In addition, the loss of interest in play may be the result of a general increase in solitary activities characteristic of this age period in most primates.

Other forms of peer interaction also change during adolescence. Grooming, an important part of juvenile and adult interaction, is infrequent among male adolescents. When they are involved in grooming, males are more likely to be the groomer than the groomee (Ellefson, 1974; Goodall, 1968). Adolescent females are as apt to be the recipient as the giver of grooming behavior (Jay 1965). Goodall believes that grooming is the first step in courtship or a means by which to assuage tense and arousal-producing social situations, hence the higher rate of male adolescent grooming behavior. Adolescent males also engage in more self-grooming than individuals of other ages. During the subadult years males develop a more adult-like grooming pattern, focusing upon adult females for long periods of time.

For many males, adolescence is a time of social isolation: "He is, in many respects, an extremely marginal participant in group life" (Jay, 1965, p. 231). Total social interactions fall, and adolescents become social strangers in a familiar land. For example, pubescent male hamadryas baboons become more inhibited than they were only a few years before, and they play less and sit alone more. A subadult male is at his life's peak of sitting alone; only 18% of his resting minutes are involved in social interactions. In adulthood, 43% of his resting time will be spent in social interactions, primarily with adult females in estrus (Kummer, 1968). With the onset of puberty, a langur male, only one year earlier a playful and curious juvenile, becomes a sulky and rather noninteractive adolescent (Bernstein, 1968; Sugiyama, 1981). Relative to his former level of group participation, the pubertal male drops out. He rarely grooms or is groomed and spends most of his time on the periphery of the group, only approaching adults when they are resting (Jay, 1965).

When not alone, adolescent males are most likely to associate with other adolescent males. These all-male groups may enhance male bonding and increase individual and troop survival. Erwin, Maple, and Welles (1975) found that some social attachments that develop between male rhesus monkey peers during adolescence are persistent and can be seen even in adulthood. For example, when an adult was paired with another adult who had been a companion during adolescence, aggression was lower than when two unfamiliar adults were paired together. But this strong male bonding present during the juvenile and adolescent periods gives way to heterosexual involvement by late adolescence (Kummer, 1968).

BECOMING A PRIMATE ADULT

Puberty is a critical period in the lives of nonhuman primates. Pre-
and postpubescent nonhuman primates are not only biologically
different from each other but, at least for males, also behave in
significantly different ways. Some juvenile behaviors disappear after
puberty, while others appear for the first time. More commonly,
juveniles express a form of many postpubescent adolescent behaviors
that are transformed during puberty. In this section the author attempts to integrate into a few general themes the many behavioral
changes already described.

Two themes run through the descriptions of nonhuman primate
growth and development between childhood and adolescence. First,
during puberty the mother-child relationship is transformed: Mothers
and offspring spend less time together, offspring are less attached to
and dependent upon their mothers, and maternal care-giving declines. After puberty, mothers and their offspring continue to support
and comfort each other, but less intensely. A second theme is the
gradual integration of the postpubescent animal into its society. This
integration is different for males and females. Becoming an adult male
often means leaving one's troop, aggressively establishing a place in
a new troop's dominance hierarchy, and gaining sexual access to adult
females. For females, adulthood means pregnancy and motherhood.

Mother-offspring separation and the attainment of adult status in
nonhuman primates does not suddenly occur after puberty. The
transition is gradual, although not uniform across the life span. It
begins with weaning, but is not completed until after puberty. The
developmental road to adulthood is quite different for males and
females, however, and it is impossible to describe a single developmental path.

The social development of most primate males falls into four periods, each characterized by a different social orientation. First, an
infant male is entirely dependent upon his mother for survival, and
his orientation completely centers on her. This close bond is ruptured
at weaning, which usually corresponds to the birth of a new sibling.

During the second period, which starts with weaning and includes
juvenilehood, the young male's behavior centers on mixed-sex, same-
age peer play groups. These groups are open and fluid, unlike the
all-male groups of the next period. Play during this time is relatively
nonaggressive. A male during this period still associates with his

mother and may return to her each night to sleep or count on her to be an ally during intense aggressive interaction with another juvenile.

When the juvenile male begins to mature sexually and enters adolescence, the third period begins. It is characterized by peripheralization, solitarization, and formation of all-male groups. Finally, some time after the onset of sexual capability, a young adult male typically emigrates from his troop into another or begins a new life with a captured female. He competes with other adult males in his new troop for the right of access to females. Eventually he establishes his position in the dominance hierarchy, becoming an adult in his troop.

In females, separation from mother and achievement of adult status proceed along a different route. Before weaning, female infants and their mothers are completely oriented to each other. Infancy lasts somewhat longer for females than for males, and females are weaned at a later time.

During the juvenile period, male and female behavior diverge noticeably. Prepubescent females are members of mixed-sex, same-age peer play groups but, unlike males, show a strong orientation to yearlings. During this period most females actively engage in aunting. Before puberty, their interests shift entirely from play groups to aunting infants, and young females are likely to be found in the company of infants and mothers rather than female peers. Juvenile females associate closely with their mothers and have relatively good relations with them.

Once a juvenile female reaches puberty, she begins to focus on the adult males in her troop, and males turn their attentions to her. Not long after the start of her estrus cycle, she copulates and, when the adolescent sterility period ends, becomes pregnant and gives birth. A female with an infant of her own is an adult.

CONCLUSIONS: WHY ADOLESCENCE EXISTS

Adolescence, including subadulthood, can be defined in several ways: the time between puberty and the attainment of adult status; a period of behavioral discontinuity between childhood and adulthood; or a period of storm and stress. However it is defined, the evidence now available suggests that subadulthood and probably adolescence does not truly exist for females in most species of nonhuman primates, although both exist for males. Females become sexually active soon after the onset of puberty and quickly become pregnant and give birth, attaining adult status. Furthermore, the behavior of postpubescent and prepubescent females is more similar than dissimilar. What changes do occur after puberty are gradual rather than discontinuous with prepubescent behavior. Pubescent females do not experience much storm and stress in relations with their mothers, peers, and adult males.

In contrast to females, an adolescent period clearly exists for males. Males are denied adult status, that is, sexual access to females, often for many years past puberty, until they aggressively seize a place in a male dominance hierarchy. Moreover, the frequency of expression (quantity) and form (quality) of many prepubescent behaviors is significantly altered after puberty. Pubescence is a stormy period of life for males in most primate species. For example:

> [Adolescence] is a period of social development during which there is most stress and tension for the young animal. . . . This varies with different species but the transition from subadult to adult for the male is likely to be one of the most dangerous and traumatic stages in his life. (Dolhinow, 1972, p. 383)

Why does a true adolescent period exist for males but not females, and why is pubescence more stressful for males than females? These questions cannot be answered definitely, but speculation is possible. During late juvenilehood and early adolescence, the adult forms of many male and female behaviors first emerge (Lancaster, 1971; Pereira, 1988). For males, achievement of adulthood means primarily completion of physical growth and establishment of one's social position. Adolescence is a period when aggressive skills are learned and sharpened, and unfit or weak individuals are relegated to low-status positions with little access to fertile females. Being a primate male is dangerous, and adolescents must aggressively demonstrate their prowess before they can contribute to the gene pool of their troop.

Being a nonhuman primate adult female means bearing and successfully raising offspring. A species is advantaged when females have many offspring who survive past infancy. Delaying the onset of sexuality past puberty reduces the frequency of pregnancy and is disadvantageous for species survival. In addition to fecundity, appropriate mothering is essential for species survival. As maternal behavior must be in place before the birth of the first offspring, these behaviors probably have a biological basis in most species or are learned before puberty. An adolescent period need not exist for females, because adult female behaviors necessary for species survival are either wired in or learned before puberty.

Tanner (1962) also speculates about the evolutionary development of an adolescent period. He offers a reason why adolescence only appears in the life cycle of relatively advanced primates. He notes that the prolongation of preadulthood is closely tied to the importance of learned behavior in the primate order. Adolescence allows time for individuals to learn the skills necessary to survive in a complex social world. Thus, higher primates, with their complex social arrangements, are more likely to have an adolescent period than lower primates. Along these same lines, the absolute and proportional amount of their lives spent in preadulthood increases as one moves from lower to higher primates. For example, the lemur, considered the most primitive group of primates, which implies a predominance of innate over learned behavior, spends 14% (two years) of its expected life span in preadulthood; the chimpanzee, with its humanlike learning abilities, spends 30% (12 years) of its expected life in preadulthood. In humans, the figure is also 30%, or 21 years, in length.

Regardless of its length, adolescence in nonhuman primates is characterized by a wide range of old and new behaviors. For example, juvenile behavior among tamarins is more bivalent than intermediate, combining infantile and adult behavior patterns (Moynihan, 1970). In a study of vervets, adolescent males were the most unpredictable animals of any age group, spending much of their time alone one day and the next day intensely involved in intragroup activities (McGuire, 1974). In a study of lemurs, Budnitz and Dainis (1975) gave the following description of one male adolescent:

Some days he would comport himself like a dominant male, swaggering and occasionally winning in spats with other males. At other times he was submissive and would spat and retreat if another animal as much as looked at him. Most of the time he vacillated between these two extremes. (p. 231)

Adolescence and subadulthood, then, is a period marked by both continuity and fluctuation. Although adolescence is chronologically midway between juvenilehood and adulthood, it is not just an intermediary point between the two—it is a unique stage of life that includes components of both.

REFERENCES

Albrecht, H., & Dunnett, S. C. (1971). *Chimpanzees in Western Africa*. Munchen: R. Piper & Co.

Altmann, J. (1986). Adolescent pregnancies in nonhuman primates: An ecological and developmental perspective. In J. B. Lancaster & B. A. Hamburg (Eds.), *School-age pregnancy and parenthood* (pp. 247-262). Hawthorne, NY: Aldine De Gruyter.

Baldwin, J. D. (1968). The social behaviour of adult male squirrel monkeys *(Saimiri sciureus)* in a seminatural environment. *Folia Primatologica, 9*, 281-314.

Baldwin, J. D. (1969). The ontogeny of social behaviour of squirrel monkeys *(Saimiri sciureus)* in a seminatural environment. *Folia Primatologica, 11*, 35-79.

Baldwin, J. D., & Baldwin, J. I. (1977). The role of learning phenomena in the ontogeny of exploration and play. In S. Chevalier-Skolnikoff & F. E. Poirier (Eds.), *Primate biosocial development* (pp. 343-406). New York: Garland.

Bernstein, I. S. (1968). The lutong of Kuala Sclangor. *Behaviour, 32*, 1-16.

Bernstein, I. S., & Ehardt, C. (1986). The influence of kinship and socialization on aggressive behaviour in rhesus monkeys *(Macaca mulatta)*. *Animal Behavior, 34*, 739-747.

Boggess, J. (1982). Immature male and adult male interactions in bisexual langur *(Presbytis entellus)* troops. *Folia Primatologica, 38*, 19-38.

Budnitz, N., & Dainis, K. (1975). *Lemur catta*: Ecology and behavior. In I. Tattersall & R. W. Sussman (Eds.), *Lemur biology* (pp. 219-235). New York: Plenum.

Chandler, C. F. (1975). Development and function of marking and sexual behavior in the Malagasy prosimian primate, *Lemur fulvus*. *Primates, 16*, 35-47.

Cheney, D. L. (1978). Interactions of immature male and female baboons with adult females. *Animal Behaviour, 26*, 389-408.

Coe, C. L., Kayashi, K. T., & Levine, S. (1988). Hormones and behavior at puberty: Activation or concatenation. In M. R. Gunnar & W. A. Collins (Eds.), *Development during the transition to adolescence* (pp. 17-41). Hillsdale, NJ: Lawrence Erlbaum.

Dixon, A. F. (1980). Androgens and aggressive behavior in primates: A review. *Aggressive Behavior, 6*, 37-67.

Dixon, A. F. (1983). The owl monkey *(Aotus trivirgatus)*. In J. Hearn (Ed.), *Reproduction in new world primates* (pp. 69-113). Hingham, MA: MTP Press.

Dolhinow, P. (Ed.). (1972). *Primate patterns*. New York: Holt, Rinehart, & Winston.

DuMond, F. V. (1968). The squirrel monkey in a seminatural environment. In L. A. Rosenblum & R. W. Cooper (Eds.), *The squirrel monkey* (pp. 87-145). New York: Academic Press.

Dunbar, R., & Dunbar, P. (1975). *Social dynamics of gelada baboons. Contributions to primatology* (Vol. 6, pp. 1-158). Basel, Switzerland: S. Karger.

Ellefson, J. O. (1974). A natural history of white-handed gibbons in the Malayan Peninsula. In D. M. Rumbaugh (Ed.), *Gibbon and siamang* (Vol. 3, pp. 1-136). Basel, Switzerland: S. Karger.

Epple, G., & Katz, Y. (1983). The saddle back tamarin and other tamarins. In J. Hearn (Ed.), *Reproduction in new world primates* (pp. 115-148). Hingham, MA: MTP Press.

Erwin, J., Maple, T., & Welles, J. F. (1975). Responses of rhesus monkeys to reunion. In S. Kondo, M. Kawai, & A. Ehara (Eds.), *Contemporary primatology: Proceedings of the fifth international congress of primatology*. Basel, Switzerland: S. Karger.

Fedigan, L. M. (1982). *Primate paradigms: Sex roles and social bonds.* Montreal: Eden Press.

Fossey, D. (1979). Development of the mountain gorilla *(Gorilla gorilla beringei):* The first thirty-six months. In D. A. Hamburg & E. R. McCown (Eds.), *The great apes* (pp. 139-184). Menlo Park, CA: Benjamin/Cummings.

Fossey, D. (1982). Reproduction among free-living mountain gorillas. *American Journal of Primatology, 1,* 97-104.

Galdikas, B. M. F. (1981). Orangutan reproduction in the wild. In C. E. Graham (Ed.), *Reproductive biology of the great apes* (pp. 281-300). New York: Academic Press.

Gingerich, P. D. (1972). The development of sexual dimorphism in the body pelvis of the squirrel monkey. *Anatomical Record, 172,* 589-594.

Glick, B. B. (1980). Ontogenetic and psychobiological aspects of the mating activities of male *Macaca radiata.* In D. G. Lindburg (Ed.), *The macaques: Studies in ecology, behavior and evolution* (pp. 345-369). New York: Van Nostrand.

Goodall, J. (1968). The behavior of free-living chimpanzees in the Gombe Stream Reserve. *Animal Behaviour Monographs, 1,* 161-311.

Goodall, J. (1986). *The chimpanzees of Gombe.* Cambridge, MA: Harvard University Press.

Hanby, J. (1976). Sociosexual development in primates. In P. P. G. Bateson & P. H. Klopfer (Eds.), *Perspectives in ethology* (Vol. 2, pp. 1-67). New York: Plenum.

Harcourt, A. H., Stewart, K. J., & Fossey, D. (1976). Male emigration and female transfer in wild mountain gorilla. *Nature, 263,* 226-227.

Harcourt, A. H., Stewart, K. J., & Fossey, D. (1981). Gorilla reproduction in the wild. In C. E. Graham (Ed.), *Reproductive biology of the great apes* (pp. 265-279). New York: Academic Press.

Hasegawa, T., & Hiraiwa-Hasegawa, M. (1983). Opportunistic and restrictive matings among wild chimpanzees in the Mahale Mountains, Tanzania. *Journal of Ethology, 1,* 75-85.

Hausfater, G. (1972). Intergroup behavior of free-ranging rhesus monkeys *(Macaca mulatta). Folia Primatologica, 18,* 78-107.

Hayaki, H. (1985). Copulation of adolescent male chimpanzees, with special reference to the influence of adult males, in the Mahale National Park, Tanzania. *Folia Primatologica, 44,* 148-160.

Hayaki, H. (1988). Association partners of young chimpanzees in the Mahale Mountains National Park, Tanzania. *Primates, 29,* 147-161.

Hrdy, S. B. (1976). Care and exploitation of nonhuman primate infants by conspecifics other than the mother. In J. S. Rosenblatt, R. A. Hinde, E. Shaw, & C. Beer (Eds.), *Advances in the study of behavior* (Vol. 6, pp. 101-158). New York: Academic Press.

Hrdy, S. B. (1977). *The langurs of Abu.* Cambridge, MA: Harvard University Press.

Jay, P. C. (1965). The common langur of North India. In I. DeVore (Ed.), *Primate behavior* (pp. 197-249). New York: Holt, Rinehart, & Winston.

Johnson, J. A. (1987). Dominance rank in juvenile olive baboons, *Papio anubis:* The influence of gender, size, maternal rand and orphaning. *Animal Behavior, 35,* 1694-1708.

Jones, K. C. (1983). Inter-troop transfer of *Lemur catta* males at Berenty, Madagascar. *Folia Primatologica, 40,* 145-160.

Kano, T. (1982). The social group of pygmy chimpanzees *(Pan paniscus)* of Wamba. *Primates, 23,* 171-188.

Kawai, M. (1979). Ecological and sociological studies of gelada baboons. *Contributions to primatology* (Vol. 16). Basel, Switzerland: S. Karger.

Klopfer, P. H., & Boskoff, K. J. (1979). Maternal behavior in prosimians. In G. A. Doyle & R. D. Martin, (Eds.), *The study of prosimian behavior* (pp. 123-156). New York: Academic Press.

Koford, C. B. (1965). Population dynamics of rhesus monkeys on Cayo Santiago. In I. DeVore (Ed.), *Primate behavior* (pp. 160-174). New York: Holt, Rinehart, & Winston.

Koyama, N. (1967). On dominance rank and kinship of a wild Japanese monkey troop in Arashiyama. *Primates, 8,* 189-216.

Kummer, H. (1968). *Social organization of hamadryas baboons.* Chicago: University of Chicago Press.

Kurland, J. A. (1977). Kin selection in the Japanese monkey. *Contributions to primatology* (Vol. 12, pp. 1-145). Basel, Switzerland: S. Karger.

Lancaster, J. B. (1971). Play-mothering: The relations between juvenile females and young infants among free-ranging velvet monkeys *(Cercopithecus aethiops). Folia Primatologica, 15,* 161-182.

Lancaster, J. B. (1986). Human adolescence and reproduction: An evolutionary perspective. In J. B. Lancaster & B. A. Hamburg (Eds.), *School-age pregnancy and parenthood* (pp. 17-37). Hawthorne, NY: Aldine De Gruyter.

Lindburg, D. G. (1971). The rhesus monkey in North India: An ecological and behavioral study. In L. A. Rosenblum (Ed.), *Primate behavior* (Vol. 2; pp. 2-106). New York: Academic Press.

Loy, J. (1971). Estrous behavior of free-ranging rhesus monkeys *(Macaca mulatta). Primates, 12,* 1-31.

Loy, J., & Loy, K. (1977). Sexual harassment among captive patas monkeys *(Erythrocebus patas). Primates, 18,* 691-699.

MacDonald, K. (1987). Biological and psychosocial interactions in early adolescence: A sociobiological perspective. In R. M. Lerner & T. T. Foch (Eds.), *Biological-psychosocial interactions in early adolescence* (pp. 95-120). Hillsdale, NJ: Lawrence Erlbaum.

MacKinnon, J. (1979). Reproductive behavior in wild orangutan populations. In D. A. Hamburg & E. R. McCown (Eds.), *The great apes* (pp. 257-273). Menlo Park, CA: Benjamin/Cummings.

McGinnis, L. M., & McGinnis, P. R. (1978). Primate behavior and the first infant. In W. B. Miller & L. F. Newman (Eds.), *The first child and family formation* (pp. 24-34). Chapel Hill, NC: Carolina Population Center.

McGuire, M. T. (1974). The St. Kitts vervet. In H. Kuhn (Ed.), *Contributions to primatology* (Vol. 2, pp. 1-199). Basel, Switzerland: S. Karger.

Meaney, M. J., Stewart, J., & Beatty, W. W. (1985). Sex differences in social play: The socialization of sex roles. In J. S. Rosenblatt, C. Beer, M. C. Busnel, & P. J. B. Slater (Eds.), *Advances in the study of behavior* (Vol. 15, pp. 1-58). New York: Academic Press.

Meikle, D. B., & Vessey, S. H. (1981). Nepotism among rhesus monkey brothers. *Nature, 294,* 160-161.

Michael, R. P., & Wilson, M. (1973). Changes in the sexual behaviour of male rhesus monkeys *(M. mulatta)* at puberty. *Folia Primatologica, 19,* 384-403.

Mitani, J. C. (1985). Mating behaviour of male orangutans in the Kutai Game Reserve, Indonesia. *Animal Behavior, 33,* 392-402.

Moynihan, M. (1970). Some behavior patterns of Platyrrhine monkeys II: *Saguinus geoffroyi* and some other tamarins. *Smithsonian Contributions to Zoology, 28,* 1-77.

Neville, M. K. (1972). The population structure of red howler monkeys *(Alouatta seniculus)* in Trinidad and Venezuela. *Folia Primatologica, 17,* 56-86.

Nishida, T. (1979). The social structure of chimpanzees of the Mahale Mountains. In D. A. Hamburg and E. R. McCown (Eds.), *The great apes* (pp. 73-121). Menlo Park, CA: Benjamin/Cummings.

Pereira, M. E. (1988). Effects of age and sex on intra-group spacing behaviour in juvenile savannah baboons, *Papio cynocephalus cynocephalus. Animal Behavior, 36,* 184-204.

Pereira, M. E., & Altmann, J. (1985). Development of social behavior in free-living nonhuman primates. In E. S. Watts (Ed.), *Nonhuman primate models for human growth and development* (pp. 217-309). New York: Alan Liss.

Pusey, A. E. (1978a). Age changes in the mother-offspring association of wild chimpanzees. In D. J. Chivers & J. Herbert (Eds.), *Recent advances in primatology* (pp. 119-123). New York: Academic Press.

Pusey, A. E. (1978b). *The physical and social development of wild adolescent chimpanzees.* Doctoral dissertation, Stanford University.

Ransom, T. W., & Rowell, T. E. (1972). Early social development of feral baboons. In F. Poirier (Ed.), *Primate socialization* (pp. 105-144). New York: Random House.

Richard, A. F., & Heimbuch, R. (1975). An analysis of the social behavior of three groups of *Propithecus verreauxi.* In I. Tattersall & R. W. Sussman (Eds.), *Lemur biology* (pp. 313-333). New York: Plenum Press.

Rosenblum, L. A. (1971). Kinship interaction patterns in pigtail and bonnet macaques. In H. Kummer (Ed.), *Proceedings of the third international congress of primatology* (pp. 79-84). Basel, Switzerland: S. Karger.

Rowell, T. E., Hinde, R. A., & Spencer-Booth, Y. (1964). "Aunt"-infant interaction in captive rhesus monkeys. *Animal Behaviour, 12,* 219-294.

Savin-Williams, R. C., & Weisfeld, G. E. (1989). An ethological perspective on adolescence. In G. R. Adams, R. Montemayor, & T. P. Gullotta (Eds.), *Biology of adolescent behavior and development* (pp. 249-274). Newbury Park, CA: Sage.

Schaller, G. B. (1963). *The mountain gorilla.* Chicago: University of Chicago Press.

Simonds, P. E. (1965). The bonnet macaque in South India. In I. DeVore (Ed.), *Primate behavior* (pp. 175-196). New York: Holt, Rinehart, & Winston.

Starin, E. D. (1981). Monkey moves. *Natural History, 90*(9), 37-42.

Steinberg, L. (1989). Pubertal maturation and parent-adolescent distance: An evolutionary perspective. In G. R. Adams, R. Montemayor, & T. P. Gullotta (Eds.), *Biology of adolescent behavior and development* (pp. 71-97). Newbury Park, CA: Sage.

Struhsaker, T. T., & Leland, L. (1979). Socioecology of five sympatric monkey species in the Kibale forest, Uganda. In J. S. Rosenblatt, R. A. Hinde, C. Beer, & M. C. Busnel (Eds.), *Advances in the study of behavior* (Vol. 9, pp. 159-228). New York: Academic Press.

Sugiyama, Y. (1981). Observations on the population dynamics and behavior of wild chimpanzees at Bossou, Guinea, in 1979-1980. *Primates, 22,* 435-444.

Tanner, J. M. (1962). *Growth at adolescence* (2nd ed.). Oxford: Blackwell Scientific Publications.

Tanner, J. M. (1978). *Fetus into man.* Cambridge, MA: Harvard University Press.

Tattersall, I. (1982). *The primates of Madagascar.* New York: Columbia University Press.

Trollope, J., & Blurton-Jones, N. G. (1975). Aspects of reproduction and reproductive behaviour in *Macaca arctoides. Primates, 16,* 191-205.

Tutin, C. E. G., & McGinnis, P. R. (1981). Chimpanzee reproduction in the wild. In C. E. Graham (Ed.), *Reproductive biology of the great apes* (pp. 239-264). New York: Academic Press.

Weisfeld, G. E., & Berger, J. M. (1983). Some features of human adolescence viewed in evolutionary perspective. *Human Development*.

Zucker, E. L., & Kaplan, J. R. (1981). A reinterpretation of "sexual harassment" in patas monkeys. *Animal Behaviour, 29,* 957-958.

2. Physical Growth and Performance During the Transitional Years (9-16)

Robert M. Malina
University of Texas

Two interrelated processes, the growth spurt and sexual maturation, make the transition from childhood to adolescence distinctive from a biological perspective. The growth spurt and sexual maturation are variable in timing and tempo, that is, when they occur and the rate at which individuals pass through them. Allowing for interindividual variation, the physiological and physical changes that characterize these processes occur between 9 and 16 years of age in most children. The initiation and coordination of somatic growth and sexual maturation are dependent upon the maturation of the hypothalamic-pituitary-gonadal axis of the neuroendocrine system (Preece, 1986; Wierman & Crowley, 1986). Consideration of the neuroendocrine regulation of growth and maturation, however, is beyond the scope of this chapter.

Significant changes in body size, proportions and composition, and in the primary and secondary sex characteristics occur during the transition from childhood to adolescence. This chapter considers first, the timing of the growth spurt and sexual maturation, and second, the changes in growth and maturation that occur during the transition from childhood to adolescence. Although the growth spurt and sexual maturation influence a variety of behaviors, physical performance is more directly affected. Hence, changes in performance during the transition are also considered.

TIMING OF THE GROWTH SPURT IN STATURE

The growth spurt in stature is the most commonly used indicator of somatic growth during the transition from childhood to adolescence. An increase in the velocity of statural growth marks the initiation of the spurt. Velocity of statural growth eventually reaches a maximum during the spurt and then gradually declines. Growth curves are fit mathematically or graphically to longitudinal records of

41

TABLE 2.1 Timing of the Adolescent Spurt in Stature in Swiss Children

	n	M	SD	Range
Age, years, at initiation of the spurt:				
Girls	110	9.6	1.1	6.6 – 12.9
Boys	112	11.0	1.2	7.8 – 13.5
Age, years, at PHV:				
Girls	110	12.2	1.0	9.3 – 15.0
Boys	112	13.9	0.8	12.0 – 15.8

SOURCE: Adapted from Largo, Gasser, Prader, Stuetzle, & Huber (1978). Parameters for individual growth curves were estimated with cubic splines.

stature for individual children to extract the change in velocity of growth and, thus, age at initiation of the spurt (age at take-off), the velocity of statural growth when it reaches its maximum (peak height velocity, PHV), and the age at which maximal growth in stature occurs (age at PHV).

Age at Take-Off. The change in velocity that marks the initiation of the growth spurt occurs relatively early in the transition from childhood to adolescence. Mean ages at initiation of the spurt in samples of North American and European children range from 8.7 to 10.3 years in girls and 10.3 to 12.1 years in boys, with standard deviations of about 1 year in most studies (Malina, Bouchard, & Beunen, 1988). Variation in mean ages is related in part to the different models and procedures used to derive them. Means are, of course, sample estimates and variation within samples is considerable (Table 2.1). Although the initiation of the growth spurt occurs, on average, earlier in girls than in boys, there is much overlap. Further, some children begin the growth spurt in stature before the age range commonly given for the transitional period from childhood to adolescence.

Age at PHV. Data for estimated age at PHV during the adolescent spurt are more extensive than those for the age at initiation of the spurt. Mean ages at PHV in samples of North American and European children range from 11.4 to 12.2 years in girls and from 13.4 to 14.4 years in boys. Most means cluster between 11.7 to 12.2 years in girls and 13.9 to 14.2 years in boys, while standard deviations for most estimates are about 1 year (Malina et al., 1988). Girls reach PHV, on average, about 2 years earlier than boys, but variation is considerable among individual children (Table 2.1).

TIMING OF SEXUAL MATURATION

Assessment of sexual maturation is based upon the development of the secondary sex characteristics, that is, breast development in girls, penis and testes (genital) development in boys, and pubic hair in both sexes. However, menarche is the most commonly reported maturity indicator of sexual maturation for girls. Each secondary sex characteristic is ordinarily rated on the 5-stage criteria described by Tanner (1962). Stage 1 indicates absence of development of the particular characteristic and Stage 2 indicates initial development. Stages 3 and 4 are intermediate stages of development, while Stage 5 indicates the mature state. Specific stages of each characteristic should be indicated, that is, Stage 2 of breast development (B 2) or Stage 3 of genital development (G 3), rather than reporting them as Tanner Stage 2 or Tanner Stage 3. Although the latter is a common practice, it is not correct.

The development of secondary sex characteristics is a continuous process upon which the stages are superimposed. Thus, the rating scales are somewhat arbitrary. For example, a boy just entering G 3 of genital development is rated the same as a boy nearing the end of G 3, that is, they are both rated as being in G 3.

The most common sequences for the development of secondary sex characteristics in girls and boys based on the mean/median ages for several samples of European and North American youth are summarized in Table 2.2. Age at PHV is also included so that the timing of secondary sex characteristic development relative to age at maximum growth can be noted. Standard deviations for each characteristic tend to be greater than those for age at PHV. Several trends should be noted in Table 2.2. First, budding of the breasts in girls (B 2) and initial enlargement of the genitalia in boys (G 2) are, on average, the first overt signs of sexual maturation in most samples. There are, however, some children in whom pubic hair development coincides with or precedes breast or genital development. Second, girls mature, on average, in advance of boys. Stages of breast and genital development, however, are not directly comparable so that comparison of ages is not warranted. Third, PHV tends to occur earlier in the pubertal sequence of events in girls than in boys. And fourth, menarche is a rather late maturational event that occurs, on average, more than 1 year after PHV.

Variation in the sequence of events at puberty is partly genuine and partly methodological. One of the major sources of variation is the

TABLE 2.2 Sequence of Pubertal Events in North American and European Girls and Boys

	Girls		*Boys*	
		Range of		*Range of*
Event	*Reported Ages*	*Event*	*Reported Ages*
B 2	10.6 – 11.4	G 2	11.0 – 12.4
PH 2	10.4 – 12.1	PH 2	12.2 – 13.4
B 3	11.2 – 12.6	G 3	12.7 – 13.4
PH 3	11.9 – 13.1	PH 3	13.1 – 13.9
PHV	11.5 – 12.1	G 4	13.4 – 14.7
PH 4	12.5 – 13.5	PHV	13.8 – 14.1
B 4	12.2 – 13.8	PH 4	13.9 – 15.1
M	12.8 – 13.5	G 5	14.6 – 17.3
PH 5	13.9 – 15.2	PH 5	14.9 – 16.1
B 5	13.7 – 15.6		

SOURCE: Adapted from Malina (1989).
NOTE: Pubertal events are as follows: B 2 – B 5, G 2 – G 5, and PH 2 – PH 5 refer to breast, genital, and pubic hair Stages 2 through 5 respectively; PHV refers to peak height velocity; M refers to menarche. Range of reported ages refers to mean or median ages (yrs) for each pubertal event.

interval between observations in longitudinal studies. For example, if the interval between observations is 6 months, it is possible that a girl might be near the end of Stage B 2 of breast development at the first examination and at B 4, 6 months later. Hence, no Stage B 3 is recorded.

The general sequence of pubertal events is based primarily on longitudinal studies, which ordinarily do not have sufficiently large samples to derive estimates for a population. Selected percentiles for ages at attaining each stage of secondary sex characteristic development in a national sample of Dutch children are given in Table 2.3.

GROWTH AND PERFORMANCE STATUS DURING THE TRANSITIONAL YEARS

The preceding focused on the timing of the growth spurt and sexual maturation. This section describes age- and sex-associated variation in body size and composition and in physical performance during the transitional years.

TABLE 2.3 Selected Percentiles for Ages (yrs) at Which Stages of Secondary Sex Characteristics Are Attained in a National Sample of Dutch Youth

| | | *Percentiles* | | |
		P 10	P 50	P 90
Girls				
Breast	B 2	9.1	10.5	12.3
	B 3	10.2	11.7	13.1
	B 4	11.4	12.9	14.5
	B 5	12.5	14.2	—
Pubic hair	PH 2	9.0	10.8	12.6
	PH 3	10.2	11.7	13.1
	PH 4	11.3	12.6	14.0
	PH 5	12.2	14.0	16.4
Menarche		11.7	13.3	14.9
Boys				
Genital	G 2	9.3	11.3	13.3
	G 3	11.6	13.1	14.5
	G 4	12.7	14.0	15.6
	G 5	13.5	15.3	18.6
Pubic hair	PH 2	9.0	11.7	13.5
	PH 3	11.7	13.1	14.5
	PH 4	12.9	14.0	15.5
	PH 5	13.5	15.0	18.4

SOURCE: Adapted from Roede & Van Wieringen (1985).

Body Size

Growth curves for stature and body weight are shown in Figure 2.1. Sex differences in body size are small late in childhood, but during the early part of the transition girls are, on average, taller and heavier than boys, as the growth spurt occurs earlier in girls than in boys. When the male growth spurt occurs, boys catch up and eventually surpass girls in body size.

Most external body dimensions (e.g., leg length, skeletal breadths, and limb circumferences) follow a similar growth pattern. There is, however, variation in rates of growth that contributes to sex differ-

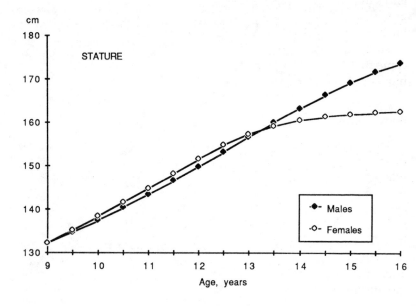

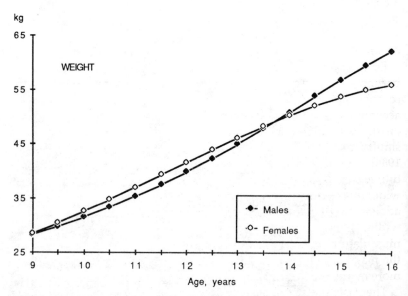

Figure 2.1 Mean Stature and Body Weight from 9 Through 16 Years of Age in American Children. Drawn from data of the U.S. Health Examination Survey (Hamill, Drizd, Johnson, Reed, & Roche, 1977).

ences in physique. For example, boys experience considerably more growth in shoulder breadth than girls, while both sexes attain similar hip breadths. Thus, boys have, on average, not only absolutely broader shoulders than girls, but also have relatively broad shoulders compared to their hips. Girls, on the other hand, have relatively broad hips compared to their shoulders.

Body Composition

Body composition is most often viewed in a two-compartment model: Body Weight = Fat Free Mass + Fat Mass. Fat free mass (FFM) follows a growth pattern like that of stature and weight. Boys have, on average, a larger FFM than girls at all ages. Both boys and girls experience a growth spurt in FFM, but the magnitude of the gain in boys is about twice as large as that in girls; hence, the sex difference in FFM is magnified at this time. On the other hand, girls increase in fat mass (FM) at a greater rate than boys from childhood through adolescence, while FM appears to reach a plateau near the time of the growth spurt in boys (Malina et al., 1988).

On a relative basis, at all ages girls have a greater percentage of body weight as fat than boys. Relative fatness increases gradually from late childhood through adolescence in girls, while it is, on average, rather stable in boys until the growth spurt, when relative fatness gradually declines.

Estimates of body composition within the context of the two-compartment model treat the body as a whole. Regional variation in body composition occurs during the transitional years. For example, boys accumulate proportionally more subcutaneous fat on the trunk than on the extremities, while girls accumulate subcutaneous fat at a similar rate on both the trunk and extremities (Malina & Bouchard, 1988). Muscle tissue also shows regional variation (Figure 2.2). Sex differences, though apparent, are small in late childhood, boys having wider muscles in the arm and calf. By about 11 years, girls begin their adolescent spurt and have a temporary size advantage in calf muscle width. There is, however, no temporary size advantage for girls in arm musculature, and boys have an adolescent spurt that is almost twice the magnitude of that in girls. The sex difference in muscularity is more marked in the arm than in the calf.

The basic pattern of sexual dimorphism in size, relative proportions, and body composition is established during the transition from childhood to adolescence. Descriptive statistics for age- and sex-

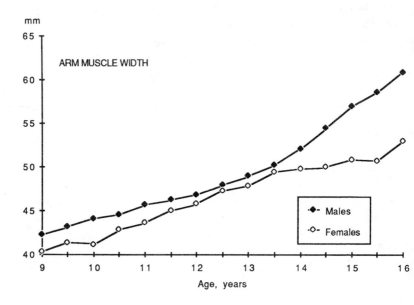

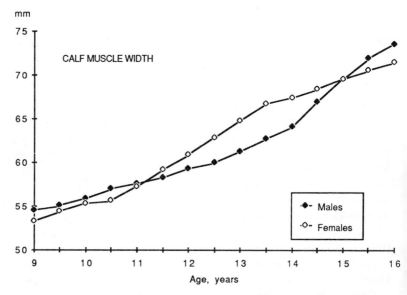

Figure 2.2 Mean Widths of Muscle Tissue on the Arm and Calf from 9 Through 16 Years in British Children. Drawn from data reported by Tanner, Hughes & Whitehouse (1981).

associated variation in a variety of body dimensions of North American children and youth have been summarized elsewhere (Malina & Roche, 1983; Roche & Malina, 1983).

Performance

Strength, motor, and aerobic performance increase linearly with age from late childhood into adolescence, and at all ages, the performances of boys are, on average, greater than those of girls (Haubenstricker & Seefeldt, 1986). Further, boys show reasonably well-defined growth spurts in performance during the transition while girls do not (Beunen & Malina, 1988). Thus, the magnitude of the gains in performance during the growth spurt are considerably greater in boys as compared to girls. Muscular strength and aerobic power improve somewhat during the growth spurt in girls, but motor performance tends to reach a plateau.

GROWTH SPURTS IN OTHER DIMENSIONS

Although most emphasis is placed upon the growth spurt in stature, other bodily dimensions experience growth spurts during the transition from childhood to adolescence. Variation in the timing and magnitude of growth spurts in different dimensions illustrates the differential nature of growth during the transition and contributes to sexual dimorphism.

Estimated ages at peak velocity for stature, body weight, estimated leg length, and sitting height in several longitudinal studies are summarized in Table 2.4. Maximum growth in leg length generally occurs, on average, before PHV, while maximum growth in weight and sitting height occur after PHV.

Peak velocity of growth in arm muscle occurs about 3 to 6 months after PHV in boys and girls. Boys, however, have a spurt in arm muscle that is approximately twice the magnitude of that for girls. Peak gain in calf muscle occurs at PHV in boys, while there is no clear peak in girls. In contrast to the arm, peak gain in calf muscle during the growth spurt is only slightly greater in boys than in girls (Tanner, Hughes & Whitehouse, 1981).

Longitudinal data for Czechoslovak boys indicate a gain of about 7.5 kg FFM/year and of 0.8 kg FM/year at PHV, but a decline in relative fatness of about −0.4% fat/year at PHV (Parizkova, 1976).

TABLE 2.4 Mean Ages (yrs) at Peak Velocity for Stature, Body Weight, Estimated Leg Length and Sitting Height in Several Samples of North American and European Youth

	Leg Length	Stature	Sitting Height	Weight
Girls				
California	11.0	11.7	11.8	12.2
England	11.6	11.9	12.2	12.9
Poland	11.2	11.7	12.2	12.4
Boys				
California	13.6	14.1	14.5	14.5
Belgium	14.0	14.2	14.3	14.6
England	13.6	13.9	14.3	14.3
Poland	13.6	14.0	14.4	14.2

SOURCE: Based on Malina, Bouchard, & Beunen, (1988) which includes sample sizes, methods of estimating ages, and standard deviations. Most standard deviations approximate ±1 year.

When estimates of FFM and FM collated from the literature are viewed from the years around the time of PHV (i.e., about 11 to 13 years in girls and 13 to 15 years in boys) estimated annual increases in FFM are about 7.2 kg/year for boys and 3.5 kg/year for girls during the interval of PHV, while estimated increases in FM at this time are about 0.7 kg/year in boys and 1.4 kg/year in girls. Corresponding estimates for relative fatness during the interval of PHV are about −0.5%/year in boys and +0.9%/year in girls (Malina et al., 1988). Thus, during the interval of the growth spurt in stature, boys gain in FFM at a rate that is almost double that of girls, while girls gain almost twice as much FM as boys. The marked increase in FFM of boys is such that FFM accounts for a greater percentage of body weight; hence, relative fatness declines during the growth spurt in boys.

GROWTH SPURTS IN PERFORMANCE

Most strength and motor performance tasks show reasonably well-defined spurts in boys during the transition. Results from a longitudinal sample of approximately 270 Belgian boys indicate maximal gains in strength (static-arm pull, explosive-vertical jump, functional-bent arm hang) after PHV, and maximal gains in speed (shuttle run and plate tapping) and flexibility (sit and reach) prior to PHV (Beunen, Malina, Van't Hof, Simons, Ostyn, Renson, & Van Gerven, 1988). In contrast, data for a smaller sample of Canadian boys indicate maximum increments for the standing long jump (explosive strength) and the bent arm hang in the year of PHV (Ellis, Carron, & Bailey, 1975). The somewhat variable results probably reflect analytical differences. Nevertheless, the two studies indicate definite performance spurts during the transition from childhood to adolescence in boys. In contrast, there does not appear to be a clear spurt in trunk strength or abdominal muscular endurance as measured by leg lifts (Beunen et al., 1988) and bent knee situps (Ellis et al., 1975) in boys.

In contrast to clear spurts in the strength and motor performance of boys during the transition, limited information suggests little evidence for corresponding performance spurts in girls. For example, a composite strength score based on the sum of right and left grip, pushing and pulling strength in American girls from California shows considerable variation relative to the growth spurt in stature (Faust, 1977). In contrast, arm pull strength in Dutch girls indicates a clear spurt in the year after PHV, which is consistent with the trend for boys (Kemper, 1985). The peak gain in arm strength of girls, however, is only about one-half that for Dutch boys. Data relating motor performance to PHV in girls are not available. When performance is related to menarche, there is no tendency for performance to peak before, at, or after menarche. Changes in performance over this span tend to be, on average, relatively small (Espenschade, 1940).

Longitudinal studies of Canadian, European, and Japanese boys and girls indicate a maximal gain in aerobic power near the time of PHV (Beunen & Malina, 1988), and estimated velocities of $\dot{V}O_2$ max at PHV are greater in boys than girls (Mirwald & Bailey, 1986). Absolute $\dot{V}O_2$ max (1/min) increases, on average, several years prior to PHV and continues to increase through the growth spurt in boys and girls. The increase in $\dot{V}O_2$ max reflects growth in body size at this time. On the other hand, when $\dot{V}O_2$ max is expressed relative to body weight, it tends to decline a year or so prior to PHV and continues to decline several years after PHV (Beunen & Malina, 1988). The decline in relative maximal aerobic power reflects the rapid growth in body mass during the adolescent spurt, so that per unit body mass, oxygen uptake declines during the growth spurt.

STABILITY OF GROWTH AND PERFORMANCE

Given individual variability in growth and maturation, the stability of measures of growth and performance is of interest. Does the individual maintain the same relative position in the group from one observation to another or over the age span that comprises the transition? Correlations between measurements made at one stage of growth with outcomes later in growth or in adulthood are used most often in studies of stability. A correlation of +0.5 is suggested as a criterion for a minimum level of consistency over at least a 1-year interval (Bloom, 1964). Nevertheless, correlation is a group statistic, and some individuals may be more or less stable than indicated by the magnitude of the correlation. Further, a correlation of 0.5 over a 5-year period implies that only 25% of the variance in one of the measurements is accounted for by variance in the other. Although such a correlation indicates greater consistency than expected by chance, it also implies variability.

In general, the closer the time span between measurements, the higher the correlation and the greater the stability. As the interval between observations increases, interage correlations generally decline, that is, there is less stability and, conversely, greater likelihood of change.

Body Size

Correlations between stature during childhood and adult stature reach about 0.8, but there is a slight decline during the growth spurt attributable to individual variation in the timing, duration, and magnitude of the spurt. Correlations for body weight during growth and young adult weight are slightly lower (0.6 to 0.8) than those for stature (Tanner & Whitehouse, 1982). Thus, stature and weight are reasonably stable during the early part of the transition.

Body Composition

Longitudinal data for estimates of fat free mass (FFM) and fat mass (FM) are limited. Correlations between FFM at 11 and 15 years and at 11 and 18 years of age in boys are moderately high (0.7 and 0.6), while those for FM are lower (0.5 and 0.2) (Parizkova, 1977). Interage analyses of radiographic and skinfold measurements of subcutaneous fat from seven longitudinal studies in the United States and Australia indicate a significant tendency to retain quartile rank during the transition from childhood to adolescence (Roche, Siervogel, Chumlea, Reed, Valadian, Eichorn, & McCammon, 1982). Children in the fourth or fattest quartile thus have a moderate or high risk of remaining at the fourth quartile at subsequent ages. Using 16 years as the upper age limit, correlations between subcutaneous fatness during childhood and at 16 years of age are generally stable until puberty, decline during pubescence, and then increase to 16 years. On the other hand, interage correlations for the relative distribution of subcutaneous fat on the trunk and limbs in boys are low (Beunen, Claessens, Ostyn, Renson, Simons, Lefevre, & Van Gerven, 1986), which indicates that fat distribution changes significantly in boys.

Performance

Stability of muscular strength varies among the muscle groups tested. Correlations taken at intervals of 5 to 6 years during childhood (7 and 12 years) and adolescence (12 and 17 years) or over 10 years (7 and 17 years) range from low to moderately high (0.0 to 0.8) (Rarick & Smoll, 1967), and sex differences are not consistent. Lower extremity strength tends to be more stable than upper extremity strength. This may be related to weight bearing and locomotor functions of the lower extremities. Composite strength scores tend to be somewhat more stable across male adolescence than the specific measurements, and expressing strength per unit body weight does not alter the correlations (Carron & Bailey, 1974). Interage correlations for motor performance also vary among tasks and age interval, but relatively few reach 0.5 (Rarick & Smoll, 1967; Ellis, Carron, & Bailey, 1975; Branta, Haubenstricker, & Seefeldt, 1984).

Between 11 and 14 years, correlations for absolute aerobic power indicate reasonable stability in active boys (0.7) and girls (0.6), but correlations for relative aerobic power are negative (Malina, Eveld, & Woynarowska, no date). The apparent instability of relative aerobic power may reflect individual variation in timing of growth spurts in weight and maximal oxygen consumption. Correlations for absolute and relative aerobic power measured at 11 and 18 years of age in boys approximate only 0.3 (Sprynarova & Parizkova, 1977), which suggests little stability across the transitional period. Similar long term data are not available for girls.

Thus, the stability of physical performance is quite low compared to that for overall body size and FFM. Many correlations for performance over intervals of 5 or more years do not reach 0.5, and thus have limited predictive utility.

"ADOLESCENT AWKWARDNESS" IN BOYS

Mean velocities for several motor performance tasks during the growth spurt in stature are positive in boys, which would suggest that there is no temporary period of "adolescent awkwardness," or of a boy "outgrowing his strength." Such a temporary slow down or period of clumsiness in strength and motor performance of some, but not all, adolescent boys has often been suggested in the general child development literature (see Beunen & Malina, 1988). It may be related to the time during the growth spurt when leg length increases rapidly early in the spurt or when trunk length increases late in the spurt prior to the attainment of full mass and strength of the musculature. The net result may be temporary problems with balance, which may affect performance in some tasks and give the impression of awkwardness or clumsiness.

Although the available longitudinal data that relate the motor performances of boys to the growth spurt do not support the notion of adolescent awkwardness, there may be individual boys who experience temporary problems in performance. This was considered in the longitudinal sample of Belgian boys (Beunen et al., 1988; Beunen & Malina, 1988), which identified boys whose performance in any of 6 motor tasks declined during the year of PHV. Although some boys declined in performance during the growth spurt, the decline did not occur in all tasks for the same individual. Interestingly, boys who declined in motor performance at the time of PHV were generally good performers at the beginning of the interval of PHV. Further, those who declined in performance did not differ, on the average, from those who improved in performance at the time of PHV in both the timing and magnitude of the growth spurt. This would suggest that maturity-associated variation in size and strength (discussion follows) or the temporary disproportion of leg and trunk lengths relative to overall body size are not significant factors that distinguish boys who decline from those who gain in motor performance at the time of PHV. Thus, a factor or factors that account for a temporary decline in the motor performance of some boys during the interval of PHV is not immediately apparent. Variation in motivation or changing attitudes toward performance may be important factors, but they are difficult to specify. Change in body image or self-concept during the period of rapid growth is an additional factor that may influence the motivation to perform or performance per se.

MATURITY-ASSOCIATED VARIATION IN
GROWTH AND PERFORMANCE

Children function in a society that is based on chronological age. For example, youth sports programs have age limits during the transitional years, and maturity-associated variation in size can be a significant factor in some sports. Thus, how do children of contrasting maturity status within a given chronological age group compare in growth and performance?

Children within a given age group can be subdivided by stage of secondary sex characteristic development or on the basis of age of attainment of a developmental landmark such as menarche or PHV. Skeletal age is an additional maturity criterion that has been used, but use of radiographs in surveys of growth and performance is presently quite limited. When maturity indicators with an assigned age are used, children are commonly classified as advanced in maturity status for chronological age (early maturers), average in maturity status for chronological age, or delayed in maturity status for chronological age (late maturers).

Body Size. Within a given chronological age group, children advanced in biological maturity status are, on average, taller and heavier (Figure 2.3). Although maturity-associated differences are apparent prior to the adolescent spurt, they are most pronounced between 11 and 13 years in girls and 13 and 15 years in boys, which reflects individual variation in the timing of the spurt. These are also the years of peak participation in youth sports programs. Late maturing children generally catch up in stature, but differences in body weight persist into adulthood. These trends reflect physique differences between early and late maturers (Tanner, 1962; Malina & Bouchard, 1990).

Body Composition. Estimates of the body composition in children grouped by maturity status are limited. Within a given age group, boys advanced in genital maturation are not only larger in body size, but also have a greater FFM (Figure 2.4). The maturity-associated differences in FFM are more apparent among boys in the later stages of genital maturation and probably reflect increased production of testosterone at this time. In contrast to FFM, differences in estimated

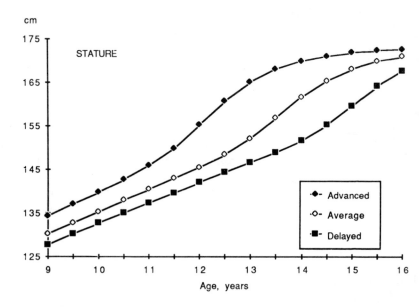

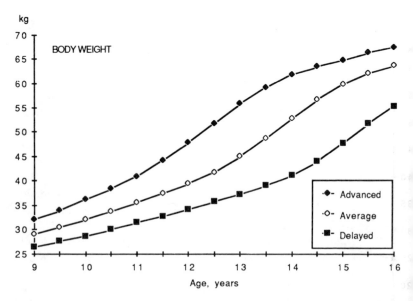

Figure 2.3 Mean Statures and Weights of Boys (left) and Girls (right) Classified As Advanced (early), Average, and Delayed (late) in Age at Maximum Growth in Stature. Drawn from data reported by Shuttleworth (1939).

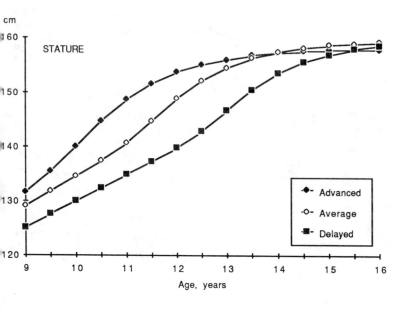

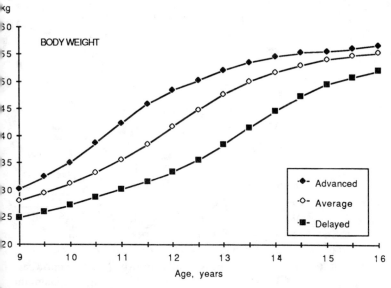

Figure 2.3 Continued

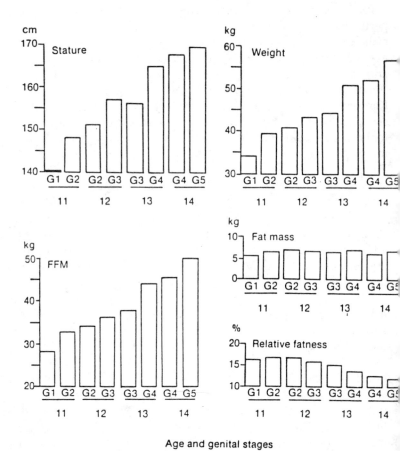

Age and genital stages

Figure 2.4 Body Composition (mean values) of Boys Grouped by State of Genital Maturation Within Single Age Groups. Calculated from data reported by Haschke (1983).

FM are small among boys differing in maturity status, but FM comprises a lesser percentage of body weight in boys in the later stages of genital maturation. Corresponding data for the gross body composition of girls differing in maturity status are not available. However, measurements of muscle, bone, and fat widths on standardized radiographs of the extremities indicate similar trends (Malina & Bouchard, 1989).

Performance. Variation in maturity status also influences physical performance, but, to some extent, does so differentially in boys and girls. Among boys, those advanced in maturity status within a given age group tend to be stronger, to perform better on gross motor tests, and to have greater aerobic power, especially between 13 and 15 years (Jones, 1949; Beunen, Ostyn, Simons, Renson, & Van Gerven, 1980; Kemper, Verschuur, & Ritmeester, 1986). The differences relate to the size advantage of early maturing boys. When performance is adjusted for body size, differences between the maturity groups in strength and motor performance are reduced, but are not completely eliminated. The performance advantage of early maturing boys tends to persist at most ages during the transition after size and age variation are statistically controlled (Beunen et al., 1980; Malina & Bouchard, 1990). Nevertheless, in the world of adolescents, size variation is real and influences performance, especially in those tasks requiring strength and power. Late maturing boys, on the other hand, tend to have a greater maximal oxygen intake per unit body weight, which reflects their lighter body weight (Kemper et al., 1986).

Differences in physical performance among girls of contrasting maturity status are less apparent. Early maturers tend to be slightly stronger early in the transition from childhood to adolescence, but the differences between maturity groups are reduced considerably with age (Jones, 1949) and when adjusted for body size (Malina & Bouchard, 1990). Early maturing girls also have greater absolute aerobic power, but late maturing girls have greater maximal oxygen uptake per unit body weight (Kemper et al., 1986). In contrast, there is little consistent difference in the motor performance of early and late maturing girls (Espenschade, 1940; Beunen, Ostyn, Renson, Simons, & Van Gerven, 1976), although better performing girls tend to be late maturing (Malina, 1983).

IMPLICATIONS

Although the growth spurt and sexual maturation are biological processes, they do not occur in a vacuum. The outcomes of these processes (i.e., changes in size, proportions, body composition, and sexual maturation) are one aspect of many changes that occur during the transition from childhood to adolescence. Children also develop in a variety of behavioral domains, social, emotional, and cognitive.

Interactions and interrelationships between biological and behavioral changes can influence the child's self-concept as he or she moves from childhood to adolescence. Physical performance is, to some extent, a composite of biological and behavioral changes that occur during the transition. On one hand, performance per se is influenced by size, body composition, and maturity status. On the other hand, the child's social and emotional development influence his or her motivation to perform, habits of physical activity, interests, and so on.

Individual variation in biological maturation and associated changes in size and body composition is the backdrop against which children evaluate and interpret their own growth, maturation, and social status among peers. Physical performance can be an important aspect of the evaluative process and is especially apparent in youth sports. For example, as the late maturing boy begins to catch up to the early maturer in size and strength, the disadvantage faced previously by the former may be considerably reduced and, in turn, contribute to success in sports (Malina, 1988). Similar interactions between biological maturation and social circumstances influence success in sports among young girls. In contrast to boys, among whom the early maturer's size and strength advantage more often leads to success in youth sports, it is the late maturing girl who more often experiences success in sports and persists in sports through the transition from childhood to adolescence (Malina, 1983).

REFERENCES

Beunen, G., & Malina, R. M. (1988). Growth and physical performance relative to the timing of the adolescent spurt. *Exercise and Sport Sciences Reviews, 16,* 503-540.

Beunen, G., Malina, R. M., Van't Hof, M. A., Simons, J., Ostyn, M., Renson, R., & Van Gerven, D. (1988). *Adolescent growth and motor performance: A longitudinal study of Belgian boys.* Champaign, IL: Human Kinetics.

Beunen, G., Claessens, A., Ostyn, M., Renson, R., Simons, J., Lefevre, J., & Van Gerven, D. (1986). *Stability of subcutaneous fat patterning in adolescent boys.* Paper presented at the 5th Congress of the European Anthropological Association, Lisbon.

Beunen, G., Ostyn, M., Renson, R., Simons, J., & Van Gerven, D. (1976). Skeletal maturation and physical fitness of girls aged 12 through 16. *Hermes, 10,* 445-457.

Beunen, G., Ostyn, M., Simons, J., Renson, R., & Van Gerven, D. (1980). Motorische vaardigheid, somatische ontwikkeling en biologische maturiteit. *Geneeskunde en Sport, 13,* 36-42.

Bloom, B. S. (1964). *Stability and change in human characteristics.* New York: Wiley.

Branta, C., Haubenstricker, J., & Seefeldt, V. (1984). Age changes in motor skills during childhood and adolescence. *Exercise and Sport Science Reviews, 12,* 467-520.

Carron, A. V., & Bailey, D. A. (1974). Strength development in boys from 10 through 16 years. *Monographs of the Society for Research in Child Development, 39*, Serial No. 157.

Ellis, J. D., Carron, A. V., & Bailey, D. A. (1975). Physical performance in boys from 10 through 16 years. *Human Biology, 47*, 263-281.

Espenschade, A. (1940). Motor performance in adolescence including the study of relationships with measures of physical growth and maturity. *Monographs of the Society for Research in Child Development, 5*, Serial No. 24.

Faust, M. S. (1977). Somatic development of adolescent girls. *Monographs of the Society for Research in Child Development, 42*, Serial No. 169.

Hamill, P. V. V., Drizd, T. A., Johnson, C. L., Reed, R. B., & Roche, A. F. (1977). NCHS growth curves for children birth-18 years, United States. *Vital and Health Statistics*, Series 11, No. 165.

Haschke, F. (1983). Body composition of adolescent males. *Acta Paediatrica Scandinavica*, Supplement 307.

Haubenstricker, J., & Seefeldt, V. (1986). Acquisition of motor skills during childhood. In V. Seefeldt (Ed.), *Physical activity and well-being* (pp. 41-102). Reston, VA: American Alliance for Health, Physical Education, Recreation and Dance.

Jones, H. E. (1949). *Motor performance and growth.* Berkeley: University of California Press.

Kemper, H. C. G. (Ed.) (1985). *Growth, health and fitness of teenagers.* Basel: Karger.

Kemper, H. C. G., Verschuur, R. V., & Ritmeester, J. W. (1986). Maximal aerobic power in early and late maturing teenagers. In J. Rutenfranz, R. Mocellin, & F. Klimt (Eds.), *Children and exercise XII* (pp. 213-225). Champaign, IL: Human Kinetics.

Largo, R. H., Gasser, Th., Prader, A., Stuetzle, W., & Huber, P. J. (1978). Analysis of the adolescent growth spurt using smoothing spline functions. *Annals of Human Biology, 5*, 421-434.

Malina, R. M. (1983). Menarche in athletes: A synthesis and hypothesis. *Annals of Human Biology, 10*, 1-24.

Malina, R. M. (1988). Biological maturity status of young athletes. In R. M. Malina (Ed.), *Young athletes: Biological, psychological, and educational perspectives* (pp. 121-140). Champaign, IL: Human Kinetics.

Malina, R. M. (1989). Growth and maturation: Normal variation and the effects of training. In C. V. Gisolfi & D. R. Lamb (Eds.), *Perspectives in exercise science and sports medicine, Volume 2. Youth, exercise, and sport* (pp. 223-265). Indianapolis, IN: Benchmark Press.

Malina, R. M., & Bouchard, C. (1988). Subcutaneous fat distribution during growth. In C. Bouchard & F. E. Johnston (Eds.), *Fat distribution during growth and later health outcomes* (pp. 63-84). New York: Liss.

Malina, R. M., & Bouchard, C. (1990). *Growth and physical activity* (in press). Champaign, IL: Human Kinetics.

Malina, R. M., Bouchard, C., & Beunen, G. (1988). Human growth: Selected aspects of current research on well-nourished children. *Annual Review of Anthropology, 17*, 187-219.

Malina, R. M., & Roche, A. F. (1983). *Manual of physical status and performance in childhood. Volume 2. Physical performance.* New York: Plenum.

Malina, R. M., Eveld, D. J., & Woynarowska, B. (no date). Growth in body size and aerobic power in active children 11 through 14 years of age. In preparation.

Mirwald, R. L., & Bailey, D. A. (1986). *Maximal aerobic power.* London, Ontario: Sport Dynamics.

Parizkova, J. (1976). Growth and growth velocity of lean body mass and fat in adolescent boys. *Pediatric Research, 10*, 647-650.

Parizkova, J. (1977). *Body fat and physical fitness*. The Hague: Martinus Nijhoff.

Preece, M. A. (1986). Prepubertal and pubertal endocrinology. In F. Falkner & J. M. Tanner (Eds.), *Human Growth. Volume 2. Postnatal growth, neurobiology* (pp. 211-224). New York: Plenum.

Rarick, G. L., & Smoll, F. L. (1967). Stability of growth in strength and motor performance from childhood to adolescence. *Human Biology, 39*, 295-306.

Roche, A. F., & Malina, R. M. (1983). *Manual of physical status and performance in childhood. Volume 1. Physical status*. New York: Plenum.

Roche, A. F., Siervogel, R. M., Chumlea, W. C., Reed, R. B., Valadian, I., Eichorn, D., & McCammon, R. W. (1982). *Serial changes in subcutaneous fat thicknesses of children and adults*. Basel: Karger.

Roede, M. J., & van Wieringen, J. C. (1985). Growth diagrams 1980: Netherlands third nation-wide survey. *Tijdschrift voor Sociale Gezondheidszorg, 63* (supplement).

Shuttleworth, F. K. (1939). The physical and mental growth of girls and boys age six to nineteen in relation to age at maximum growth. *Monographs of the Society for Research in Child Development, 4*, Serial No. 22.

Sprynarova, S., & Parizkova, J. (1977). La stabilite de differences interindividuelles des parametres morphologiques et cardiorespiratoires chez les garcons. In H. Lavalle & R. J. Shephard (Eds.), *Frontiers of activity and child health* (pp. 131-138). Quebec: Pelican.

Tanner, J. M. (1962). *Growth at adolescence*. Oxford: Blackwell Scientific Publications.

Tanner, J. M., & Whitehouse, R. H. (1982). *Atlas of children's growth: Normal variation and growth disorders*. New York: Academic Press.

Tanner, J. M., Hughes, P. C. R., & Whitehouse, R. H. (1981). Radiographically determined widths of bone, muscle and fat in the upper arm and calf from 3-18 years. *Annals of Human Biology, 8*, 495-517.

Wierman, M. E., & Crowley, W. F., Jr. (1986). Neuroendocrine control of the onset of puberty. In F. Falkner & J. M. Tanner (Eds.), *Human growth. Volume 2. Postnatal growth, neurobiology* (pp. 225-241). New York: Plenum.

3. Physiological Processes: What Role Do They Play During the Transition to Adolescence?

Roberta L. Paikoff
Educational Testing Service

Jeanne Brooks-Gunn
Russell Sage Foundation
Educational Testing Service

The transition to adolescence is a unique phase of life in that it involves physical changes within an organism capable of reflecting upon and giving meaning to these changes. Additionally, the physical changes that occur during this transition (unlike those of infancy) are laden with social and cultural meaning concerning the development of an adult body[1] (Brooks-Gunn, Petersen, & Eichorn, 1985; Brooks-Gunn & Warren, 1988). The role of such physical changes in accounting for behavioral change at puberty has recently been the focus of much research (Lerner & Foch, 1987; Gunnar & Collins, 1988; Brooks-Gunn, Petersen, & Eichorn, 1985; Petersen & Taylor, 1980; Adams, Montemayor, & Gullotta, 1989). Investigators have also begun to examine the role that internal physiological processes (or changes in hormone concentration or fluctuation) may play in behavioral transformations during the transition to adolescence. In this chapter, we explore hormonal change during the transition to adolescence as a potential contributor to some of the behavioral change during this age period. This chapter is a bit different from others in this volume, because we know that physiological changes differentiate adolescence from childhood. Thus, our question here becomes whether or not these physiological changes contribute to psychological transformations from childhood to adolescence.

AUTHORS' NOTE: *This chapter was written while the first author was a Postdoctoral Fellow at Educational Testing Service and the second author was a Visiting Scholar at the Russell Sage Foundation. The research support of the National Institutes of Health (NICHD) and the W. T. Grant Foundation is greatly appreciated. We wish to thank Christy Miller Buchanan, Megan R. Gunnar, Raymond Montemayor, Michelle P. Warren, and an anonymous reviewer for their helpful comments, and Rosemary Deibler, Adele Lechowicz, and Rhoda Harrison for their assistance in manuscript preparation.*

Interest in the relation between physiological change and psychological functioning has characterized the field of early adolescent developmental psychology since its inception (A. Freud, 1948; Hall, 1904). From a psychoanalytic perspective, hormonal changes were speculated to cause the libidinal (or sexual instinctual) transformations of puberty and to account for a host of psychological defense mechanisms (A. Freud, 1948) used by young adolescents to combat these overwhelming libidinal drives. Hall (1904) viewed the physical and psychological changes of puberty as inherently stressful and riddled with conflict; he thought of adolescence as a period of "Sturm und Drang", or Storm and Stress. Interest in whether "Storm and Stress" appropriately characterizes young adolescents persists to this day (Holmbeck & Hill, 1988).

Until very recently, however, effects of physiological change upon behavior during the transition to adolescence were studied by examining visible pubertal change rather than endocrinological change. Because the physical changes of puberty require prior endocrine changes, we consider associations between these physical changes and adolescent behavior to be mediated or indirect effects, while associations between endocrinological changes and adolescent behavior would be direct effects. Both types of effects may be examined during adolescence, but it is important to remember that direct physiological effects constituted the earliest theoretical inquiries into adolescent psychology, that these effects are just beginning to be put to empirical test, and that secondary sex characteristics carry social stimulus value along with physiological process changes and thus cannot be considered "pure" physiological effects.

Our plan is as follows: First, we review basic information pertinent to the endocrinological changes of puberty. Then we discuss some of the major methodological issues still being worked out in this area. Our third section focuses on a number of models being used (either explicitly or implicitly) in this area, reviewing for evidence for each model as we go along. Finally, we conclude by discussing the literature as it supports or refutes the proposition that physiological processes play an integral role in behavioral transformations during early adolescence.

ENDOCRINOLOGICAL CHANGES OF PUBERTY

The endocrinological and physical changes associated with puberty have been extensively studied and so are relatively easy to describe. The mechanisms responsible for these changes, however, are not well understood (Katchadourian, 1977; Grumbach & Sizonenko, 1986). Two processes, *adrenarche* and *gonadarche*, result in increased sex steroid secretion in the prepubertal and pubertal periods. *Adrenarche* involves the production of androgens by the adrenal gland, and *gonadarche* involves reactivation of the hypothalamic-pituitary-gonadotropin-gonadal system that has been quiescent since the fetal period and first few months of life. Adrenarche precedes gonadarche by approximately two years, and the two are controlled by different mechanisms and operate independently of one another.

The maturation of the reproductive endocrine system, which normally culminates in production of sex steroids and sperm or ova by fertile adults is regulated at multiple sites: (a) *higher central nervous system:* cerebral cortex and limbic system, complex neurotransmitter systems modulating hypothalamic function; (b) *hypothalamus:* the arcuate nucleus and its transducer neurosecretory neurons produce a gonadotropin releasing hormone (GnRH) in an oscillatory manner; (c) *pituitary gonadotropes:* cellular site of synthesis and storage of luteinizing hormone (LH) and follicle stimulating hormone (FSH) in response to continued stimulation by GnRH; (d) *gonads (ovaries and testes):* both are sites of sex steroid (androgen and estrogen) and gamete (sperm, ova) production; (e) *hypothalamic pituitary corticotrope unit:* produces ACTH and other adrenal stimulating hormones which enhance androgen production by the zona reticularis of the adrenal cortex (Brooks-Gunn & Reiter, 1989; see also Reiter, 1987).

The hypothalamic-pituitary-gonadal system undergoes a period of sex steroid activity during the first few months after birth. The dynamics and functions of this activity are not clear. After this initial period, the system is suppressed to a low level of activity for almost a decade and is reactivated during late childhood (Kaplan, Grumbach, & Aubert, 1976). Once the gonad's dampening effect upon the hypothalamic-pituitary axis is released in middle childhood, increases in the amplitudes and frequency of pulses of luteinizing-hormone releasing hormones (LHRH) and the responsiveness of gonadotropins to LHRH occur. In addition, secretion of FSH and LH increases, with nocturnal rises in the secretion of both in a pulsatile fashion. There is increased responsiveness of the gonads to the pulses of LH and FSH; increases in the secretion of gonadal hormones occur as well (Grumbach & Sizonenko, 1986; for more basic information on the sex steroids and their functions, the reader is referred to Goy & McEwen, 1980, or Katchadourian, 1977).

As in any new area of study, methodological problems and issues abound in the study of hormone behavior links at early adolescence. We will essentially list what we perceive as the major issues affecting interpretation of data in this area (see Buchanan & Eccles, 1989, or Paikoff, Buchanan, & Brooks-Gunn, in press, for a slightly different approach to these issues).

First, there is a problem with study variation—the current studies differ in many respects: age and pubertal range, gender, number of adolescents seen, methods used to collect and analyze pubertal hormones, and measurement of psychological variables. In addition to the problem of comparison across studies, all researchers examining the effects of pubertal hormones on adolescents face common methodological concerns and decisions, such as timing and nature of endocrine assessment, problems of assessment and measurement of female gonadotropins in menstrual young women, the high intercorrelations between hormones, questions of the nature of associations between hormones and secondary sex effects, and bidirectionality of effects. Additionally, certain developmental questions regarding the nature of hormone-behavior relations remain unanswered (e.g., the influence of adrenarche, and pulsatile surges of LH and FSH on behavior).

We suggest that endocrinological change could promote other developmental changes in at least two ways. On the one hand, endocrinological changes could contribute to behavioral transformations from childhood to adolescence through enhancing or serving to clarify interindividual variation on a particular behavior within an adolescent population (a "within groups" change, if you will). Such a contribution might distinguish groups of adolescents in terms of their reactivity to hormones, thus creating more individual variation than was the case prior to adolescence. On the other hand, rises in pubertal hormones could provoke a general developmental change in adolescent behavior, in essence creating new forms of behavior or affecting prevalence rates or manifestation level of certain behaviors in adolescents as distinguished from children (a cross-sectional, or "between groups" change). Hormonal changes thus could effect the level of depression or aggression in all adolescents, so that prevalence rates rise while level of variation stays constant. Finally, endocrinological change could promote both "within group" and "between group" change at early adolescence. While most pubertal research to date has focused on the within-group rather than the between-group question, we will speculate on the possibilities for both types of physiological contributions after reviewing the evidence.

Models for Approaching Physiological-Behavioral Links at Early Adolescence

At least six models may be used to study possible physiological effects upon development during early adolescence (see Figure 3.1). These are models examining:

A. Direct organizational effects, or effects of prenatal or early infancy hormone concentrations on behavioral transformations from childhood to adolescence;

B. Mediated organizational effects whereby hormonal concentrations early in life effect hormonal concentrations or secondary sex characteristics at puberty; in turn effecting behavioral transformations;

C. Direct activational effects with changes in hormonal concentration or fluctuation at puberty affecting adolescent behavior;

D. Mediated pubertal *or* social effects where hormonal effects are mediated through either: (1) social factors, or (2) secondary sex characteristic development;

E. Mediated pubertal *and* social effects where hormone changes are sensitive or reactive to social-environmental changes, and both secondary sex characteristics and these social changes serve as mediators; and

F. Cumulative effects whereby the sheer number of changes during the transition to adolescence contributes to behavioral change.

We now review the data collected using each model.[2]

Direct Organizational Effects Model

As mentioned earlier, investigators positing an organizational effects model suggest that early concentrations of hormones effect brain organization and development, setting in place a trajectory

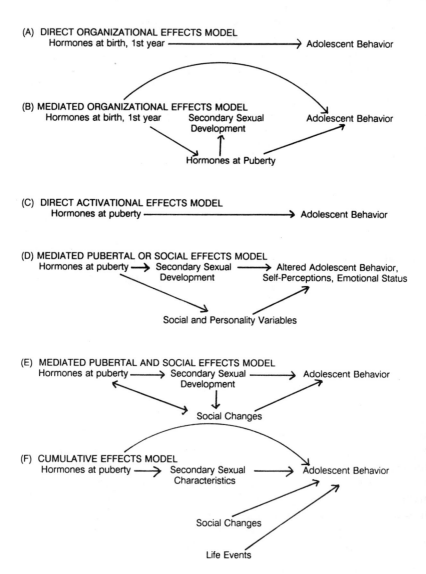

Figure 3.1 Biological Models for Studying Adolescent Development

for behavioral and affective development from adolescence through adulthood. The majority of such studies have involved nonhuman primates (Coe, Hayashi, & Levine, 1988; Goy, 1970). This area will not be reviewed extensively, and interested readers are referred to the Coe, Hayashi, and Levine (1988) paper.

Work on organizational effects of hormones on behavior during the transition to human adolescence could, however, have important implications for the question of distinctiveness of the adolescent life phase. If hormones present early in life (and *not* hormones at puberty) are associated with later behavioral transformations at early adolescence, then early adolescence is not a unique life phase from a physiological-process perspective. Organizational effects, however, may be mediated, as discussed below.

Mediated Organizational Effects Model

This second model examines mediated organizational effects of pubertal hormones upon behavior. Prenatal or early infancy hormone exposure may sensitize the brain to homotypic pubertal hormones, as well as desensitizing the brain to other sex hormones (Reinisch, Gandelman, & Spiegel, 1979). This area will also not be reviewed extensively, as the majority of studies have been conducted with clinical populations, and so have limited implications for the transition to adolescence when puberty proceeds normally.

Direct Activational Effects Model

This model has been the primary model of influence in current research programs that posit direct associations between adolescent physiological processes and other developments during the early adolescent years. Therefore, this constitutes the meatiest section of our review. Results will be discussed separately by the three major domains investigated: (a) aggressive and delinquent behavior; (b) sexual arousal and behavior; and (c) negative affect and mood lability.

Aggressive-Delinquent Behavior

An association between hormonal status, specifically testosterone, and aggressive or delinquent behavior has been hypothesized from early psychoanalytic writing (Deutsch, 1944) into the present day (Inoff-Germain, Arnold, Nottlemann, Susman, Cutler, & Chrousos,

1988; Olweus, Mattsson, Schalling, & Low, 1980; 1988). Reasons include: (a) the large literature on gender differences in the development of aggressive and delinquent behavior (Cantor, 1982; Maccoby & Jacklin, 1980); (b) the purported increases and changes in aggressive behavior from childhood to early adolescence (Cairns, Cairns, Neckerman, Ferguson, & Gariepy, 1989); and (c) the relatively strong associations between androgens and dominance and aggressive behavior in nonhuman primates (Rose, Holaday, & Hernstein, 1971). We might expect, then, that androgens would be associated with aggressive feelings and behavior as well as delinquent behavior in adolescents, and that these links would be stronger for boys than for girls.

The earliest work investigating links between pubertal hormones and adolescent male aggressive behavior is that of Olweus and his colleagues (Olweus et al., 1980, 1988). While no association between testosterone and aggression or antisocial behavior was found, they did report direct testosterone effects on provoked aggressive behavior, as well as indirect effects (via increased impatience and irritability) on aggressive-destructive behavior (Olweus et al., 1980, 1988). Higher levels of circulating testosterone were associated with increases in boys' impatience and irritability, which in turn increased their propensity toward aggressive-destructive behavior. No effects of pubertal status on aggressive behavior or responses to provocation were found.[3] In the NIMH/NIH sample, estradiol levels were negatively and androstenedione levels positively associated with parent reports of aggression in boys (measured by Child Behavior Checklist; Inoff-Germain, 1986). Additionally, lower quantities of testosterone-estradiol binding globulin,[4] and of estradiol as well as higher level of adrenal androgens, especially androstenedione, were related to aggressive attributes in boys (Susman, Inoff-Germain, Nottlemann, Loriaux, Cutler, & Chrousos, 1987). When verbal aggression was coded for a subsample of these adolescents (30 boys and 30 girls) observed interacting with their parents, no hormone-behavior associations for boys were found (Inoff-Germain et al., 1988).

In addition to studies examining aggressive behavior, several studies have examined effects of pubertal hormones on the related (but not equivalent) construct of delinquent behavior. Testosterone has been positively and testosterone-estradiol binding globulin negatively associated with boys' norm-violating behavior, with pubertal status effects mediated by testosterone level (Udry, 1987). Susman et al. (1987) report a strong negative relation between estradiol and delinquent behavior in boys, as well as a positive association between androstenedione and delinquency for boys.[5]

Both DHEA and DHEAS are negatively associated with aggressive behavior in girls (Brooks-Gunn & Warren, 1989; Susman et al., 1987). Androstenedione and estradiol were positively associated with verbal aggression in girls as measured by observer ratings of dominance, defiance, and anger at parents (Inoff-Germain et al., 1988).[6] In our own sample of 103 adolescent girls, increases in aggressive behavior and decreases in impulse control were reported at the time of initial hormonal change (including estradiol, LH, and FSH) between categories[7] 1, 2, and 3, but not thereafter (Warren & Brooks-Gunn, 1989). High progesterone and low testosterone have also been significantly associated with reports of impatience in girls ($p<.05$; Eccles et al., 1988). Pubertal status was neither examined nor controlled for in this last study. Udry and Talbert (1988) also report a positive association between progesterone and aggression in their sample of 78 12- to 16-year-old females. In the three studies looking at pubertal hormones and delinquent behavior in girls, no significant associations have been reported (Paikoff, Brooks-Gunn, & Warren, in press; Susman et al., 1987; Udry, 1987; Udry & Talbert, 1988).

Sexual Behavior

The endocrinological changes that occur at puberty affect fertility and reproductive maturity in both sexes. Do pubertal hormones influence adolescent sexual motivations, behavior, and coital activity directly? Level of "free" (circulating) testosterone has been found to play a role in a variety of sexual behavioral and motivational factors for boys. Free testosterone was a significant predictor for all sexual behaviors (including coital activity) and arousal, with effect sizes in the .30's. Once free testosterone was included in a regression equation, none of the other pubertal hormones assessed nor pubertal status nor age added significantly to predicting sexual behavior (Udry, 1988; Udry, Billy, Morris, Groff, & Raj, 1985). For girls, however, the adrenal androgens (free testosterone, DHEA, DHEAS, and androstenedione) were the most frequent hormone predictors of noncoital sexual behavior and arousal (e.g., masturbation, thinking about sex) and sexual motivation (future intentions). Masturbation but not coital activity was predicted by both pubertal status and pubertal hormone level. Pubertal development (but not pubertal hormone level) was a significant predictor of coital activity in girls, along with a variety of social factors (Udry, 1988; Udry & Billy, 1987).

Negative Affect and Depression

Overall, negative emotional expression appears to increase from childhood to adolescence, especially in clinical populations (Rutter, Graham, Chadwick, & Yule, 1976). Whether or not adolescent depressive affect is qualitatively different from earlier childhood depression or from later adult depression, however, remains a much disputed issue (Buchanan & Eccles, 1989; Kovacs, 1989). This potential rise in depressive affect during the adolescent period is important both in developmental and pragmatic terms (because of its link with suicide, a major cause of death in 13 to 18 year-olds). Hypotheses concerning associations between negative affect and pubertal hormones arise in part due to these behavioral increases, as well as the research literature on menstrual-linked affective changes in adult women (Haemmerlie & Montgomery, 1987; Rossi & Rossi, 1980).

Less clear-cut evidence exists concerning pubertal hormonal associations with negative or depressive affect than in previously discussed behavioral domains. The NIMH/NIH group (Susman et al., 1987) found that higher concentrations of testosterone-estradiol binding globulin and lower concentrations of androstenedione were associated with more positive emotional tone in boys (Susman et al., 1987). For females, however, no significant associations between pubertal hormones and affective states were found (Susman et al., 1987). In our own work, estradiol has been associated with girls' reports of depressive affect (Brooks-Gunn & Warren, 1989; Paikoff, Brooks-Gunn & Warren, in press). An increase in depressive affect occurs between what we have categorized as hormonal levels 1 and 3 but not at level 4 (considered an adult level of estradiol).[7] Using these same categories, hormonal levels are associated with depressive affect a year later (when reported by girls but not by mothers; Paikoff, Brooks-Gunn, & Warren, in press). This finding holds constant when prior depressive affect is entered into our regression models, although prior level of affect accounts for a substantially larger amount of variation in the girls' responses than do hormonal levels. Pubertal status and age were entered into our regression equations with no significant effects.

Mood Lability

Perhaps the most popular belief about early adolescence is that this life phase is characterized by rapid mood swings, or mood lability. Little empirical data exist to substantiate this belief. Rather, the picture that emerges suggests that mood variability itself varies substantially across adolescents, with the majority exhibiting fairly stable and predictable mood changes over time while a minority experience true "storm and stress"—wildly fluctuating, unpredictable mood swings (Csikszentmihalyi & Larson, 1984; Savin-Williams & Demo, 1984). How much of the variation in mood lability can be explained by pubertal hormonal changes?

To date, only the Michigan Early Adolescence Project has directly examined effects of hormonal status on mood shifts at early adolescence in a doctoral thesis as yet unpublished. The effects of hormone concentration and variability upon females' (N = 24) mood intensity (relative to sample) and mood variability was examined for a day, as well as over a month (Buchanan, 1989). High FSH variability was associated with moodiness within a day, $r^2 = .23$ and high FSH concentration was associated with moodiness over a month, $r^2 = .32$. No perceived pubertal status effects were found for total moodiness scores within a day or over a month; however, pubertal status was related to overall mood intensity. This tantalizing finding clearly needs to be replicated.

Mediated Pubertal or Social Effects Model

Mediated biological or social effects of pubertal hormones on behavior encompass our fourth model. This model suggests that the influence of pubertal hormones on adolescent behavior is largely indirect, and mediated through secondary sexual development at puberty (Petersen & Taylor, 1980), or possibly through social or personality factors (Buchanan & Eccles, 1989). Secondary sexual development is thought to signal incipient maturity to the child and her or his social world, and thus to alter the child's self-perceptions, as well as others' perception of the child. An example of this type of mediation is found in our work on delinquent behavior, where initial hormonal effects wash away when pubertal status is entered into regression equations (Paikoff, Brooks-Gunn, & Warren, in press). The literature on psychological effects of physical change at puberty suggests that psychological effects for the most part occur in different behavioral domains than those discussed here. Effects of physical change have been reported in girls' self-definitions and self-concepts (Brooks-Gunn & Warren, 1988) and in their relationships with parents and peers (Hill, 1988; Simmons & Blyth, 1987). Effects of physical change on boys have seldom been studied; however changes in relationships with parents (Steinberg & Hill, 1978), and positive reactions to spermarche (initial ejaculation) have been reported (Gaddis & Brooks-Gunn, 1985).

Social and personality factors (such as temperament) could also influence associations between hormones and behavior during the transition to adolescence. For example, studies of infancy have found associations between physiological and psychological reactivity when cortisol is considered (Gunnar, Mangelsdorf, Larson, & Hertsgaard, 1989). Additionally, culture and ethnicity may be important factors, although these are more likely to influence associations between behavior and secondary sex characteristics (because of variations in the meaning of pubertal events) than hormonal associations. Most research in this area has sampled White, middle-class adolescents, so little information is available to address this intriguing possibility.

Mediated Social and Pubertal Effects

This model suggests that the pubertal and social changes of adolescence may act in concert such that if a social change occurs at a certain point during puberty, it may have a stronger effect on the adolescent than it would either before pubertal changes began or after they are complete. For example, suppose that the hormonal changes of puberty were found to increase excitability or arousability. If a social change (such as a family problem, school transition, or the onset of dating) occurs coincidentally with such a hormonal change, the social change is likely to have a greater effect on the adolescent, because of his or her increased excitability or arousability.

Social changes also may act in concert with the secondary sexual changes of puberty. For example, young adolescent girls with more advanced breast development report having more close friends than girls who have not yet begun to develop (Brooks-Gunn, Samelson, Warren, & Fox, 1986). If later maturation is accompanied by a social change (such as family problems), the prepubertal girl may find herself without a social network to assist her with the change, and depression or social withdrawal may result. This final model projects the most complicated effects of pubertal change upon adolescent behavior and has been least systematically investigated of all the models. In the one study examining such effects (Brooks-Gunn & Warren, 1989), physiological factors (i.e., hormonal levels) accounted for only 4% of the variance in explaining girls' negative affect while social factors accounted for between 8% and 18% of the variance in girls' depressive and aggressive affect, respectively.

Cumulative Effects Model

Cumulative effects models also have been used to examine behavioral change in early adolescence. For example, Simmons and her colleagues (Simmons, Burgeson, Carlton-Ford, & Blyth, 1987) have demonstrated that the simultaneity of life event changes (including pubertal, school, peer, and family changes), rather than any particular change, predicts lowered school achievement and poor social competence in seventh graders. We have reported similar findings for depressive affect in a four-year longitudinal study of girls (Baydar, Brooks-Gunn, & Warren, 1989). This model follows the adult literature, which is replete with examples of the untoward negative effect of the occurrence of (potentially stressful) multiple life events. Young adolescents experience a high number of life events, which seems to contribute to increases in depressive affect at this time. Delayed pubertal development (breast growth in girls) may act as a protective factor in this association (Baydar, Brooks-Gunn, & Warren, 1989).

CONCLUSIONS

It should be clear from this review that the study of association between direct physiological processes and adolescent behavior and affect is just emerging. The "oldest" hormone-behavior study of a nonclinical adolescent sample was published in 1980. Thus, what may be said is limited by the small number of studies and the need for replication.

What conclusions, then, can we finally draw about the impact of physiological processes upon development at early adolescence? Is there enough evidence here to suggest that something unique happens during the pubertal period which affects psychological development? We believe there is (though we certainly invite the readers to draw their own conclusions) and suggest that it is only in combination with the physical and social changes of this life phase that the true distinctiveness of the adolescent period can be viewed.

For male sexual and aggressive behavior, direct associations with pubertal hormones are found (Olweus et al., 1980, 1988; Udry, 1987). For females, the picture is less clear. At the time that estrogen and other hormones (LH and FSH) increase, a small rise in reports of aggressive affect appears in one but not another study (Brooks-Gunn & Warren, 1989; Susman et al., 1987). Both studies, however, find a negative association between DHEA and self-reported aggressive feelings and behavior. Females' noncoital sexual behavior and sexual motivations appear to be associated with pubertal hormone levels, but social and pubertal developmental factors also play a role (Udry, 1988). As in human adult models of aggression (Mazur, 1983) and sexual behavior (Bancroft & Shakkebak, 1978), testosterone and the adrenal androgens appear to be implicated most frequently in these associations. Because these associations are reported concurrently, causality cannot be determined; however, effects suggest that the hormonal associations described are activational, not organizational in nature. Thus, evidence supports the direct activational model of biological influence on interindividual variation in male aggressive and sexual behavior, although no good tests of organizational models have been made.

For both males and females, contextual factors may play a role in the interplay between hormones and behavior at early adolescence. For example, Olweus et al. (1988) find that hormonal factors contribute to aggressive behavior under provoking circumstances. Thus, the interplay between these factors could be affected by individual variation in provoking circumstances, or in perception of these circumstances. Such contextually based models may also be important in considering other behavioral domains (see Buchanan & Eccles, 1989).

Both sexual and aggressive behavior increase dramatically in males during the early adolescent period. The nature and meaning (and certainly the potential consequences) of sexual behavior are speculated to change during early adolescence (Paikoff & Brooks-Gunn, in press), while this is not necessarily the case for aggression. Although no cross-sectional data are available to answer this question, we suspect that increases in testosterone contribute to the increase in aggressive and sexual behavior seen in some adolescent males, as well as being related to individual variation in aggressive and sexual behavior during adolescence.

In terms of depressive affect, no evidence exists for an association between hormonal status and depressive affect in males. Data for females are in conflict although the association found in our data has not been tested in the NIMH/NIH sample. Data do, however, provide limited support for the activational model of pubertal hormonal influence upon depressive affect in young adolescents (the possibility of bidirectionality has not been tested). As in other domains, we speculate that increased pubertal hormone concentration may be related to a general increase in depressive affect at early adolescence, as well as to individual variation in depressive affect. The specific nature of the processes of influence upon these between-groups differences, however, is even less clear than those discussed for within-groups differences, because of the continued controversy over the association of depressive affect with age (Buchanan & Eccles, 1989).

In a few studies of adult women, high levels of estrogens have been associated with positive affect, or feelings of well-being. Our findings suggest that initial rises of estradiol, LH, and FSH in early puberty may have the opposite effect. These findings are not incompatible with the adult literature if one considers them an "adjustment effect" (Buchanan & Eccles, 1989). In other words, the early pubertal surge in hormones may necessitate psychological as well as physical adaptation. If this is true, then our effect should not persist; we are in the process of instituting new longitudinal analyses to examine this issue.

In the area of mood lability and variability, no conclusive evidence in support of pubertal hormone effects is found, and no adult comparison data are available. In one study, mood intensity was associated primarily with perceived physical status, but mood variability was associated with hormonal status (Buchanan, 1989).

Current research suggests that physiological processes during the early adolescence life phase contribute to interindividual variation in aggressive affect and sexual behavior and arousal (with findings stronger for boys than for girls), and possibly in the areas of depressive affect and mood lability as well. While research has not directly assessed the contribution of physiological processes to overall increases in sexual behavior, aggressive or depressive affect and behavior, the mere rise in prevalence of such behavior during the early adolescent years suggests to us that processes of physiological change may be implicated. The precise nature of such mechanisms awaits

future investigation. Additionally, social factors appear to be impli
cated in many hormone-behavior associations during the transition
to adolescence and in some cases, account for more variance than do
physiological processes (Brooks-Gunn & Warren, 1989). Thus, we may
expect direct physiological effects to be small. When the effects of both
direct and indirect physiological processes are considered in context
however, the consistency of such effects and their pervasiveness lends
credibility to the notion that physiological change does in fact con
tribute to the distinctiveness of the adolescent life phase, as well as to
the appropriateness of the characterization of early adolescence as a
time of change. Research testing some of the more ambitious cumula
tive, interactive, and bidirectional ideas presented in this chapter will
be necessary in order to determine the precise nature of physiological
social, or contextual contributions during the transition to adoles
cence, as well as possible mediational relations between these process
es. As the research projects mentioned in this chapter all continue to
flourish, we look forward to the next generation of findings.

NOTES

1. Pregnancy would be another such change, although it is not as universal nor as
time-linked to a developmental phase as is early adolescence.
2. We acknowledge that we have been guided in our pairing of data to model by our
interpretations of the author's intentions, via the data that is present as well as that
which is absent. Other models, and other pairings of the data presented here to these
models, could certainly have been possible.
3. It should be noted, however, that the boys studied ranged in age from 15 to 17,
and tended to fall in the late pubertal status categories; 95% in Tanner 4 and 5. Therefore
the full range of pubertal status effects could not be examined.
4. Since testosterone-estradiol binding reduces the amount of free testerone in the
bloodstream by binding it to protein molecules, it would be expected to be associated
negatively with aggressive behavior.
5. As all studies report data from "normal" samples, the term *delinquent behavior*
must be interpreted cautiously.
6. The possibility of outlier effects was examined and ruled out in these analyses
(Inoff-Germain, 1989, personal communication); additionally, no effects of pubertal
status were reported.
7. The categories used are as follows:

Level	Estradiol Amount	Effect
1	0 - 25.00 pg/ml	-minimal
2	25.01 - 50.00 pg/ml	-early secondary sexual development; vaginal development
3	50.00 - 75.00 pg/ml	-mid to late puberty; endometrial growth and breast development
4	75.01 pg/ml - high value	-mature, associated with female cyclicity

REFERENCES

Adams, G. R., Montemayor, R., & Gullotta, T. R. (1989). *Advances in adolescent development, Volume 1.* Beverly Hills, CA: Sage.

Bancroft, J., & Shakkebak, N. (1978). Androgens and human sexual behavior. In *Ciba Foundation Symposium 62 (new series),* pp. 209-226. Amsterdam: Excerpta Medica.

Baydar, N., Brooks-Gunn, J., & Warren, M. P. (1989). *Determinants of depressive symptoms in adolescent girls: A four-year longitudinal study.* Unpublished manuscript, Educational Testing Service, Princeton, New Jersey.

Brooks-Gunn, J., Petersen, A. C., & Eichorn, D. (1985). The study of maturational timing effects in adolescence. *Journal of Youth and Adolescence, 14*(3), 149-161.

Brooks-Gunn, J., & Reiter, E. O. (1989). The role of pubertal processes in the early adolescent transition. In S. Feldman, & G. Elliot (Eds.), *At the threshold: The developing adolescent.* Cambridge: Harvard University Press.

Brooks-Gunn, J., Samelson, M., Warren, M. P., & Fox, R. (1986). Physical similarity of and disclosure of menarcheal status to friends: Effects of age and pubertal status. *Journal of Early Adolescence, 6*(1). 3-14.

Brooks-Gunn, J., & Warren, M. P. (1988). The psychological significance of secondary sexual characteristics in 9- to 11-year-old girls. *Child Development, 59,* 161-169.

Brooks-Gunn, J., & Warren, M. P. (1989). Biological contributions to affective expression in young adolescent girls. *Child Development, 60,* 372-385.

Buchanan, C. M. (1989). *Hormone concentrations and variability: Associations with self-reported moods and energy in early adolescent girls.* Paper presented at the biennial meetings of the Society for Research in Child Development, Kansas City, MO.

Buchanan, C. M. & Eccles, J. S. (1989). Evidence for activational effects of hormones on moods and behavior at adolescence. University of Michigan, unpublished manuscript.

Cairns, R. B., Cairns, B. D., Neckerman, H. J., Ferguson, L. L., & Gariepy, J. L. (1989). Growth and Aggression: I. Childhood to Early Adolescence. *Developmental Psychology, 25*(2), 320-330.

Cantor, R. J. (1982). *Family Correlates of male and female delinquency (Revised).* Project report of the Institute of Behavioral Science, Boulder, Colorado.

Coe, C. L., Hayashi, K. T., & Levine, S. (1988). Hormones and behavior at puberty. Activation or concatenation? In M. Gunnar & W. A. Collins (Ed.), *Minnesota Symposia on Child Development, vol. 21* (pp. 17-41). Hillsdale, NJ: Erlbaum.

Csikszentmihalyi, M., & Larson, R. (1984). *Being adolescent: Conflict and growth in the teenage years.* New York: Basic Books.

Deutsch, H. (1944). *The psychology of women, Vol. 1.* New York: Grune & Stratton.

Eccles, J. S., Miller, C., Tucker, M. L., Becker, J., Schramm, W., Midgley, R., Holmes, W., Pasch, L. & Miller, M. (1988, March). *Hormones and affect at early adolescence.* Paper presented at the Biannual Meeting of the Society for Research on Adolescence, Alexandria, VA.

Freud, A. (1948). *The ego and the mechanisms of defense.* New York: International Universities Press.

Gaddis, A., & Brooks-Gunn, J. (1985). The male experience of pubertal change. *Journal of Youth and Adolescence, 14*(1), 61-69.

Goy, R. W. (1970). Experimental control of psychosexuality. In G. W. Harris, & R. G. Edwards (Eds.), *A discussion on the determination of sex* (pp. 149-162). London: Philosophical Transactions of the Royal Society.

Goy, R. W., & McEwen, B. S. (1980). *Sexual differentiation of the brain.* Boston: MIT Press.

Grumbach, M. M., & Sizonenko, P. C. (Eds.), (1986). *Control of the onset of puberty II.* New York: Academic Press.

Gunnar, M. R. & Collins, W. A. (Eds.). (1988). *Development during the transition to adolescence: Minnesota symposia on child psychology Vol. 21.* Hillsdale, NJ: Erlbaum.

Gunnar, M. R., Mangelsdorf, S. C., Larson, M., & Hertsgaard, L. (1989). Attachment, temperament, and adrenocortical activity in infancy: A study of psychoendocrine regulation. *Developmental Psychology, 25*(3), 355-363.

Haemmerlie, F. M., & Montgomery, R. L. (1987). Psychological state and menstrual cycle. *Journal of Social Behavior and Personality, 2*(2), 233-242.

Hall, G. R. (1904). *Adolescence: Its psychology and its relations to psychology, anthropology, sociology, sex, crime, religion and education.* Englewood Cliffs, NJ: Prentice-Hall.

Hill, J. P. (1988). Adapting to menarche: Familial Control and Conflict. In M. R. Gunnar & W. A. Collins (Eds.), *Development during the transition to adolescence.* Vol. 21 (pp. 43-77). Hillsdale, NJ: Erlbaum.

Holmbeck, G. N., & Hill, J. P. (1988). Storm and stress beliefs about adolescence: Prevalence, self-reported antecedents, and effects of an undergraduate course. *Journal of Youth and Adolescence, 17*(4), 285-306.

Inoff-Germain, G. (1989). Personal communication.

Inoff-Germain, G. (1986, March). *Hormones and aggression in early adolescence.* Paper presented at the first biennial meeting of the Society for Research on Adolescence, Madison, Wisconsin.

Inoff-Germain, G., Arnold, G. S., Nottlemann, E. D., Susman, E. J., Cutler, G. B., & Chrousos, G. P. (1988). Relations between hormone levels and observational measures of aggressive behavior of young adolescents in family interactions. *Developmental Psychology, 24*(1), 129-139.

Kaplan, S. L., Grumbach, M. M., & Aubert, M. L. (1976). The ontogenesis of pituitary hormones and hypothalamic factors in the human fetus: Maturation of the central nervous system regulation of anterior pituitary function. *Rec Prog Horm Res, 32,* 161-243.

Katchadourian, H. (1977). *The biology of adolescence.* San Francisco, CA: W. H. Freeman.

Kovacs, M. (1989). Affective disorders in children and adolescents. *American Psychologist, 44*(2), 209-215.

Lerner, R. M., & Foch, T. T. (1987). *Biological psychosocial interactions in early adolescence.* Hillsdale, NJ: LEA.

Maccoby, E. E. & Jacklin, C. N. (1980). Sex differences in aggression: A rejoinder and reprise. *Child Development, 51,* 961-980.

Mazur, A. (1983). Hormones, aggression, and dominance in humans. In B. Svare (Ed.), *Hormones and aggressive behavior.* New York: Plenum Press.

Olweus, D., Mattsson, A., Schalling, D., & Low, H. (1980). Testosterone, aggression, physical and personality dimensions in normal adolescent males. *Psychosomatic Medicine, 42*(2), 153-169.

Olweus, D., Mattsson, A., Schalling, D., & Low, H. (1988). Circulating testosterone levels and aggression in adolescent males: A causal analysis. *Psychosomatic Medicine, 50.* 261-272.

Paikoff, R. L., & Brooks-Gunn, J.(in press). Taking fewer chances: Teenage pregnancy prevention programs. *American Psychologist.*

Paikoff, R. L., Brooks-Gunn, J., & Warren, M. P. (in press). Effects of girls' hormonal status on affective expression over the course of one year. *Journal of Youth and Adolescence.*

Paikoff, R. L., Buchanan, C. M., & Brooks-Gunn, J. (in press). Methodological issues in the study of hormone-behavior links at puberty. R. M. Lener, A. C. Peterson, & J. Brooks-Gunn, (Eds.), *The encyclopedia of adolescence.* New York: Garland.

Petersen, A. C., & Taylor, B. (1980). The biological approach to adolescence: Biological change and psychological adaptation. In J. Adelson (Ed.), *Handbook of Adolescent Psychology,* (pp. 117-155). New York: Wiley.

Reinisch, J. M., Gandelman, R., & Spiegel, F. S. (1979). Prenatal influences on cognitive abilities: Data from experimental animals and human genetic and endocrine syndromes. In M. A. Wittig, & A. C. Peterson (Eds.), *Sex-related differences in cognitive functioning* (pp. 215-239). New York: Academic Press.

Reiter, E. O. (1987). Neuroendocrine control processes. *Journal of Adolescent Health Care,* 8(6), 479-491.

Rose, R. M., Holaday, J. W., and Bernstein, I. S. (1971). Plasma testosterone, dominance rank, and aggressive behavior in male rhesus monkeys. *Nature, 231,* 366-368.

Rossi, A., & Rossi, P. (1980). Body time and social time: Mood patterns by menstrual cycle phase and day of week. In J. Parsons (Ed.), *The psychobiology of sex differences and sex roles* (pp. 269-304). New York: McGraw-Hill.

Rutter, M., Graham, P., Chadwick, O. F., & Yule, W. (1976). Adolescent turmoil: Fact or fiction. *Journal of Child Psychology and Psychiatry, 17,* 35-56.

Savin-Williams, R., & Demo, D. H. (1984). Developmental change and stability in adolescent self-concept. *Developmental Psychology, 20(6) 1100-1110.*

Simmons, R. G., and Blyth, D. A. (1987). *Moving into adolescence: The impact of pubertal change and school context.* New York: Adline De Gruyter.

Simmons, R. G., Burgeson, R., Carlton-Ford, S., & Blyth, D. (1987). The impact of cumulative change in early adolescence. *Child Development, 58(5),* 1220-1234.

Steinberg, L. D. & Hill, J. P. (1978). Patterns of family interaction as a function of age, the onset of puberty, and formal thinking. *Developmental Psychology, 14,* 683-684.

Susman, E. J., Inoff-Germain, G., Nottlemann, E. D., Loriaux, D. L., Cutler, G. B., & Chrousos, G. P. (1987). Hormones, emotional dispositions, and aggressive attributes in young adolescents. *Child Development, 58(4),* 1114-1134.

Udry, J. R. (1987). *Biosocial models of adolescent problem behaviors.* Unpublished manuscript.

Udry, J. R. (1988). Biological predispositions and social control in adolescent sexual behaviors. *American Sociological Review, 53,* 709-722.

Udry, J. R., & Billy, J. O. G. (1987). Initiation of coitus in early adolescence. *American Sociological Review, 52,* 841-855.

Udry, J. R., & Billy, J. O. G., Morris, N. M., Groff, T. R., & Raj, M. H. (1985). Serum androgenic hormones motivate sexual behavior in adolescent boys. *Fertility and Sterility, 43(1),* 90-94.

Udry, J. R., & Talbert, L. M. (1988). Sex hormone effects on personality at puberty. *Journal of Personality and Social Psychology, 54(2),* 291-295.

Warren, M. P., & Brooks-Gunn, J. (1989). Mood and behavior at adolescence: Evidence for hormonal factors. *Journal of Clinical Endocrinology and Metabolism, 69 (1),* 77-83.

PART II

EXAMINING DEVELOPMENT IN SOCIAL CONTEXT

4. Parent-Child Relationships in the Transition to Adolescence: Continuity and Change in Interaction, Affect, and Cognition

W. Andrew Collins
Institute of Childhood Development,
University of Minnesota

Changes in parent-child relationships in the transition from childhood to adolescence are a key instance of a central problem in developmental psychology; namely, the nature of the linkage between developmental changes in individuals and changes in the interpersonal relationships of which they are a part. Although this linkage could be examined at several periods of especially marked growth and shifts in social contexts (e.g., in the second year of life; at the time of entry into school), the maturational changes and age-graded social patterns at the beginning of the second decade of life provide an opportunity to examine relationships in connection with especially frequent, salient, and multiply determined growth patterns. The focus of this chapter is the nature and extent of changes in parent-child relationships during the transition from childhood to adolescence and some initial steps toward understanding the processes by which these changes occur.

Since the mid-1970s, a major shift has occurred in the premises of research in this area, and with it the nature of the family context of development during the second decade of life has come to be viewed in a new way. For much of its history, research on adolescents has emphasized the disruptive, disjunctive effect of the developmental changes of adolescence on attachment to parents. Influenced both by popular impressions and by psychological theories, particularly those influenced by psychoanalytic formulations (e.g., Blos, 1979; A. Freud, 1958, 1969), researchers focused primarily on the extent of generational disparity in values, declining parental influence, and debilitating conflicts. Research findings, however, have generally indicated a more multifaceted view of changes experienced by families during the transition to adolescence. Currently, two general premises underlie research in this area:

First, changes are now viewed as part of a process of adaptation, through which families adjust to the changing characteristics of one of its members. Terms such as *transformation* and *realignment* are used to refer to this process by which close, warm relationships are maintained, at the same time that modes of interaction and patterns of influence are gradually adjusted to the changing knowledge, skills, and predilections of adolescent offspring. Although these changes may be accompanied by dissension and decreased interdependency in the interactions between parents and children, such perturbations are hypothesized to be temporary and relatively benign in the perspective of the long-term attachments of parents and offspring to each other (for reviews, see Hill, 1987; Montemayor, 1983; Rutter, 1980; Steinberg, in press). For the majority of families, warm and pleasant relationships in which parents continue to influence their children's development appear to be the norm (e.g., Kandel & Lesser, 1972; Offer, Ostrov, & Howard, 1981; Rutter, Graham, Chadwick, & Yule, 1976). Of the families that do encounter difficulties during this period, many appear to have had a history of problems prior to their offspring's entry into adolescence (Montemayor, 1983; Offer, 1969; Offer et al., 1981; Rutter et al., 1976). Thus, changes in relationships should be examined in conjunction with similarities from one age period to another, in order to understand the nature and course of adaptations as children move into adolescence (Collins, 1988).

Second, the changes in family relationships are considered to have functional significance for the development of adolescents. Although there is presently no direct evidence on this point, the parallels between studies of the correlates of parent-child relations in adolescence and those in other periods of life are suggestive. For example, family interaction patterns that foster both individuation and connectedness in relationships have been found to be associated with adolescents' status on measures of identity exploration, role-taking skills, and ego development (e.g., Grotevant & Cooper, 1985, 1986; Hauser, Powers, Noam, Jacobson, Weiss, & Follansbee, 1984). To date, there has been no temporal dimension or tie to developmental change in these studies, although these findings are conceptually related to the linkage between authoritative rearing patterns and prosocial competence in early and middle childhood (e.g., Baumrind, 1968, 1973) and to the functional role of secure attachment in longitudinal studies covering the first five years of life (see review by Waters, Hay, & Richters, 1986). A significant question is: What *processes* account for transformations in relationships during ontogenetic change so as to sustain the functional impact of parents on individual development?

In this chapter, these two premises serve as a point of departure for examining current research on continuity and change in parent-child relationships during the first half of the second decade of life (roughly ages 10 to 15). The chapter is divided into three main sections. First, the major findings regarding age differences and age-related changes in parent-child relationships associated with the transition to adolescence are reviewed. The focus of the review will be the characteristic patterns of relations between parents and their offspring, rather than the socializing influences and effects of parents on adolescents. Second, one possible process by which normative changes in parent-child relationships may occur during this period is considered. Finally, initial studies in a program of research on processes of change in parent-child relationships during the transition to adolescence are described.

RELATIONSHIPS BETWEEN ADOLESCENTS AND PARENTS

A useful framework for delineating dimensions of parent-child relationships comes from recent formulations in both social and developmental psychology regarding the nature of close relationships (e.g., Hinde, 1979; Hinde & Stevenson-Hinde, 1987; Kelley, Berscheid, Christensen, Harvey, Huston, Levinger, McClintock, Peplau, & Peterson, 1983). These proposals are based on a hierarchical view in which group (e.g., family) relationships are comprised of interconnected dyadic relationships (i.e., mother-child, father-child, mother-father, etc.), each of which in turn is made up of specific exchanges with characteristic patterning. In general, descriptions of these exchanges include information about *interactions, affect,* and *perceptions and cognitions* pertaining to the relationship and the individuals who comprise it. In this section, these dimensions will serve as organizing rubrics for research findings on parent-child relationships in the transition to adolescence. Because relatively little longitudinal data exists, the findings are drawn from (1) comparisons of groups of different ages in middle childhood and adolescence or (2) comparisons of individuals of the same age or grade in school who differ in pubertal statuses.

CHANGES IN INTERACTIONS

The frequency of interaction between adolescents and their parents is lower in adolescence than in earlier life periods (Hill & Stafford, 1980) and further declines occur between early (grades 6-7) and middle (grades 8-12) adolescence (Montemayor & Brownlee, 1987). Perceived engagement in family activities appears to vary with pubertal status. In studies of seventh-grade girls (Hill, Holmbeck, Marlow, Green, & Lynch, 1985a), parents reported lower involvement by daughters who had begun to menstruate within the past six months, compared to daughters who were premenarcheal, and by daughters who had been menstruating for more than a year (early-maturing girls). In a parallel study with seventh-grade boys (Hill, Holmbeck, Marlow, Green, & Lynch, 1985b), mothers perceived the lowest levels of engagement for sons who were at the apex of pubertal change. Despite these differences in engagement, there are clear similarities in how parents and children spend their time together in the two age periods. In childhood, most joint time is spent in caretaking activities; in adolescence, most parent-child time occurs in the context of family work activities. In both age periods, more father-child time than mother-child time involves play and recreation (Montemayor & Brownlee, 1987).

The most extensive data on parent-child interactions pertain to modes and content of exchanges. As a common instance, the incidence of contentious exchanges increases and the topics of these exchanges are different in adolescence than in the preadolescent years (Carlton-Ford & Collins, 1988; Montemayor, 1983). Most disagreements between parents and adolescents occur in connection with everyday matters (e.g., performance of chores, appropriate dress), although in later adolescence there are relatively fewer "daily hassles" and more instances of conflicts about dating and alcohol use (Carlton-Ford & Collins, 1988). In general, contentiousness between adolescents and their mothers appears to be greatest at or near the time of pronounced physical change (e.g., menarche for girls, or the period of most rapid and extensive maturation for boys) (Hill, Holmbeck, Marlow, Green, & Lynch, 1985a,b; Montemayor & Hanson, 1985; Steinberg, 1987, 1988).

Degree of reciprocity and mutuality in interactions changes as a function of maturation during middle childhood and adolescence (Youniss & Smollar, 1985). Recent studies using spatial placement of figures representing different family members (e.g., Feldman & Gehring, 1988; Gehring & Feldman, 1988; Pipp, Shaver, Jennings, Lamborn, & Fischer, 1985) revealed lower perceptions of relative power in adolescence than in earlier life periods. Seventh-grade girls' self-reports of their own influence in interactions were found to be a function of pubertal status, although seventh-grade boys' perceptions were not (Hill et al., 1985a,b). In observational research (Hill, 1988; Steinberg, 1981; Steinberg & Hill, 1978), responses to being interrupted during problem-solving discussions also varied by pubertal status. When interrupted by mothers, both sons and daughters reciprocated with increased interruptions of mothers' statements; but when interrupted by fathers, sons reacted by yielding, daughters by a "passive assertiveness" in which they neither yielded to fathers nor increased their interruptions of fathers. Thus, the degree to which parents dominate discussions may change as children mature physically.

CHANGES IN AFFECTIVE EXPRESSION AND EXPERIENCE

That feelings between parents and children remain generally positive in adolescence has been persistently documented in studies over four decades (see reviews by Hill, 1987, Steinberg, in press). At the same time, variations in pubertal status have been associated with variability in emotional expression and experience between parents and adolescents. Papini and Datan (1983) found that families whose adolescent offspring were in the midst of pubertal changes showed a higher incidence of emotional expression than did pre- or postpubertal families. The incidence of positive emotional expressions appears to be lower the nearer adolescents are to the apex of pubertal maturation, although there is no evidence that negative expressions increase. Adolescents (in this case, seventh-grade girls) also report varying feelings of acceptance in relationships with both mothers and fathers as a function of menarcheal status. Daughters who had experienced menarche within the previous six months reported lower acceptance compared to those who were premenarcheal. Perceived acceptance was significantly higher in mother-daughter relationships for girls who had experienced menarche 6-12 months before, but not for those who had been menstruating for more than one year (Hill, 1988; Hill et al., 1985a). Whether pubertal changes are the only factors in these perceptions is not clear. The finding that adolescents' perceptions of acceptance by parents declined monotonically as a function of age between middle childhood and adolescence (Armentrout & Burger, 1972; Johnson, 1987) implies that a variety of factors associated with the transition to adolescence should be considered as potential determinants of affective change.

Feelings about relationships and relationship partners also fluctuate with pubertal status and with age (Feldman & Gehring, 1988; Hill, 1988; Papini & Sebby, 1987; Steinberg, 1981, 1988). Steinberg (1988) found that parents' reports of closeness with their adolescent offspring were inversely associated with pubertal maturation. The deleterious effects of pubertal onset on perceived closeness may be especially pronounced for daughters (Hill, 1988; Steinberg, 1988), although correlations between puberty and closeness appear to be more transitory for mothers and daughters than for fathers and daughters (Hill, 1988). Cross-sectional age comparisons showed lower perceived cohesion between 18-year-olds and their parents than between 15-year-olds and their parents; there was little difference between the perceptions of 12- and 15-year-olds, although these are ages at which adolescents in the United States undergo marked pubertal changes. Findings of emotional perturbations are consistent with Steinberg's (1988, 1989) hypothesis of increased distance between parents and children at puberty, but it is unclear whether it is pubertal maturation or other aspects of social and behavioral changes that precipitates emotional distancing in adolescence.

CHANGES IN PERCEPTION AND COGNITION

A final dimension of relationships concerns cognitions with regard to each other's traits, perspectives, and respective roles and the degree of congruency or discrepancy among these cognitions (Hinde, 1979, pp. 119-130). General incongruency between parents' and adolescents' actual and presumed views of each other, their relationships, and family functioning has been widely documented (e.g., Alessandri & Wozniak, 1987; Hess & Goldblatt, 1957; Olson, McCubbin, Barnes, Larsen, Muxen, and Wilson, 1983; Thurnher, Spence, & Lowenthal, 1974). Age-related patterns of discrepancy between parents' and children's perceptions vary, depending on the content of perceptions in question. Alessandri & Wozniak (1987) found that middle adolescents (age 15 to 16) perceived their parents' beliefs about them more accurately than preadolescents (age 10 to 11) did. Early adolescents were not included in this study. By contrast, in a study of parents' and adolescents' concepts regarding jurisdiction over adolescents' behavior, Smetana (1988) found an increase across ages 10 to 18 in the tendency to view issues with moral and conventional ramifications as under personal jurisdiction. In short, the limited research to date implies that, in different aspects of their relationships, both the direction and the degree of cognitive and perceptual discrepancies between parents and children may be altered in the transition to adolescence.

SUMMARY

Family relationships remain a primary context for development well into the adolescent years, and adolescents typically remain positive toward their parents and warmly engaged with their families. At the same time, changes occur in modes or styles of interaction. These changes entail possibly transitory increases in contentiousness and likelihood of incongruent perceptions on issues of common concern, as well as decreases in adolescents' perceptions of acceptance and parents' perceptions of their engagement in family activities and in expressions of positive affect and perceived closeness and cohesion. Both age and pubertal status have been associated with these changes, although neither the relative contributions of each nor the interplay between them has been adequately addressed in previous studies. Neither have apparent gender differences in either parent or offspring generations been systematically examined. Nevertheless, the evidence of both continuity and change in research findings implies that family relationships undergo an adaptation or *transformation*, rather than the disjunction that is often implied by stereotypes of the transition to adolescence. A pressing need is a better understanding of the nature and determinants of change processes in the relationships between parents and children during this period.

CHANGE PROCESSES IN PARENT-ADOLESCENT RELATIONSHIPS

The remaining sections of the chapter are focused on some processes that might account for change in parent-adolescent relationships. First one view of change processes, drawn from the close relationships perspective is outlined. This view emphasizes the role of age-related changes in cognitions and perceptions in mediating changes in the interactional and affective components of relationships. Second, a program of research designed to examine some hypotheses derived from this view is described.

ADAPTATION TO DEVELOPMENTAL CHANGE: THE ROLE OF EXPECTANCIES

The basic premise of the analysis of close relationships proposed by Kelley et al. (1983) is that such relationships are comprised of highly interdependent action sequences. In the case of parents and children, these interdependencies are natural products of their shared histories and complementary roles in earlier life periods. From this premise, several corollaries can be drawn concerning parent-child relationships in the transition to adolescence. First, the interdependencies of parent-child relationships form the basis for *expectancies* that affect the perception and interpretation of other persons' behavior and, therefore, guide their actions and reactions toward one another. Second, the transition to adolescence is a time when violations of these expectancies are especially likely to occur, (1) because multiple, rapid changes in the child make past behavior an unreliable basis for predicting actions and responses and (2) because these changes elicit new expectancies that may not yet be appropriate. Third, consistent with the view of several researchers in this area (e.g., Steinberg & Silverberg, 1986), it is assumed that these violations of expectancies serve as an impetus toward new expectancies that are appropriate for interactions between parents and adolescents. More specifically, discrepancies between parents' expectancies and their perceptions of their offspring's behavior and those between adolescents' expectancies and perceptions of parental behavior are assumed to contribute to a *bilateral realignment* of expectancies.

Expectancy is not a new construct, but serves as a general label for a category of influential ideas concerning the nature and organization of knowledge about common experiences. For example, constructs such as scripts, prototypes, schemas, behavioral norms, and rules are categories of representations (Markus & Zajonc, 1984) that are relevant to the expectancies that underlie interactions between parents and children. In the approach described here, perceptions and expectancies of others' behavior are viewed as significant mechanisms whereby multiple changes—biological, social, emotional, and cognitive—affect parent-child relationships.

RESEARCH ON EXPECTANCIES AND RELATED PROCESSES

An initial question in understanding the role of expectancies in parent-adolescent relationships is whether and in what ways the perceptions of each other held by parents and their offspring differ across age groups during the transition to adolescence. A second question is whether perceptions deviate from *expected* patterns of behavior to a greater extent at some points in this developmental transition than others. Finally, it is interesting to ask whether and in what ways discrepancies between expectancies and perceptions of actual behavior are linked to the affective and interactive dimensions of the relationships between parents and adolescents during this period. In the research program described below, cross-sectional studies have been conducted to examine discrepancies between perceptions and expectancies held by parents and children at different ages during the transition to adolescence.

Adolescents and Parents' Perceptions Regarding the Other's Behavior

The first step is to ask whether, within the relatively short period encompassing the transition to adolescence, children and adolescents of different ages and parents whose offspring are different ages perceive each others' behavior in distinctive ways.

Adolescents' Perceptions of Parents' Behavior. Johnson and Collins (1988) recently addressed this question in a sample of 385 subjects in grades 5, 8, and 11 (ages 11, 14, and 17) in a middle-class community in the Midwest. In this sample more than 95% of the adolescents were Caucasian and 81% came from families in which the parents were the original marriage partners. The sample was limited in this way to provide a relatively restricted set of social and cultural conditions under which the patterns of expectancies and correlates of parent-child relationships in different age groups could be studied.

The measure of perceptions of parent behavior was the Child's Report of Parent Behavior (Schaefer, 1965). This inventory required children and adolescents to respond to 56 items about both mothers' and fathers' childrearing practices, affect, and typical responses to offspring. Factor analyses of responses, using a principal-factors approach with varimax rotation, yielded essentially the same as factors that have emerged in studies using the Schaefer measure with larger numbers of items: *Acceptance* (e.g., "Always listens to my ideas and opinions," "Often speaks of the good things I do"); *Psychological Autonomy* (versus Psychological Control) (e.g., "Speaks to me in a cold, matter-of-fact voice when I offend her/him"; "Almost always wants to know who phoned me or wrote to me and what they said"); *Firm Discipline* (e.g., "Does not insist I obey if I complain or protest"; "Doesn't tell me what time to be home when I go out"). To calculate perception scores for each subject for each of the three factors, responses to the items were keyed in a positive direction, and mean scores for each factor were taken. Analyses of variance were computed in which grade level and sex were between-subject factors and sex of parent was a within-subject factor.

Comparing across three age groups that mark roughly the beginning, middle, and end of the transition to adolescence, there was considerable similarity in the degree of positive affect shown toward parents and in perceptions of parents' attempts to control behavior. Group means for perceptions of parents consistently fell above the midpoints on all three scales, perhaps reflecting the homogeneous and relatively affluent sample. These findings thus complement the results of previous studies showing that adolescents generally feel positively toward parents (see review by Hill, 1987) by indicating that such affectively positive perceptions occur consistently across several age levels during the transition from middle childhood to adolescence. Our subjects also perceived their parents to exercise roughly the same degree of psychological control over them and to impose firm discipline to about the same extent across the three age groups.

At the same time, preadolescents and adolescents at each successive grade level were less likely to perceive their parents as accepting of their behaviors and as warmly engaged with them emotionally. These group differences, together with similarities across age in general positivity of perception of parents and in perceptions of psychological autonomy and firmness, imply a differentiation in adolescents' perceptions that is consistent with both continuity and change in relationships with parents. An additional and somewhat unexpected differentiation is that, regardless of age and gender, these subjects perceived their mothers to be more accepting toward them than they perceived their fathers to be. In this respect, our findings differ from research findings on mother-child and father-child relations in early life, where the emphasis has been on the ways in which mothers and fathers are similar (e.g., as persons with whom infants can form secure, stable attachments, and as competent caregivers). However, the differences are consistent with recently reported results in middle-childhood and adolescence in which mothers' interactions with and responses to children differ from fathers' in both kind and frequency (Collins & Russell, 1988; Gjerde, 1986).

Parents' Perceptions of Adolescents' Behavior. In a related project, Schoenleber and Collins (1988) studied 69 pairs of parents whose children had participated in the previous study (22-24 pairs in each of the three grades). All parents completed the Behavior Expectancies Inventory, an instrument developed for use in this project to assess expectancies regarding behaviors that are commonly thought to change between the ages of 11 and 16. Each parent separately completed the inventory with respect to their *own* son or daughter. There were four response options: "rarely," "occasionally," "frequently," and "very frequently." A combination of conceptual and empirical criteria was used to aggregate responses to the inventory items. First, separate factor analyses were computed for mothers' and fathers' responses. Three highly similar factors emerged for mothers and fathers, and these corresponded to categories of issues that are addressed in most theoretical formulations about parent-child relationships in the transition to adolescence: *Compliance* (e.g., "Does what parents want even if he/she doesn't like it"; "Responds in a sarcastic manner to parents' comments"); *Communicativeness* (e.g., "Doesn't want to answer questions about school and/or friends"; "Likes to do things with the family"); and *Task Independence* (e.g., "Uses his/her own judgment about most things"; "Depends on you to decide things for him/her"). Scores were computed and analyses conducted in parallel to the study with adolescents.

As in the findings with adolescents, parents' perceptions of their children's behavior were more differentiated than would be expected from theoretical formulations about parent-child relationships in this period. Perceptions were generally positive, always falling above the midpoint on the three scales. At the same time, parents perceived their offspring differently from one grade to another, with mothers' and fathers' perceptions differing somewhat with respect to the dimensions on which differences occurred. Mothers of eighth graders perceived less communicativeness and less compliance in their own children than did mothers of fifth and eleventh graders, whereas fathers' perceptions of communication and compliance for these same children were similar at all three grades. Both mothers and fathers more strongly perceived independence in performing certain tasks at eleventh grade than at eighth grade and, in turn, at eighth grade than at fifth grade.

These comparisons may reflect markedly different knowledge of base rates of certain interpersonal behaviors for children, despite apparent social changes in the involvement of fathers in childrearing. There may also be important differences in mothers' and fathers' concepts of the meaning and significance of behaviors of children and adolescents (Collins & Russell, 1988). The findings are also consistent with popular beliefs and a growing body of research evidence that perturbations in parent-child relationships may be most keenly experienced by mothers (e.g., Hetherington, 1989; Hill, 1988; Patterson, 1982).

Taken together, these two studies indicate that both similarities and differences mark parents' and adolescents' perceptions of their relationships across ages during the transition to adolescence. The two self-report inventories were specifically chosen to assess perceptions that might be expected to affect responses of parents and adolescents toward each other in family interactions; they were not presumed to give a veridical account of the actual behavior of either. A significant question is whether and how these perceptions might be associated with violations of expectancies about behavior and, in turn, with perturbations in the interactional and affective dimensions of relationships between these adolescents and their parents.

Discrepancies Between Perceptions and Expectancies

The possibility that violations of expectancies might be especially likely at times of marked changes, such as the transition to adolescence, is of particular interest. Several theorists have hypothesized that a powerful predictor of negative feelings about family interactions and family atmosphere for both parents and offspring would be the degree to which the other generation violated expectancies. In the case of adolescents, the critical discrepancy has been thought to arise from children's idealizations of parent behavior or their beliefs about how typical parents would behave and their judgment that their own families do not conform to these expectancies. This discrepancy has been considered to be particularly likely in early adolescence, because of incomplete cognitive transitions associated with the achievement of formal reasoning capacities (Elkind, 1967) or because sharper differentiations are being made between one's own parents and the image of ideal individuals to which their behaviors have previously been assimilated (Blos, 1979). In the case of parents, the hypothesis is that perceived variance from highly valued socialization goals or perceptions of the norms would be interpreted as an indication of failure in their parental responsibilities.

To test these discrepancy hypotheses, two categories of expectancies of parent/offspring behavior were examined. One, *category-based expectancies*, refers to normative expectancies associated with membership in a particular age group or social-role category; for example, being 13 years old evokes expectancies in many societies, regardless of an individual's previous behavior. The second, *value or goal-based expectancies*, consist of implicit standards of behavior derived from general values or goals for socialization, without regard to individual history or the typicality of behavior (e.g., the distinction between values of conformity and values of self-direction [Kohn, 1963]).

To assess expectancies, subjects completed the measures of perceptions four additional times. Adolescents completed the Child's Report of Parent Behavior once each while imagining *typical* mothers and *typical* fathers (measures of categorical expectancies) and the *ideal* mother and the *ideal* father (measures of value or goal-based expectancies). In the study with parents, a similar scheme was followed, asking parents to complete the Behavior Expectancies Inventory for a typical child and for the ideal child of the age and sex of their own child. These additional measurements were taken in a different testing session than the measures of perceptions of actual behavior. Order of the typical and ideal responses were counterbalanced across subjects and were separated by intervening activities to break set.

For both children and their mothers, findings were consistent with the hypothesis that perceptions of actual behavior are more likely to violate expectancies about ideal behavior in adolescence than in preadolescence. Discrepancies between perceptions of actual parent behavior and expectancies regarding ideal behaviors were greater for adolescents (14- and 17-year-olds) than for preadolescents (11-year-olds) on the acceptance and psychological autonomy factors. Expectancies regarding typical parents, however, were not discrepant from perceptions of actual behavior; that is, subjects in all three age groups perceived their parents as conforming to their expectancies regarding the behavior of typical parents.

For parents, ideal scores were consistently higher than perceptions on the dimensions of compliance and communication; for mothers, but not fathers, the discrepancies were greater at eighth grade than at fifth and eleventh grades. Grade differences in discrepancies on the independence dimension were negligible. Both mothers' and fathers' perceptions of their own child were more positive than their expectancies regarding the typical child of the same age and gender as their own offspring at grades five and eleven, but the differences was nonsignificant at grade eight. In short, negative discrepancies between parents' perceptions and their expectancies regarding ideal behavior appear to be greater in early adolescence than in preadolescence or middle adolescence.

Expectancies, Interactions, and Affect in Parent-Child Relationships

A related question concerns how perceptions and violations of expectancies are related to parents' and adolescents' interactions. Although these initial studies were not designed to answer this question, it was possible to examine the relation between perceptions and expectancies and self-reports of family functioning as a basis for further research on actual parent-child interactions.

One approach involved having adolescents and each member of the 69 pairs of parents in our study separately rate their families on the Family Assessment Measure (Skinner, Steinhauer, & Santa-Barbara, 1983). This inventory was derived from a process model of family functioning and included subscales dealing with conflict and problem-solving, communication, affective expression; role performance, affective involvement, control, and values and norms. Although disruption in early adolescence is widely implied in popular and theoretical discourse, there were few differences between grades in this sample.

In order to predict family functioning from parents' and adolescents' perceptions and expectancies, multiple regressions were computed in which perceptions of own parents or own offspring were entered first, followed by expectancies of either typical or ideal parent/offspring. If a discrepancy between perceptions of own child or parent and expectancies regarding ideal child or parent were creating negative feelings about family relationships, then ideal expectancies should subsume a significant portion of the variance over and above that accounted for by perceptions of actual behavior.

Perceptions of own parents or own offspring alone—and not the discrepancy between this perception and expectancies regarding typical or ideal members of the category—were the important cognitions about parent-child relationships in predicting perception of family functioning. For adolescents, perceptions of one's own parents on the factors of Acceptance and Psychological Autonomy/Control accounted for 20%-36% of the variance in perceptions of family functioning. For parents, perceptions of one's own offspring accounted for a significant, but relatively small proportion of the variance in reports of family functioning (10%). In the cases of both parents and adolescents, adding ideal or typical expectancies improved prediction of family functioning only slightly.

A second approach (Schoenleber, 1988) involved asking parents to complete the Behavior Expectancies Inventory indicating how important each behavioral item was to them as parents and how frequently each item had been a source of conflict between themselves and their child during the past week. Two different types of conflict were rated: *overt* conflict, in which arguments actually occurred between parent and child; and *covert conflict*, in which parents felt dissatisfaction, anger, or tension, but did not engage in open argument about the provocation. Although these two types of conflict were significantly intercorrelated for both mothers and fathers, the patterns of correlates for the two were different enough that they were treated separately in analyses. An index of overt/covert conflict style was also constructed, based on the differences between overt and covert conflict.

Using these measures of conflict, we first computed a regression analysis similar to that reported for the Family Assessment Measurement. Perceptions of compliance and communication from one's child predicted both overt and covert conflict and conflict style, but expectancies for the ideal and the typical child did not improve the prediction. Next, we formed four clusters of parents based on all possible combinations of high and low covert and overt conflict (low overt/low covert; low overt/high covert; high overt/low covert; and high overt/high covert). Mothers and fathers who showed a pattern of high overt and high covert conflict perceived their child's compliance more negatively than do parents in the other three groups. Mothers in the low overt/high covert conflict group also describe a significantly more negative view of their child than mothers in the low/low and high/low groups. These patterns were strongest for the items that parents had rated as highly important to them, although the effect was apparent even on the less highly important items.

The null findings on the key hypothesis that discrepant expectations are linked to family perturbations may reflect several limitations of this first attempt to link cognitive discrepancies to relationship indicators. It may be attributable (1) to the impaired power in the small sample with which we were working; (2) to the restricted range of scores in a sample that was remarkably homogeneous and well functioning; or (3) to our reliance on very global measures of expectancies and conflict, rather than measures in connection with specific instances in which violation-conflict relationships might be especially likely. Microanalytic analyses of observed interactions over time are needed to address these limitations.

The Expectancy Construct and Future Research

Returning to the questions that originally inspired this line of work, some issues remain to be addressed. The questions of interest concerned the nature and course of adaptation in close relationships to the physical, social, and cognitive changes of the transition to adolescence. These initial studies have demonstrated that some broad, general dimensions of parent and child perceptions differ from one age period to another, whereas others were quite similar across age groups. Furthermore, the perceptions are associated with global assessments of family functioning. The next step is to identify perceptions that may influence specific expectancies in interactions between parents and children and, thus, mediate their actions toward each other. A longitudinal design is needed to trace changes across time in family interaction and in the nature and role of expectations held by both parents and child.

To date, only one aspect of violated expectancies has been examined: the discrepancy between perceptions of actual (past) behavior and normative or desired behavioral expectancies. Other cognitions might also be pertinent to the linkage between expectancies and interactions. For example, age-related changes may elicit different *attributions* about the causes of child behaviors than parents have made at earlier points in development. Dix, Ruble, Grusec, & Nixon (1986) compared adults' responses to hypothetical misbehaviors by children and adolescents and found that the older the child, the more likely parents were to infer that the child understood that certain behaviors are wrong, that the transgression was intentional, and that the behavior indicated negative dispositions in the child. Furthermore, when parents inferred that the child was capable of self-control and that the misbehavior was intentional, they were more upset with the child, and they thought punishment, rather than discussion and explanation, was a more appropriate response. Clearly, transgressions by adolescents have a different significance than transgressions by younger children; they trigger a complex of parental judgments and responses to behavior that effectively change the environment.

ISSUES FOR RESEARCH ON CHANGES IN PARENT-ADOLESCENT RELATIONSHIPS

Three broad issues remain to be addressed in research about the process of change in parent-child relationships.

First, there is a need to examine systematically the dimensions of individual change in adolescence that may be most significant. At present, pubertal status has been considered the dimension of adolescent developmental changes that is most likely to elicit different expectations from parents and to color perceptions of family functioning. Several precedent studies (e.g., Hill, 1988; Steinberg, 1981) have yielded correlations between disruptions in parent-child interactions and changes in pubertal status, although no longitudinal studies have adequately assessed the relative strength of the associations between both age and pubertal-status changes and changes in parent-child relationships. Other determinative factors in psychosocial and relationship perturbations at adolescence (e.g., school changes) should also be considered in connection with family changes (Simmons & Blyth, 1987). The need is for a longitudinal study of parent-child transformations in which significant life events, including pubertal changes, are tracked in conjunction with information about relationships per se. An approach similar to that used in studies of stress and coping in children and adolescents (e.g., Garmezy, Masten, Tellegen, 1984; Simmons, Burgeson, & Reef, 1988) may be more likely than current formulations to identify the proximal factors in relationship perturbation and change.

Second, consideration must be given to variations across the diversity of families in the United States in responses to the physical, cognitive, and social changes of adolescence. Most studies of adolescents and their families, including studies of change in parent-child relationships, have been done with white, two-parent, middle-class families; little is known about Afro-American, Native-American,

Asian-American, or Hispanic-American adolescents and their relations with parents (Hill, 1987). The twin demands of explicating the
processes involved in family transformations in response to individual development in adolescence and in understanding the variations
across families in the nature and course of these processes underscore
the need for systematic cooperative research efforts directed toward
adolescents and their families.

Third, the study of change processes in family relationships requires a bilateral focus. For the most part, research on parent-adolescent relations has taken a unilateral focus on changes in the younger
generation. In this chapter, the author has suggested a *bilateral*, or
two-sided, change process, such that both generations change to
adapt to new capacities and predilections in the younger generation.
Other recent work indicates that this bilateral view must take account
of the adult developmental changes that influence the parents' responses to changes in the child, as well (e.g., Aldous, 1978; Rossi, 1987;
Silverberg & Steinberg, 1987). The research model advocated above
would provide information about life events of parents, as well as
children, and would therefore provide a more extensive base than in
previous studies for incorporating parent-change variables into research on parent-adolescent relationships.

CONCLUSION

The study of changes in parent-child relationships represents a new
perspective on the long-standing interest in the family context of
individual development. Up to now, most research has focused on the
impact of variations in families on children's personality characteristics and social and intellectual competence (Maccoby, 1984). As a
result, the question of how families adapt to the changing capacities
and needs of their offspring has received little attention. The growing
body of research on parent-child relationships during the transition
to adolescence indicates that the process of adaptation is a gradual,
rather than precipitous, one. Changes in some aspects of interaction,
affect, and cognitions regarding relationships now appear to be bal-
anced by significant continuities in the bonds between parents and
children and in the functions served by families in individual development.

It seems likely that the development of relationships in this period
involves a process in which the changing physical, cognitive, and

social characteristics of adolescents provide an impetus for parents and children to generate and coordinate altered patterns of interaction that are appropriate to the greater maturity of the child and the different ways in which parents and children must interact as the child moves toward adulthood. By studying parents and children during major developmental transitions such as this, scholars may be able to illuminate a central question about the role of relationships in development: How do parents and their offspring create new modes of interaction, while maintaining the social and emotional bonds between them?

REFERENCES

Aldous, J. (1978). *Family Careers: Developmental Change in Families.* New York: John Wiley.

Alessandri, S. M., & Wozniak, R. H. (1987). The child's awareness of parental beliefs concerning the child: A developmental study. *Child Development, 58,* 316-323.

Armentrout, J., & Burger, G. (1972). Children's reports of parental child-rearing behavior at five grade levels. *Developmental Psychology, 7,* 44-48.

Baumrind, D. (1968). Authoritarian vs. authoritative control. *Adolescence, 3,* 255-272.

Baumrind, D. (1973). The development of instrumental competence through socialization. In A. D. Pick (Ed.), *Minnesota symposia on child psychology,* (Vol. 7, pp. 3-46). Minneapolis: University of Minnesota Press.

Blos, P. (1979). *The Adolescent Passage.* New York: International Universities Press.

Carlton-Ford, S., & Collins, W. A. (1988, August). *Family conflict: Dimensions, differential reporting, and developmental differences.* Paper presented at the annual meeting of the American Sociological Association, Chicago, Illinois.

Collins, W. A. (1988). Research on the transition to adolescence: Continuity in the study of developmental processes. In M. Gunnar & W. A. Collins (Eds.), *Development during the transition to adolescence: The Minnesota symposia on child psychology,* (Vol. 21, pp. 1-15). Hillsdale, NJ: Erlbaum.

Collins, W. A., & Russell, G. (1988). *Mother-child and father-child relationships in middle childhood and adolescence.* Unpublished manuscript, University of Minnesota.

Dix, T., Ruble, D., Grusec, J., & Nixon, S. (1986). Social cognition in parents: Inferential and affective reactions to children of three age levels. *Child Development, 57,* 879-894.

Elkind, D. (1967). Egocentrism in adolescence. *Child Development, 38,* 1025-1034.

Feldman, S. S., & Gehring, T. M. (1988). Changing perceptions of family cohesion and power across adolescence. *Child Development, 59,* 1034-1045.

Freud, A. (1958). Adolescence. In R. Eissler, A. Freud, H. Hartman, & M. Kris (Eds.), *Psychoanalytic study of the child* (Vol. 13). New York: International Universities Press.

Freud, A. (1969). Adolescence as a developmental disturbance. In G. Caplan & S. Lebovici (Ed.), *Adolescence: Psychological perspectives.* New York: Basic Books.

Garmezy, N., Masten, A., & Tellegen, A. (1984). The study of stress and competence in children: A building block for developmental psychopathology. *Child Development, 55,* 97-111.

Gehring, T. M., & Feldman, S. S. (1988). Adolescents' perceptions of family cohesion and power: A methodological study of the Family Systems Test. *Journal of Adolescent Research, 3,* 33-52.

Gjerde, P. (1986). The interpersonal structure of family interaction settings: Parent-adolescent relations in dyads and triads. *Developmental Psychology, 22,* 297-304.

Grotevant, H., & Cooper, C. (1985). Patterns of interaction in family relationships and the development of identity exploration in adolescence. *Child Development, 56,* 415-428.

Grotevant, H., & Cooper, C. (1986). Individuation in family relationships. *Human Development, 29,* 82-100.

Hauser, S., Powers, S., Noam, G., Jacobson, A., Weiss, B., & Follansbee, D. (1984). Familial contexts of adolescent ego development. *Child Development, 55,* 195-213.

Hess, R., & Goldblatt, I. (1957). The status of adolescents in American society: A problem in social identity. *Child Development, 28,* 459-468.

Hetherington, E. M. (1989). Coping with family transitions: Winners, losers, and survivors. *Child Development, 60,* 1-14.

Hill, C., & Stafford, F. (1980). Parental care of children: Time diary estimate of quantity, predictability and variety. *Journal of Human Resources, 15,* 219-239.

Hill, J. (1987). Research on adolescents and their families: Past and prospect. In W. Damon (Ed.), *New directions in child psychology* (pp. 13-31). San Francisco: Jossey-Bass.

Hill, J. (1988). Adapting to menarche: Familial control and conflict. In M. Gunnar & W. A. Collins (Eds.), *Development during the transition to adolescence: The Minnesota symposia on child psychology,* (Vol. 21, pp. 43-77). Hillsdale, NJ: Erlbaum.

Hill, J., & Holmbeck, G. (1987). Disagreements about rules in families with seventh graders. *Journal of Youth and Adolescence, 16,* 312-319.

Hill, J., Holmbeck, G., Marlow, L., Green, T., & Lynch, M. (1985a). Menarcheal status and parent-child relations in families of seventh grade girls. *Journal of Youth and Adolescence, 14,* 314-330.

Hill, J., Holmbeck, G., Marlow, L., Green, T., & Lynch, M. (1985b). Pubertal status and parent-child relations in families of seventh-grade boys. *Journal of Early Adolescence, 5,* 31-44.

Hinde, R. A. (1979). *Towards understanding relationships.* London: Academic Press.

Hinde, R. A., & Stevenson-Hinde, J. (1987). Interpersonal relationships and child development. *Developmental Review, 7,* 1-21.

Johnson, B. M., & Collins, W. A. (1988). *Developmental differences in perceptions and expectations: Implications for family relationships and psychosocial functioning in the second decade of life.* Unpublished manuscript, University of Minnesota.

Kandel, D., & Lesser, G. (1972). *Youth in two worlds.* San Francisco: Jossey-Bass.

Kelley, H., Berscheid, E., Christensen, A., Harvey, J., Huston, T., Levinger, G., McClintock, E., Peplau, L., & Peterson, D. (1983). (Eds.), *Close relationships.* New York: W. H. Freeman.

Kohn, M. (1963). Social class and parent-child relationships. *American Sociological Review, 68,* 471-480.

Maccoby, E. (1984). Middle childhood in the context of the family. In W. A. Collins (Ed.), *Development during middle childhood: The years from six to twelve* (pp. 184-239). Washington, DC: National Academy of Sciences Press.

Markus, H., & Zajonc, R. (1984). The cognitive perspective in social psychology. In G. Lindzey & E. Aronson (Eds.), *Handbook of social psychology.* Reading, MA: Addison Wesley.

Montemayor, R. (1983). Parents and adolescents in conflict: All families some of the time and some families most of the time. *Journal of Early Adolescence, 3,* 83-103.

Montemayor, R., & Brownlee, J. (1987). Fathers, mothers, and adolescents: Gender-based differences in parental roles during adolescence. *Journal of Youth and Adolescence, 16,* 281-291.

Montemayor, R., & Hanson, E. (1985). A naturalistic view of conflict between adolescents and their parents and siblings. *Journal of Early Adolescence, 5,* 23-30.

Offer, D. (1969). *The psychological world of the teenager.* New York: Basic Books.

Offer, D., Ostrov, E., & Howard, K. (1981). *The adolescent: A psychological self-portrait.* New York: Basic Books.

Olson, D. H., McCubbin, H. I., Barnes, H. L., Larsen, A. S., Muxen, M. J., & Wilson, M. A. (1989). *Families: What makes them work* (updated edition). Newbury Park, CA: Sage.

Papini, D., & Datan, N. (1983, April). *Transitions into adolescence: An interactionist perspective.* Paper presented at the biennial meetings of the Society for Research in Child Development, Detroit, Michigan.

Papini, D., & Sebby, R. (1987). Adolescent pubertal status and affective family relationships: A multivariate assessment. *Journal of Youth and Adolescence, 16,* 1-15.

Patterson, G. (1982). *Coercive family processes.* Eugene, OR: Castalia Press.

Pipp, S., Shaver, Pl, Jennings, S., Lamborn, S., & Fischer, K. W. (1985). Adolescents' theories about the development of their relationships with parents. *Journal of Personality and Social Psychology, 58,* 991-1001.

Rossi, A. (1987). Parenthood in transition: From lineage to child to self-orientation. In J. Lancaster, J. Altmann, A. Rossi, & L. Sherrod (Eds.), *Parenting across the life span: Biosocial dimensions* (pp. 31-81). New York: Aldine de Gruyter.

Rutter, M. (1980). *Changing youth in a changing society.* Cambridge, MA: Harvard University Press.

Rutter, M., Graham, P., Chadwick, O., & Yule, W. (1976). Adolescent turmoil: Fact or fiction? *Journal of Child Psychology and Psychiatry, 17,* 35-56.

Schaefer, E. (1965). Children's reports of parental behavior: An inventory. *Child Development, 36,* 413-424.

Schoenleber, K. (1988). *The effects of expectations on parent-child conflict and relationship satisfaction.* Unpublished doctoral dissertation, University of Minnesota.

Schoenleber, K., & Collins, W. A. (1988). *Parental perceptions, conflict, and family satisfaction in preadolescence and adolescence.* Unpublished manuscript, Institute of Child Development, University of Minnesota, Minneapolis.

Silverberg, S., & Steinberg, L. (1987). Adolescent autonomy, parent-adolescent conflict, and parental well-being. *Journal of Youth and Adolescence, 16,* 293-312.

Simmons, R., & Blyth, D. (1987). *Moving into adolescence: The impact of pubertal change and school context.* New York: Aldine de Gruyter.

Simmons, R., Burgeson, R., & Reef, M. (1988). Cumulative change at entry to adolescence. In M. Gunnar & W. A. Collins (Eds.), *Development during the transition to adolescence: Minnesota symposia on child psychology,* (Vol. 21, pp. 123-150). Hillsdale, NJ: Erlbaum.

Skinner, H., Steinhauer, P., & Santa-Barbara, J. (1983). The Family Assessment Measure. *Canadian Journal of Community Mental Health, 2,* 91-105.

Smetana, J. (1988). Adolescents' and parents' conceptions of parental authority. *Child Development, 59,* 321-335.

Steinberg, L. (1981). Transformations in family relations at puberty. *Developmental Psychology, 17,* 833-840.

Steinberg, L. (1987). Impact of puberty on family relations: Effects of pubertal status and pubertal timing. *Developmental Psychology, 23,* 451-460.

Steinberg, L. (1988). Reciprocal relations between parent-child distance and pubertal maturation. *Developmental Psychology, 24,* 122-128.

Steinberg, L. (1989). Pubertal maturation and parent-adolescent distance: An evolutionary perspective. In G. R. Adams, R. Montemayor, & T. P. Gullotta (Eds.), *Biology of adolescent behavior and development* (pp. 71-97). Newbury Park, CA: Sage.

Steinberg, L. (in press). Interdependency in the family: Autonomy, conflict, and harmony in the parent-adolescent relationship, In S. S. Feldman (Ed.), *Normal adolescent development.* Washington, DC: Carnegie Council on Adolescent Development.

Steinberg, L., & Hill, J. (1978). Patterns of family interaction as a function of age, the onset of puberty, and formal thinking. *Developmental Psychology, 14,* 683-684.

Steinberg, L., & Silverberg, S. (1986). The vicissitudes of autonomy in early adolescence. *Child Development, 57,* 841-851.

Thurnher, M., Spence, D., & Lowenthal, M. (1974). Value confluence and behavioral conflict in intergenerational relations. *Journal of Marriage and the Family, 36,* 308-319.

Waters, E., Hay, D., & Richters, J. (1986). Infant-parent attachment and the origins of prosocial and antisocial behavior. In D. Olweus, J. Block, & M. Radke-Yarrow (Eds.), *Development of antisocial and prosocial behavior: Research, theories, and issues* (pp. 97-126). New York: Academic Press.

Youniss, J., & Smollar, J. (1985). *Adolescents' relations with mothers, fathers, and friends.* Chicago: University of Chicago Press.

5. The Preadolescent's Contributions to Disrupted Family Process

G. R. Patterson
L. Bank
M. Stoolmiller
Oregon Social Learning Center
Eugene, Oregon

Bronfenbrenner (1988) and other developmental theorists enjoin the investigator to view the family as a system undergoing a metamorphizing process over time. As they point out, a study of family process requires that one conceptualize both stability and change. The present report examines one set of variables that are related to the long-term *maintenance* of deviant family processes. It also examines a set of variables that contribute to the start of deviancy processes. One set of variables consists of the youth's own behaviors and the other of measures of significant transitions in the life of early adolescent boys. The relationships are expressed in the form of structural equation models. In both models, the youth is more than a passive recipient. He is presented as actively engaged in altering the processes of which he is a part.

A longitudinal study of families with boys first assessed at grade 4 (the data base for this report), using multiple-agent and multiple-method measures of family-management practices, showed them to be surprisingly stable during the years immediately preceding entry into adolescence (Patterson & Bank, 1989). The findings raise the question: What contributes to such stability? The hypothesis considered in the present report is that one of the significant contributors to continuing disrupted family-management practices is the adolescent himself. Specifically, it is assumed that earlier measures of the

AUTHORS' NOTE: *Support for the research presented in this chapter was provided by Grant Nos. MH 37940 and MH 17126, Center for Studies of Antisocial and Violent Behavior, NIMH, U.S. PHS; Grant No. MH 37911, Mood, Anxiety, and Personality Disorders Research Branch, Division of Clinical Research, NIMH, US. PHS; Grant No. HD 22679, Center for Research for Mothers and Children, NICHD, U.S. PHS; and Grant No. DA 05304, National Institute of Drug Abuse, U.S. PHS.*

preadolescent's antisocial behavior will contribute to future disruptions of parenting practices.

The authors choose to think of this as an example of a homeostatic feedback loop. In the present context, status as a homeostatic loop requires a sequence of two significant findings. First, it must be shown that parenting practices are significant potential determinants for child antisocial behaviors. Second, it must be shown that earlier child antisocial behaviors are associated with disruptions in future parenting practices. This report is, in part, a description of a methodology for investigating the general case for homeostatic loops in developmental processes. The family is enmeshed in a dynamic process that generates many outcomes, some of which alter the future course of the process itself. But how does one set about identifying such loops embedded in family process? And how can loops associated with maintenance, or stability, be differentiated from those associated with initiation, or change?

The literature is rich in discussions of developmental transitions that might in turn relate to the initiation of new family processes. For example, most developmental theorists view the passage into adolescence as defining a critical shift in context for the youth (e.g., Magnusson, 1988). The step from middle school to high school is thought to be another profound shift in context, particularly if this is concurrent with pubescence. Moving or non-normative shifts within the school (being held back) are also significant. The authors hypothesize, and will test later in this report, that the impact of each of these transitions is mediated by accompanying disruptions in peer relations.

All three transitions are combined here to form a *risk score* reflecting disturbances in the early adolescent's context. The sample for the present study are young boys first assessed when 10 to 11 years old, then reassessed at 12 to 13. During this span, many youths experienced more than one transition. The hypothesis is that these shifts will have a profound effect on the quality of the social exchanges that take place between the youth and members of his or her family. These upheavals disrupt good parenting practices, and thereby initiate deviancy-amplifying processes in the family.

The sample characteristics and assessment battery are briefly reviewed in the next section. The section thereafter examines the case for a feedback loop that might maintain a deviant process. The last section makes a case for transition variables as possible initiators for a deviancy process.

METHOD

Subjects

Three major school districts in a medium-sized (pop. 150,000) metropolitan area agreed to participate in the study providing the data base for this report. Using juvenile court data for the frequency of delinquent episodes reported by the police, 15 high-risk schools were targeted; 14 agreed to participate. The 10 highest risk schools were randomly ordered, and of these, the first 6 schools were recruited for the study.

Each school provided a list of families of grade 4 boys and their addresses. Of these, 21 families were declared ineligible because they moved out of state, they moved before contact, they were foreign speaking, or for other reasons. Of the eligible families, 77% agreed to participate in the study ($N = 206$). Of the 30 families who refused, most said they were too busy or not interested. Each family was paid up to $300 for participating in the full assessment battery. The details of the recruitment procedures and sample characteristics for those who participated and those who did not are reported in Capaldi and Patterson (1987).

Assessment

Data were collected as part of an ongoing longitudinal study. Each family participated in over 20 hours of assessment that included office interviews, daily telephone interviews, home observations, questionnaires, videotaped family problem-solving tasks, teacher ratings, and peer nominations. All of the measures taken in the first wave (grade 4) were repeated again two years later in the third wave (grade 6) of data collection using the same procedures. The intensive assessment battery was designed to facilitate the use of multimethod, multiagent indicators for use in building each of the constructs in the models. This strategy is discussed in Patterson and Bank (1986, 1987).

A strenuous effort was made to parallel construct definition between grades 4 and 6, but when building the assessment battery at grade 6, new indicators were added to strengthen the definitions for some of the constructs. When a variable or indicator was added at grade 6, it had to survive both the itemetric and the factor analyses. In some cases this resulted in changes for one or two variates in an indicator.

Constructs

The procedures for building constructs involve a series of steps beginning with a definition for the construct. The definition is used to construct a priori scales that are then examined for internal consistency; the weaker items are dropped from the scale. The set of possible scales is then used in an exploratory factor analysis constrained to a single solution. Scales that do not load significantly are then dropped. Finally, surviving indicators are used in a confirmatory factor analysis to demonstrate that a given construct can be differentiated from other constructs used in our models (i.e., do the resulting data provide both convergent and discriminative validity?).

Child Antisocial Behavior construct. This construct was defined by five indicators to provide a moderate amount of flexibility in testing the various models employing it. Three subscales comprised the parent report, including the Child Behavior Checklist (CBC), Oregon Child Aggression (OCA), and daily telephone interviews with parent. Two were obtained from data collected at the schools: the teachers report on the Child Behavior Checklist and peer nominations. The TAB score is based on observed child aversive behavior in the home, and one scale was based on child telephone self-report.

A small sample (about 20) of families were asked to respond to the scales again after an interval of six to eight weeks. The test-retest reliabilities for the parent score on the OCA was .83 ($p<.001$) and for the CBC it was .68 ($p<.001$). The mother and father ratings were standardized to form a single score. The report from Capaldi and Patterson (1988) for the combined cohorts in the at-risk sample showed that the kurtosis and skewness values for parent indicator, the child telephone interview, and peer nomination data were all less than 1.96. The kurtosis value for the teacher indicator was 3.31. The values for the composite score was less than 2.00.

Monitoring construct. This construct was defined by three indicators: child interview questions, interviewer impressions, and daily parental telephone reports. The alpha values for the mother interview was .69 and for the father interview .78. The interviewer impressions consisted of two ratings made by the staff interviewing the two parents and separately for the staff interviewing the child. All of the skewness and kurtosis values for these indicators and for the composite score were less than 1.0.

Good Discipline construct. Two of the indicators were based on home observations and a third was based on mother interview data (combined with father interview data in wave 3). The 13-item interview scale for the mother had an alpha value of .75; and a test-retest reliability of .92. The kurtosis and skewness value were normal.

At the end of each of three observations in the home, the observers rated the consistency and follow through for the discipline confrontations. The test-retest reliability for this indicator was .67 for the combined parent score; both values were within the normal range for kurtosis and skewness.

The third indicator, nattering, was based on sequential observation data, and describes the likelihood of parental aversive behavior, given they were interacting with the child. The test-retest reliability for this score was .37 for fathers and .41 for mothers. The skewness for the combined parent score was 1.5 and the kurtosis 2.5. The skewness for the Good Discipline composite score was −1.16 and for kurtosis 2.38.

Transition risk score. This variable consisted of an average of the following five standardized variables:

1. number of residence changes between grade 4 and grade 6
2. number of family structure changes up to grade 6
3. number of nonnormative school changes between grade 4 and grade 6
4. number of normative school changes between grade 4 and grade 6
5. level of pubertal maturation.

The number of residence changes was a simple count of the times a family moved during the two data collection points. The number of family structure changes up to grade 6 was a count of the number of divorces, remarriages, or live-in partner changes. The number of non-normative school changes was a simple count of the number of times a child changed schools not including normative changes. In this study a normative school change was defined as the transition from elementary to middle school. Because of the ages of the boys in the study, this was the only normative change possible. The sample is still too young to be entering high school. The normative school changes variable was scored so that failing to make the change resulted in a score of 1, and making the change sometime during the two data collection points was scored as 0.

The level of pubertal maturation was based on the reports of the mother, father, interviewer, and observer. Items used for all four reporting agents were as follows:

1. facial features
   face round in shape   1
   angular face, but no facial hair or acne   2
   small amount of facial hair and/or acne   3

2. body proportion
   body well proportioned, but soft and rounded, not muscular   1
   arms and legs too long for body   2
   body well proportioned, and muscles well defined   3

3. coordination
   coordinated but childlike walk   1
   gawky and uncoordinated walk   2
   coordinated and adultlike walk   3

4. voice
   high pitched, childlike voice   1
   voice beginning to change   2
   deep adult voice   3

In addition to the above, items used only for mother and father were as follows:

1. body hair
   body hair fine and childlike   1
   body hair more coarse and noticeable;
       small amount of pubic and underarm hair   2
   pubic and underarm hair fully developed;
       possibly some chest hair   3

2. has your child recently had a growth spurt?
   yes   1
   no   2

A global pubescence score was computed for the observer and the interviewer by taking the average of the four individual items. Cronbach's standardized alphas were .76 and .68 for observer and interviewer respectively. The score was computed separately for mothers and fathers by standardizing and taking the average of the six items. Cronbach's standardized alphas were .58 and .50 for mothers and fathers respectively. This global mother and father score was then combined to get a parental global indicator of level of physical maturity. The scores for mothers and fathers correlated .24. The global scores for interviewer, observer, and parent were then standardized and averaged to form a single indicator of level of physical maturity. Cronbach's standardized alpha for these three items was .60.

Coercive child construct. Three indicators defined this construct; all were based on data collected during the three home observation sessions. The data were recorded in sequential form on a hand-held computer by highly trained observers. The code and the psychometric studies are described in the report by Dishion, Gardner, Patterson, Reid, and Thibodeaux (1983). Each of the three conditional probabilities describes the likelihood of the target child's aversive reaction to a family member. The synchronicity indicators describe the likelihood of an aversive reaction given an immediately preceding aversive act by a family member. There are two synchronistic indicators: one for reactions to mothers and the other for reactions to siblings. The third indicator, start-up, describes the likelihood of an aversive reaction given the sibling was previously engaged in a neutral or prosocial behavior. As yet, none of the test-retest or skewness and kurtosis studies have been completed for this construct.

ANTISOCIAL BEHAVIOR AS A DISRUPTOR VARIABLE

Homeostatic Feedback Loops

The authors propose that products generated by the coercion process serve as feedback mechanisms maintaining or exacerbating the already disrupted state of affairs. Thus far, a number of variables that might serve this function have been examined. The strategy followed in the search has been the same in each case; and it is also the one followed here. The authors begin by selecting some event measured at two points as the "target." The function of the model is to understand what variables are associated with the maintenance of the target event over time. Next, the target construct is measured at two points in time as a basis for estimating stability. Then variables are selected that seem, a priori, to be reasonable determinants for either the maintenance or alteration in occurrence for the target event. For example, from the perspective given by the coercion model, Patterson, Reid, and Dishion (in press) speculate that for 10-year-old boys, failure in his peer relations, low self-esteem, or failure in school might all contribute to the significant maintenance of the boys in the coercion process.

The next step is to construct models that describe how these outcomes occur. The models summarized in Patterson et al. (in press) showed that the child's antisocial behavior covaried significantly with all three outcomes. Furthermore, findings from several other longitudinal studies have shown that antisocial problems *precede* the later development of failures in achievement (Tremblay, 1988) and rejection by peers (Coie & Kupersmidt, 1983; Dodge, 1983). This part of the link required for a homeostatic loop seems quite robust.

The third step defining a loop requires that the product produced by the process at time-1 correlate with the target event measured at time-2. The authors agree with the Gollop and Reichardt (1987) formulation, that the feedback variable must make a significant contribution to the target event measured at time-2 relative to what is contributed by the *prior measure* of the *target variable*. In a model, the stability coefficient describes the *relative* contribution of the prior measure for the target event in comparison with the relative contribution for the potential feedback variable.

Introducing the feedback variable in conjunction with information about the stability for the target event may actually produce a *reduction* in the stability coefficient estimated alone. For example, in the study by Patterson and Bank (1989) peer relations measured at grade 4 made a highly significant contribution to antisocial behavior measured two years later (as shown by the path coefficient of .46). Adding the cross-lagged correlation did *not* increase the amount of variance accounted for beyond that explained by the prior estimates for stability alone. This finding was interpreted as an explanation for why some boys remain antisocial: Presumably, antisocial boys who were also rejected by peers were more likely to be maintained in the process.

A comparable set of analyses was carried out by Bank and Stoolmiller (1989) for the Self-Esteem construct as a feedback variable. While both the target Antisocial Behavior construct and the Self-Esteem construct were shown to be stable over time, the cross-lagged coefficient from Self-Esteem to Child Antisocial Behavior was not. The authors' unpublished effort to test the status of an Academic Achievement construct met a similar fate. Neither the Academic Achievement nor the Self-Esteem constructs met the requirement for status as homeostatic loops.

Patterson and Forgatch (in press) used a sample of divorced mothers to demonstrate that constructs measuring maternal stress were highly stable when measured over a 12-month interval. The Child Antisocial Behavior construct measured at time-1 showed a cross-lagged correlation with Maternal Stress measured at time-2. The path coefficient was of borderline significance ($p<.10$) but the finding was consistent with the hypothesis that products generated by family process can serve as feedback loops associated with future disruptions.

Child Antisocial Behavior as a Maintenance Variable

The authors hypothesize that, in practicing coercive skills, the antisocial child disrupts parental efforts to discipline and to monitor their child's whereabouts. For example, simply saying "No, don't do that" constitutes a less effective sanction for problem boys than for nonproblem boys (Patterson, 1982; Snyder, 1977). Similarly, asking about where he is going that evening is unlikely to lead to information that would make it possible for parents to monitor his whereabouts. Clinical experience suggests that as the child becomes increasingly antisocial, parents tend to avoid reasonable discipline confrontations or monitoring attempts.

As noted earlier, the first step in establishing antisocial behavior as a feedback loop is to demonstrate that there is a significant link between some aspect of the process and the antisocial behavior itself. Patterson (1986) showed a significant covariation between constructs measuring parent discipline and monitoring practices and child antisocial behavior. The effect was replicated by Forgatch (1988) for a sample of boys from divorced families and for a sample of boys referred for treatment for antisocial problems. That study and the study of the accompaniments of longitudinal changes in parenting practices by Patterson and Bank (1987) support the causal status of discipline and monitoring practices on child adjustment. In both studies, changes in parenting practices were associated with changes in child behaviors.

The next step requires a significant relation between an earlier product, antisocial behavior, and later disruptions in parental discipline and monitoring practices. Specifically, the authors hypothesize that measures of antisocial behavior obtained at grade 4 will correlate with both parental discipline and monitoring practices measured at grade 6. Presumably, the significant contribution will hold even when evaluated within the context of the general stability of the parenting practices. As noted earlier, simply demonstrating that such a path is significant is not sufficient: the cross-lagged contribution to later parenting practices must be significant *relative* to the information contained in stability coefficients for parenting practices.

Correlation Matrix

The data collected for the at-risk sample at grades 4 and 6 were used to test this hypothesis. Table 5.1 outlines the pairwise correlation matrix. All coefficients in the matrix were based on 186 or more data points. In that the skewness and kurtosis values for the 17 indicators were minimal, the data were thereby judged to meet the assumptions underlying statistical tests in structural equation modeling (SEM).

Most convergent correlations (those correlations among indicators within a construct) fall between .25 and .40, but several unusually high convergent correlations are noteworthy. For example, within the Discipline construct, the correlations of the observational variables with the Observers' Impressions were high. The simplest explanation for this occurrence is that the observer, by and large, forms his or her impressions from the same behavior that is being coded in real time.

Within the Child Antisocial Behavior construct, the correlation between the teacher's report and peer nominations for child antisocial behavior is considerably higher than the other convergent correlations. In this case, it would appear that the common setting (the classroom and playground) and an extended period of contact (the school year) results in teachers and peers agreeing to a greater extent than might agents from across settings.

Among the discriminant correlations, those correlations among indicators across constructs, the largest tend to be associated with the same agent or method. This is most obvious in measures that are taken at two points in time with the same agent (e.g., the mother). Some of these oversized discriminant correlations are associated with error covariance terms in the structural models, but none are so large that they create problems such as nonconvergence or improper solutions.

A Strategy for the Use of SEM in Hypothesis Testing

The strategy employed in general for modeling is to start by fitting a measurement model in which the constructs are allowed to freely

Table 5.1 Intercorrelations of Indicators for Discipline (grades 4 & 6), Monitoring (grades 4 & 6), and Child Antisocial Behavior (grade 4 only)

	Discipline^1			Monitoring^1			Antisocial^1					Monitoring^2			Discipline^2		
	Mother Int'view	Natter-ing	Observer Impres-sions	Child Int'view Rules	Int'viewer Impres-sions	Parent Report #Hours	Parent Report Antisocial	Teacher CBC	TAB Score	Child Phone Int'view	Peer Nomi-nation	Child Int'view Rules	Parent Report #Hours^a	Int'viewer Impres-sions	Mother Int'view	Observer Impres-sions	Natter-ing
Discipline^1																	
Mother Interview	1.00																
Nattering	-.266	1.00															
Observer Impressions	.221	-.581	1.00														
Monitoring^1																	
Child Interview: Rules	.147	-.077	.079	1.00													
Interviewer Impressions	.234	-.265	.250	.385	1.00												
Parent Report: #Hours w/Child	.136	.048	.041	.145	.244	1.00											
Antisocial^1																	
Parent Report: Child Antisocial	-.476	.349	-.185	-.147	-.273	-.203	1.00										
Teacher CBC	-.228	.400	-.284	-.116	-.271	-.060	.401	1.00									
Total Aversive Behavior Score	-.229	.444	-.306	-.159	-.186	-.060	.298	.144	1.00								
Phone Interview Child	-.041	.181	-.071	-.120	-.164	-.100	.310	.251	.142	1.00							
Peer Nomination	-.230	.390	-.334	-.148	-.315	-.083	.370	.642	.196	.209	1.00						
Monitoring^2																	
Child Interview: Rules	.177	-.088	.145	.393	.309	.113	-.229	-.102	-.118	-.220	-.178	1.00					
Parent Report: #Hours w/Child	.208	.003	.127	.179	.320	.338	-.123	-.079	-.083	.001	-.134	.298	1.00				
Interviewer Impressions	.216	-.262	.273	.184	.313	.165	-.220	-.262	-.297	-.030	-.307	.411	.271	1.00			
Discipline^2																	
Mother Interview	.583	-.235	.195	.118	.125	.182	-.415	-.274	-.150	-.08	-.213	.172	.157	.293	1.00		
Observer Impressions	.232	-.540	.597	.085	.234	.044	-.348	-.385	-.364	-.117	-.410	.156	.187	.358	.372	1.00	
Nattering	.221	-.534	.402	.029	.146	.105	-.344	-.330	-.209	-.168	-.295	.050	.063	.178	.358	.665	1.00

^{a} Contains # hours with child and single item: "Did you talk with your son about his day today?"

117

correlate. Often the measurement model will have a satisfactory fit at this point in the process, but it is also common for one or more additional covariances to be specified to adequately re-create the data matrix. This typically involves permitting one or more pairs of error terms to covary.

These steps are serial, and each dependent on the previous one(s) in fitting the measurement model. Once a measurement model with satisfactory fit is determined, then a theoretically specified path model is fit using the same measurement structure. That is, only a priori hypothesized paths and covariances are included.

A nested chi-square test is then carried out to determine if the path model adequately reproduces the measurement model. In this way, the measurement model serves as a best possible baseline fit against which the theoretical path models are compared. For more details on this approach to modeling, see Anderson and Gerbing (1988) and Bentler and Bonnett (1980).

The Measurement Model

The measurement model was initially specified with same or similar measures at two points in time having error covariance terms. This initial model did not fit by the chi-square criterion. It was then respecified to include five pairs of indicators that shared methods and agents (e.g., maternal report of discipline with parental report of antisocial behavior). This model still lacked satisfactory fit. Error covariances for four additional indicator pairs with correlations in the expected theoretical directions—but larger than would be predicted by the correlations among the latent variables and factor loadings—were allowed to covary. For example, residuals covary for interviewer impressions of monitoring at grade 4 with parental report of monitoring at grade 6. An acceptable fit was then obtained. Several of the error covariance terms associated with same or similar measures across time were nonsignificant, so they were eliminated from the final measurement model. Table 5.2 provides a listing of all error covariances estimated in the model.

Model 1: The Stability Model

The authors decided that the most conservative beginning would be to build a simplified path model that could serve as a comparison for the feedback loop model. This first model stipulated two things

Table 5.2 Error Covariance Terms Included in Model

Repeated or similar measures across time
1. Mother Report Discipline (grade 4) to Parent Report Discipline (Grade 6): .55, $t = 6.73$.
2. Nattering (grade 4) to Nattering (grade 6): $-.28$, $t = -2.41$.
3. Observer Impressions Discipline (grade 4) to Observer Impressions Discipline (grade 6): .44, $t = 2.90$.
4. Child Report Monitoring (grade 4) to Child Report Monitoring (grade 6): .32, $t = 3.76$.
5. Parent Telephone Monitoring (grade 4) to Parent Telephone Monitoring (Grade 6): .30, $t = 4.05$.

Same method, agent, or context
1. Mother Report Discipline (grade 4) to Parent Report Antisocial (grade 4): $-.40$, $t = -4.92$.
2. Parent Report Antisocial (grade 4) to Parent Report Discipline (grade 6): $-.31$, $t = -3.83$.
3. Mother Report Discipline (grade 4) to Parent Telephone Monitoring (grade 6): .12, $t = 2.12$.
4. Child Telephone Antisocial (grade 4) to Child Report Monitoring (grade 6): $-.21$, $t = -2.70$.
5. Nattering (grade 4) to TAB scores (grade 4): .28, $t = 3.01$.

Other terms
1. Interviewer Impressions Monitoring (grade 4) to Parent Telephone Monitoring (grade 6): .22, $t = 1.94$.
2. Parent Telephone Monitoring (grade 4) to Nattering (grade 6): .17, $t = 2.31$.
3. TAB scores (grade 4) to Interviewer Impressions Monitoring (grade 6): $-.19$, $t = -2.19$.

we already knew. First, the two parenting practices and child antisocial behavior at grade 4 were all interrelated. Second, it required that parental monitoring and discipline practices be highly stable over time. The model said nothing about cross-lagged or synchronous effects. But the hypothesis tested was that the stability model would account for enough of the information in the measurement model to survive. As a strategy, the expectation was that when the cross-lagged paths were included in the feedback loop model, the fit of data to the a priori model will be significantly better.

The stability coefficient was .66 for Monitoring and .77 for Discipline. This finding is consistent with the idea that parenting practices are highly stable over a two-year period (Patterson & Bank, 1987).

The overall chi-square for this model was 128.73, with 99 degrees of freedom. The probability value of .028 showed that the stability model did not fit the data. When this model was compared to the measurement model as an alternative, the resulting chi-square was highly significant. The authors concluded that the stability model, as a representation of the data, failed to satisfactorily explain the correlations among the latent variables as determined in the measurement model. The next hypothesis tested was that the addition of the cross-lagged effects would provide a better fit.

Model 2: Antisocial Behavior as a Feedback Variable

The next step included all relationships tested in the first path model, but also including a provision for the child's impact on parenting practices (i.e., estimates of the relative stabilities for the parenting constructs and estimates of the relative contribution for the effect of cross-lagged paths across time from the child's antisocial behavior to the parent's later parenting practices). The newer model is illustrated in Figure 5.1.

The general pattern of findings offer solid support for the hypothesis that antisocial child behavior may contribute to later disruptions in parenting practices. The cross-lagged path from Child Antisocial Behavior assessed at grade 4 to Monitoring assessed at grade 6 was –.29 and to Good Discipline –.36. The more extreme the antisocial score, the greater the disruption in later measures of parenting practices.

The reader might note that the relative stability coefficients for the parenting practices are now in the .4 range; considerably less than the values obtained in the first model. However, the squared multiple correlations for Monitoring and Good Discipline did *not change* substantially when the lagged paths from Child Antisocial Behavior entered the model. We interpret this to mean that the cross-lagged paths serve as partial explanations for the stability of the parenting practices. The findings are consistent with the idea that the child's antisocial behavior may indeed form a homeostatic feedback loop that disrupts parental discipline and monitoring practices.

The hypothesis finds further support when one examines the overall fit of this theoretically preferred model to the data. As shown in the figure, the fit is quite satisfactory. The chi-square value was 118.97 (p = .074). An even more conservative view can be obtained by

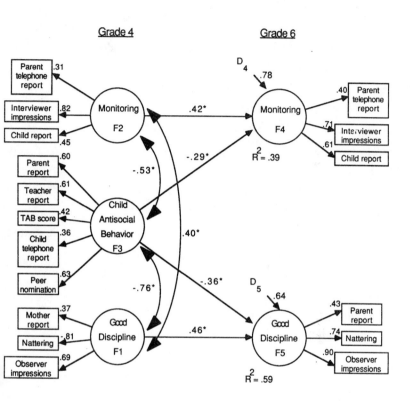

Figure 5.1 Antisocial Behavior as a Feedback Variable
NOTES: N = 206; $x^2_{(98)}$ = 118.97; p = .074; BBN = .897; BBNN = .971; $^*p < .05$

comparing this path model to the measurement model. The chi-square value was 7.33 (df = 3, n.s.). One might conclude, therefore, that the theoretically specified path model can be accepted as adequately reproducing the measurement model. On the other hand, the chi-square also implies that it might be possible to improve the model (it does not perfectly account for the measurement model).

In the general coercion model (Patterson et al., in press), it is as sumed that difficulties in discipline confrontations contribute to ineffective monitoring. The results of modeling concurrent data sets are consistent with this assumed relation between discipline to monitoring. It seemed reasonable, therefore, to include it in our present study to see if it improved the fit for the feedback loop model. As expected the addition of the path from Discipline to Monitoring at grade 6 was significant. The data also showed that a mediated model (not shown here), with the effects of Child Antisocial Behavior on Monitoring mediated through its effects on Discipline, provided a better fit than did the simple feedback model. The chi-square value was 115.05 ($p =$ .102). A chi-square comparison of this mediated model and the simple feedback models showed that the mediated model was a significant improvement. The chi-square value was 4.48 ($p<.05$). Also, the fit of the mediated model to the measurement model was now very close indeed. The chi-square comparison produced a value of 2.85 ($df = 2$ $p = .20$).

The reader should note, however, that when the mediational path from Good Discipline to Monitoring was added, the cross-lagged path from Child Antisocial Behavior to the Monitoring construct had essentially dropped to zero. While both parenting practices may be disrupted by the antisocial child, the effect seems to generalize *from* disruptions in discipline *to* disruptions in monitoring.

In summary, the results of the modeling analyses support the hypothesis that the earlier measures of child antisocial behavior are associated with significant disruptions in parenting practices two years later. The results also suggest that the effects of child antisocial behavior on parental monitoring might be mediated through disruptions of parental discipline.

CHILD STRESSORS AS DISRUPTORS FOR PARENTING PRACTICES

The reviews by Maccoby (1983) and Rutter (1983) document the effect of stress on children as well as their surprising resilience in the face of such overwhelming stressors as war, floods, and other catastrophes (Garmezy, 1983). The assumption to be examined in this section is that there are some stressors unique to children that serve the function of disrupting family processes. Because of the nature of the stressors examined in this section, the authors chose to label

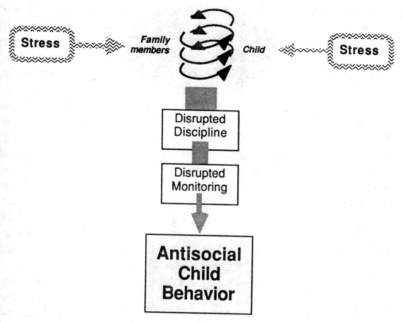

Figure 5.2 A Mediated Model for Family Stress

them as *transitional stressors:* pubescence, shifts in residence, changing schools, nonnormative shifts within school (e.g., being held back), normative shifts within school (e.g., graduating from lower to upper schools), and shifts in family structure.

In keeping with a social interactional perspective, we assume the effect of stressors on child adjustment is mediated by their effect on the child's social exchanges with family members (Patterson, 1983). These disruptions can be brought about by stressors that impinge on the parent or the child. Figure 5.2 illustrates how either avenue to disrupted social exchanges may disrupt parental efforts to discipline and monitor the child. The effect of stress on child adjustment is mediated by two different mechanisms; the first is the initial increase in irritable exchanges and the other in disrupted parenting practices.

In keeping with the disruption hypothesis, the intrasubject analyses for five mother-child dyads by Patterson (1983) showed a covariation between maternal self-reported stressors and observed irritable reactions with her child. On days characterized by high self-reported stress, mothers were observed to be more irritable in interactions with their preschool children. This effect was replicated using a larger sample of clinical cases by Wahler and Dumas (1983). More recently, Snyder (1988) has developed an elegant model demonstrating this same effect for normal dyads.

Increased irritability would presumably disrupt parental discipline efforts. This was demonstrated using SEM for cross-sectional data collected in a sample of recently divorced families (Forgatch, Patterson, & Skinner, in press). High levels of stress covaried with disruptions in discipline.

These studies, establishing that daily variations in stress are associated with commensurate variations in maternal irritability, strongly suggest that highly stressed parents are also less effective in their discipline practices. The authors hypothesize a parallel relationship for the adolescent: (1) Increases in child stressors (transitions) will be associated with increases in child coerciveness during exchanges with family members; (2) The effect of stressors on child adjustment will be mediated by their disrupting effect of parental discipline practices; and perhaps (3) Child stressors contribute *directly* to disruptions in parental disciplines and monitoring practices.

The Mediational Model for the Effect of Adolescent Stressors

The hypothesis tested was that the impact of preadolescent's stressors on parental discipline practices would be mediated by their effect on the child's coercive exchanges with family members. A matrix for the correlation among the indicators is summarized in Table 5.3. It can be seen that the transition indicators showed only marginal convergence. Given such findings, the authors have adopted the strategy of using a risk score rather than attempting to define a latent construct (Bank, Dishion, Skinner, & Patterson, in press).

The convergence for the Coercive Child construct was within acceptable limits; as noted earlier the convergence for the two parenting constructs (Good Discipline and Monitoring) was also within reasonable limits. The discriminant correlations clearly point to some shared method variance for the Good Discipline and the Coercive Child constructs. This would be expected in that both are based on data collected during or after home observation sessions.

The intercorrelations for the Coercive Child construct and Transition Risk score with the Discipline and Monitoring constructs for grades 4 and 6 are listed in Table 5.3. The intercorrelations among the family-management indicators are essentially unchanged from those n Table 5.1. Pairwise deletion was again used with computing correlations for the 206 families, but the minimum number of observations per correlation is reduced to $N = 159$ because the Coercive Child construct includes two measures requiring target child-sibling interaction. There were 37 single-child families. Goodness-of-fit tests were carried out using the more conservative $N = 206$.

The effect of the preadolescents' transition stressors on parenting practices (Monitoring and Discipline) is thought to be mediated through their effect on the youths' irritable exchanges with siblings and parents. Presumably, stressors that impinge on the preadolescents will not lead to antisocial outcomes unless by disrupting their social exchanges with family members. These disruptions will not lead to deviant outcomes unless they disrupt parental monitoring and discipline practices.

A measurement model (not shown here) was tested and fitted using the same strategy described in the preceding section. The chi-square was 137.87 ($df = 113$, $p = .056$). In order to achieve this fit, it was necessary to fix the loading for interviewer impressions on Monitoring at grade 4 at its upper bound so that it would not exceed 1.0. Six error covariances were included to estimate method/agent uniqueness across time for Good Discipline and Monitoring. Within time, error covariances were calculated for mother report on discipline and Monitoring for grades 4 and 6. One unexpected covariance was permitted between the Transition Risk score and parent synchronicity variable residuals. It is assumed that this last covariance reflects random fluctuation in the data.

Correlations among constructs in that measurement model suggested that there was a relationship between earlier parental discipline practices and later assessment of both the Coercive Child construct and the Transition Risk score measured at a later time. These omissions were rectified: the resulting post hoc model is depicted in Figure 5.3. The respecified model not only provides a satisfactory fit to the data, but the two key paths are also significant. The path coefficient of .31 from the Transition Risk score to Coercive Child was significant, as was the path from the Coercive Child to Good Discipline construct. The model provides solid support for the idea that stress influences adolescents in ways reminiscent of what happens to parents when they are stressed (i.e., they become more irritable and this disrupts discipline confrontations). For an N of 206, the fit was marginally adequate. It should be noted that if only the 159 families with target child and at least one sibling are used for the same analysis,

Table 5.3 Intercorrelations of Indicators for Coercive Child and Transition Risk with Discipline and Monitoring

		Coercive Child			Good Discipline - Grade 4				Good Discipline - Grade 6		
		Sibling Synchronicity	Sibling Startup	Parent Synchronicity	Mother Report Discipline	Nattering	Observer Impressions	Abuse Cluster	Parent Report Discipline	Observer Impressions	Nattering
Coercive Child	Sibling Synchronicity	1.000									
	Sibling Startup	.358**	1.000								
	Parent Synchronicity	.277**	.361**	1.000							
Good Discipline - Grade 4	Mother Rept: Discipline	-.001	-.085	-.149	1.000						
	Nattering	.267**	.307**	.130	-.267**	1.000					
	Observer Impressions	-.103	-.203*	-.097	.221**	-.581**	1.000				
	Abuse Cluster	.084	.182	.127	-.160	.472**	-.480**	1.000			
Good Discipline - Grade 6	Parent Rpt: Discipline	-.089	-.261**	-.186*	.583**	-.235**	.195*	-.133	1.000		
	Observer Impressions	-.193*	-.385**	-.284**	.232**	-.540**	.597**	-.387**	.372**	1.000	
	Nattering	-.345**	-.364**	-.308**	.221*	-.534**	.402**	-.324**	.358**	.665**	1.000
Monitoring - Grade 4	Child Rpt Monitoring	.044	.005	-.005	.147	-.077	.079	.050	.118	.085	.030
	Int'vwr Imp: Monitoring	.016	.071	.071	.234**	-.265**	.250**	-.173*	.125	.234**	.146
	Parent Phone Rpt	-.087	-.016	-.016	.136	.048	.041	.004	.182*	.044	.105
Monitoring - Grade 6	Child Rpt Monitoring	-.003	-.012	-.012	.177*	-.088	.145	.035	.172*	.156	.050
	Int'vwr Imp Monitoring	-.055	-.028	-.028	.216*	-.262**	.273**	-.213*	.293**	.358**	.178*
	Parent Phone Rpt	-.024	-.010	-.010	.208*	.003	.127	.024	.157	.187*	.053
	Mother Rpt: Monitoring	.004	-.125	-.125	.240**	-.060	.131	-.141	.283**	.166	.080
Transition Risk	Transition Risk Score	.169	.297**	.297**	-.070	.290**	-.240**	.151	-.072	-.230**	-.238**
	Puberty	.225*	.110	.110	.038	.075	-.073	.057	.041	-.028	-.133
	#Residence Moves	.069	.101	.101	-.040	.197*	-.166*	.074	-.042	-.168*	-.157
	Norm School Transitions	-.110	-.354**	-.354**	.119	-.164*	.078	-.054	.170*	.045	.109
	NonNorm School Trans.	.134	.218*	.218*	-.020	.274**	-.243**	.122	.028	-.240**	-.215*
	#Family transitions	-.028	.122	.122	-.060	.150	-.146	.143	-.023	-.193*	-.090
	S.D.	.116	.042	.789	.635	.450	.980	.442	.540	.784	.880

Table 5.3 (continued)

	Monitoring - Grade 4			Monitoring - Grade 6				Transition Risk					
	Child Report: Monitoring	Int'vwr Impress: Monitoring	Parent Phone Report	Child Report: Monitoring	Int'vwr Impress: Monitoring	Parent Phone Report	Mother Report Monitoring	Transition Risk Score	Puberty	Number of Residence Moves	Normative School Transit.	Nonnorm. School Transit	#Family Transitions
Coercive Child													
Sibling Synchronicity													
Sibling Startup													
Parent Synchronicity													
Good Discipline - Grade 4													
Mother Rept: Discipline													
Nattering													
Observer Impressions													
Abuse Cluster													
Good Discipline - Grade 6													
Parent Rpt: Discipline													
Observer Impressions													
Nattering													
Monitoring - Grade 4													
Child Rpt Monitoring	1.000												
Int'vwr Imp: Monitoring	.385**	1.000											
Parent Phone Rpt	.145	.244**	1.000										
Monitoring - Grade 6													
Child Rpt Monitoring	.393**	.309**	.113	1.000									
Int'vwr Imp Monitoring	.184*	.313**	.165	.411**	1.000								
Parent Phone Rpt	.179*	.320**	.338**	.298**	.271**	1.000							
Mother Rpt: Monitoring	.222*	.270**	.089	.225**	.300**	.131	1.000						
Transition Risk													
Transition Risk Score	.079	-.096	.084	-.131	-.090	-.010	-.037	1.000					
Puberty	-.045	-.049	.019	-.140	-.027	.029	.008	.385**	1.000				
#Residence Moves	.184*	.008	.084	-.022	-.017	.032	.058	.676**	.064	1.000			
Norm School Transitions	-.005	.012	-.085	.042	-.001	-.060	.040	-.609**	-.035	-.190*	1.000		
NonNorm School Trans.	.098	-.080	.009	-.032	.002	.041	.032	.750**	.027	.433**	-.531**	1.000	
#Family transitions	-.018	-.159	.044	-.144	-.225**	-.178*	-.170*	.539**	.010	.316**	-.042**	.220**	1.000
S.D.	.550	.788	2.526	.628	.796	.746	.635	.594	.745	.978	.450	1.070	1.769

* $p < .01$, ** $p < .001$

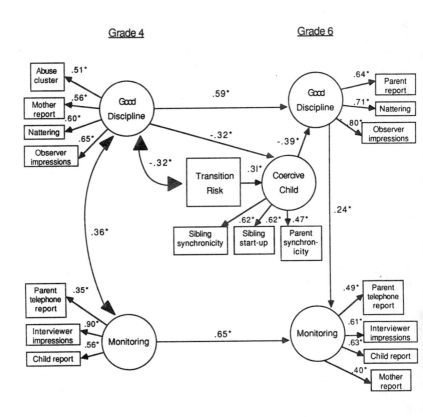

Figure 5.3 Respecified Model of Effects of Child Risk of Transition on Parenting Practices
NOTES: $N = 206$; $x^2_{(120)} = 150.34$; $p = .032$; GFI = .928; AGFI = .897; $^*p < .05$

the same results occur, but with a chi-square greater than .05. This "improved" result occurs in calculating chi-square goodness of fit when a sample size of 159 is used in lieu of the more conservative sample size of 206 for all the models presented in this chapter. The fit does not differ significantly from that of the measurement model, X^2 (difference) = 12.47, $df = .05 < p < .10$.

The findings are consistent with the hypothesis that transition stressors are disrupting to the preadolescents' social exchanges with family members. Presumably, the effect of the stress is to increase the level of irritable exchanges. The disruptions are correlated with ineffective discipline and these, in turn, to disrupted monitoring. The model offers general support for the idea that stressors impinging on the young adolescent boy contribute *indirectly* to adjustment problems.

The findings are also consistent with the idea that pubescence and other transitions are indirectly related to adjustment problems. This finding replicates the earlier findings from the longitudinal study by Magnusson (1988), who showed that early pubescent girls were at particular risk for such norm-violating behaviors as staying out late, cheating on exams, getting drunk, loitering, etc. The effect was particularly marked for girls pubescent before the age of 11. In his elegant study, he went on to demonstrate that the effect of pubescence on adjustment was mediated by the greater propensity for early involvement with older peers. The present findings suggest the possibility of a *second* mediating variable for this effect: the disrupting effect it may have on parental discipline and indirectly its effect on monitoring.

IMPLICATIONS

The findings offer consistent support for the hypothesis that certain characteristics of the child are associated with risk for future disruption in parenting practices, very much in keeping with the findings in the longitudinal study reported by Elder, Caspi, and Van Nguyen (1986). They found that the effect of economic deprivation on parenting practices varied as a function of the age, sex, and personality characteristics of the child. In the present context, data were presented that support the hypothesis that as preadolescent boys become increasingly deviant, their parents may become increasingly ineffective in their use of discipline and monitoring. Confidence in the finding is enhanced by the fact that it replicates part of the findings from the longitudinal study by Cohen and Brook (1987). They also found that earlier measures of child problem adjustment covaried significantly with later measures of parent practices.

Dishion (1988) found that about 66% of antisocial boys are rejected by members of the normal peer group. The analyses by Patterson and Bank (1989) showed that early peer rejection contributes significantly to the maintenance of future antisocial behavior; similar to studies by Coie and Kupersmidt (1983) and Dodge (1983). The possibility that peer rejection may function as a second feedback loop raises the interesting question of what the mediating mechanism might be. For the present, the authors would suppose that peer rejection contributes to a more limited selection of opportunities for learning prosocial survival skills, and that limited skills constrain the youth to remaining at continued risk.

For the third feedback loop (that a change in context produces shifts in the adolescents' behavior, which in turn lead to disruptions in family process), the analyses were somewhat less than satisfying in that they combined the effects from three rather different transitions in estimating the impact on social exchanges with family members. As our longitudinal study progresses, it will be possible to estimate the effect of transitions separately from shifts in neighborhoods or through the school systems. Doubtless each of these transitions makes an unique as well as shared contribution to changes in context.

The most reasonable conclusion seems, at this point, to be that our present tools for measurement and analysis show promise in disentangling the impact of changes in context from changes brought about by shifts within the process. It seems well within the realm of present technology to finally build the bridges designed by Bronfenbrenner and other developmental theorists. Given adequate measurement and a longitudinal design, it is indeed feasible to construct a developmental theory that is sensitive to ongoing changes in context. The models may also assist the investigator in delineating some of the complex feedback loops that emerge as products and then influence later outcomes.

These preliminary analyses also raise some interesting, albeit very complex, questions. For example, longitudinal designs require that data be collected on some prearranged, fixed schedule. But who is to say that the two-year interval used to test for peer rejection as a feedback loop is equally appropriate for the estimate of self-esteem or academic achievement on later antisocial behavior? We badly need some coherent logical basis for making an a priori guess about what the appropriate interval might be for each variable. For example, there are consistent data establishing adult chronic offending as significantly correlated with earlier school failure, as well as earlier antisocial child behavior. In spite of our present data set to prove so, we remain convinced that, when the data are available for grades 10 or 12, early school failure will be shown to function as a positive feedback loop for later chronic delinquency.

The next question concerns the necessity for differentiating among variables that contribute to the *maintenance* from those that contribute to the *change* (e.g., worsening) of a deviancy process. The format used in the present analyses do not permit such a differentiation. However, the lucid discussion of these problems by Kessler and Greenberg (1981) suggests that it may be possible to mount a systematic attack on this question. We are currently following up on their suggestion, and hope our future publications on this topic will represent a more sophisticated approach.

REFERENCES

Anderson, J. C., & Gerbing, D. W. (1988). Structural equation modeling in practice: A review and recommended two-step approach. *Psychological Bulletin, 103*, 411-423.

Bank, L., Dishion, T. J., Skinner, M., & Patterson, G. R. (in press). Method variance in structural equation modeling: Living with "glop." In G. R. Patterson (Ed.), *Aggression and depression in family interactions*. Hillsdale, NJ: Erlbaum.

Bank, L., & Stoolmiller, M. (1989). *Effects of antisocial behavior on preadolescent boys' self-esteem*. Poster paper presented at the Biannual Conference of the Society for Research on Child Development, Kansas City, Missouri.

Bentler, P. M., & Bonnett, D. G. (1980). Significance tests and goodness of fit in the analysis of covariance structures. *Psychological Bulletin, 88*, 588-606.

Bronfenbrenner, U. (1988). Interacting systems in human development: Research paradigms, present and future (pp. 25-49). In N. Bolger, A. Caspi, G. Downey, & M. Moorehouse (Eds.), *Persons in context: Developmental processes*. New York: Cambridge University Press.

Capaldi, D. M., & Patterson, G. R. (1987). An approach to the problem of recruitment and retention rates for longitudinal research. *Behavioral Assessment, 9*, 169-177.

Capaldi, D. M., & Patterson, G. R. (1988). *Psychometric properties of fourteen latent constructs from the Oregon Youth Study*. New York: Springer-Verlag.

Cohen, P., & Brook, J. (1987). Family factors related to the persistence of psychopathology in childhood and adolescence. *Psychiatry, 50*, 332-345.

Coie, J. D., & Kupersmidt, J. B. (1983). A behavioral analysis of emerging social status in boys' groups. *Child Development, 54*, 1400-1416.

Cronbach, L. J., & Meehl, P. E. (1955). Construct validity in psychological tests. *Psychological Bulletin, 52*(4), 281-302.

Dishion, T. J. (1988). *The family ecology of boys' peer relations in middle childhood*. (Available from the author, Oregon Social Learning Center, 207 E. 5th, Suite 202, Eugene, OR 97401.)

Dishion, T. J., Gardner, K., Patterson, G. R., Reid, J. B., & Thibodeaux, S. (1983). Family process code. *OSLC Technical Report*. (Available from OSLC, 207 E. 5th, Suite 202, Eugene, OR 97401.)

Dodge, K. A. (1983). Behavioral antecedents: A peer social status. *Child Development, 54,* 1386-1399.

Elder, G. H., Caspi, A., & Van Nguyen, T. (1986). Resourceful and vulnerable children: Family influences in hard times. In R. K. Silbereisen, K. Eyferth, & G. Rudinger (Eds.), *Development as action in context: Problem behavior and normal youth development* (pp. 167-186). Berlin: Springer-Verlag.

Forgatch, M. S. (1988). *The relation between child behavior, client resistance, and parenting practices.* Paper presented at the Earlscourt Symposium on Childhood Aggression, Toronto, Ontario, June 15-18.

Forgatch, M. S., Patterson, G. R., & Skinner, M. L. (in press). A mediational model for the effect of divorce on antisocial behavior in boys. In E. M. Hetherington & J. D. Arasteh (Eds.), *Impact of divorce, single parenting, and stepparenting on children.* Hillsdale, NJ: Erlbaum.

Garmezy, N. (1983). Stressors of childhood. In N. Garmezy & M. Rutter (Eds.), *Stress, coping, and development in children* (pp. 43-84). New York: McGraw-Hill.

Gollop, H. F., & Reichardt, C. S. (1987). Taking account of time lags in causal models. *Child Development, 58,* 80-92.

Kessler, R. C., & Greenberg, D. F. (1981). *Linear panel analysis: Models of quantitative change.* New York: Academic Press.

Maccoby, E. E. (1983). Social-emotional development and response to stressors. In N. Garmezy & M. Rutter (Eds.), *Stress, coping, and development in children* (pp. 217-234). New York: McGraw-Hill.

Magnusson, D. (1988). *Individual development from an interactional perspective: A longitudinal study.* Hillsdale, NJ: Erlbaum.

Patterson, G. R. (1982). *A social learning approach: 3. Coercive family process.* Eugene, OR: Castalia.

Patterson, G. R. (1983). Stress: A change agent for family process. In N. Garmezy & M. Rutter (Eds.), *Stress, coping, and development in children* (pp. 235-264). New York: McGraw-Hill.

Patterson, G. R. (1986). Performance models for antisocial boys. *American Psychologist, 41,* 432-444.

Patterson, G. R., & Bank, L. (1986). Bootstrapping your way in the nomological thicket. *Behavior Assessment, 8,* 49-73.

Patterson, G. R., & Bank, L. (1987). When is a nomological network a construct? In D. R. Peterson & D. B. Fishman (Eds.), *Assessment for decision* (pp. 249-279). New Brunswick, NJ: Rutgers University Press.

Patterson, G. R., & Bank, L. (1989). Some amplifying mechanisms for pathologic process in families. In M. Gunnar & E. Thelen (Eds.), *Systems and development: The Minnesota Symposia on child psychology (Vol. 22),* (pp. 167-210). Hillsdale, NJ: Erlbaum.

Patterson, G. R., & Forgatch, M. S. (in press). Initiation and maintenance of processes disrupting single-mother families. In G. R. Patterson (Ed.), *Depression and aggression in family interaction.* Hillsdale, NJ: Erlbaum.

Patterson, G. R., Reid, J. B., & Dishion, T. J. (in press). *A social learning approach: 4. Antisocial boys.* Eugene, OR: Castalia.

Rutter, M. (1983). Stress, coping, and development: Some issues and some questions. In N. Garmezy & M. Rutter (Eds.), *Stress, coping, and development in children* (pp. 1-42). New York: McGraw Hill.

Snyder, J. J. (1977). Reinforcement analysis of interaction in problem and nonproblem families. *Journal of Abnormal Psychology, 86,* 528-535.

Snyder, J. J. (1988). *The effect of stress on mother-child interactional sequences.* Seminar presented at the Oregon Social Learning Center, Eugene OR, August.

Tremblay, R. (1988, June). *Some findings from the Montreal studies.* Paper presented at the Earlscourt Symposium on Childhood Aggression, Toronto, Ontario.

Wahler, R. G., & Dumas, J. E. (1983). *Stimulus class determinants of mother-child coercive exchanges in multidistressed families: Assessment and intervention.* Paper presented at the Vermont Conference on Primary Prevention of Psychopathology, Bolton Valley Winter/Summer Resort, June.

6. Changes in Academic Motivation and Self-Perception During Early Adolescence

Jacquelynne S. Eccles
Carol Midgley
University of Michigan

There has been growing concern with adolescence as a time of risk. By whatever criteria one uses, a substantial portion of America's adolescents are not succeeding: Between 15% and 30% (depending on ethnic group) drop out of school before completing high school; adolescents have the highest arrest rate of any age group; and increasing numbers of adolescents consume alcohol and other drugs on a regular basis (Office of Educational Research and Improvement, 1988). Many of these problems appear to begin during the early adolescent years (Carnegie Council on Adolescent Development, 1989). Why? Is there something unique about this developmental period that puts individuals at risk as they pass through it? In this chapter, we look more closely at this question as it pertains specifically to the academic life of early adolescents. Consistent with the view elaborated by Higgins and Parsons (1983), we suggest that the unique transitional nature of early adolescence results, at least in part, from an interaction between developmental changes in the individuals and structural changes in the social environments, in particular the schools, that the individuals pass through as they move from childhood into adulthood.

Evidence from a variety of sources suggests that the early adolescent years mark the beginning of a downward spiral that leads some adolescents to academic failure and school dropout. For example, Simmons and Blyth (1987) found a marked decline in early adolescents' school grades as they move into junior high school. Further-

AUTHORS' NOTE: *This research was made possible by grants from the National Institute of Child Health and Human Development (HD31724) to the first author and the National Science Foundation (BNS-8510504) to the first author and Allan Wigfield. We wish also to thank all of our colleagues for assistance in designing, running, and analyzing the data from the studies reported herein. Special thanks go to Allan Wigfield, David Reuman, Harriet Feldlaufer, Douglas MacIver, Dave Klingel, Christy Miller Buchanan, and Jan Jacobs as well as all of the teachers, school personnel, and students who agreed to participate in these studies.*

134

more, the magnitude of this decline was predictive of subsequent school failure and drop out. Although the junior high school transition effects are not so extreme for most adolescents, there is sufficient evidence of gradual decline in various indicators of academic motivation and self-perception over the early adolescent years to make one ask why (see Eccles & Midgley, 1989, for review).

A variety of explanations have been offered to explain these negative changes: Some have suggested that declines such as these result from the intrapsychic upheaval assumed to be associated with early adolescent development (e.g., Blos, 1965). These views assume that there is something unique about early adolescence that leads to an increase in motivational and behavioral problems and that this something is located within the developing adolescent.

Others have suggested that it is the coincidence of the timing of the junior high school transition with pubertal development that accounts for the decline (e.g., Blyth, Simmons, & Carlton-Ford, 1983; Simmons & Blyth, 1987). Drawing upon cumulative stress theory, these theorists suggest that declines in motivation result from the multiple stressors of pubertal development combined with a major school transition. They suggest that pubertal development is itself stressful because it is associated with major biological, morphological, and social changes. Similarly, making a major school transition is stressful because it also involves many changes. Compounding these sources of stress is likely to result in negative motivational outcomes.

We have suggested that the quality of the junior high school environment is probably the most powerful explanation for the declines. Drawing upon Person-Environment Fit theory, we have proposed that these declines could result from the fact that junior high schools are not providing developmentally appropriate educational environments for early adolescents (Eccles, Midgley, & Adler, 1984; Eccles & Midgley, 1989). According to Person-Environment Fit theory, motivation and mental health can best be understood if one looks at the fit between the characteristics individuals bring to their social environments and the characteristics of these social environments. Specifically, the fit between the needs and motivational orientation of the individuals on the one hand, and the demands and characteristics of their social environments on the other, is assumed to influence motivation and mental health. Individuals are not likely to do very well if they are in social environments that do not fit their psychological needs. In this chapter, we use this perspective to analyze the developmental declines in academic motivation and self-perceptions associated with early adolescent development. Specifically, we suggest that there is a mismatch between the developing needs of early adolescents and the typical kinds of environmental changes they experience when they make the transition to junior high school.

Several investigators have stressed how crucial the junior high years are for individual development (Hamburg, 1974; Lipsitz, 1981) both because of the developmental tasks confronting the early adolescent and because of the amount of time early adolescents must spend in this environment. At the same time, many have bemoaned the quality of the junior high school environment: For example, according to Charles Silberman (1970), "the junior high school, by almost unanimous agreement, is the wasteland—one is tempted to say cesspool—of American education" (pg. 324). What is likely to happen when we put developing adolescents into these "wastelands"? This is the focus of this chapter.

ACADEMIC MOTIVATION, SELF-PERCEPTIONS, AND CLASSROOM ENVIRONMENTS: JUNIOR HIGH SCHOOL TRANSITION EFFECTS

General Developmental Changes

Several investigators suggest that there are general developmental declines in such motivational constructs as: interest in school (Epstein & McPartland, 1976); intrinsic motivation (Harter, 1982); self-concepts/self-perceptions (Eccles et al., 1984; Simmons, Blyth, Van Cleave, & Bush, 1979), and confidence in one's intellectual abilities, especially following failure (Parsons & Ruble, 1977; Parsons, 1982). There have also been reports of age-related increases in such negative motivational characteristics as test anxiety (Hill, 1980), learned helpless responses to failure (Rholes, Blackwell, Jordan, & Walters, 1980), focus on self-evaluation rather than task mastery (Nicholls, 1980), and truancy and school dropout (Rosenbaum, 1976). (See Eccles et al., 1984, for full review.)

Although studies of developmental changes in motivation and self-perception during the early adolescent period are not entirely consistent, several studies report that the types of developmental changes outlined above are especially marked in conjunction with the junior high school transition (Eccles et al., 1984). For example, we have found a marked discontinuity in the rate of change in attitudes toward math between grades 6 and 7 when the children moved from elementary school to junior high school: There is a dramatic drop in the adolescents' confidence in their math abilities and interest in learning mathematics. Similar discontinuities are evident in the work of Harter (1981, 1982) and Simmons and her colleagues (Simmons & Blyth, 1987). Harter (1981), for example, reports a sharp drop in students' preference for challenging as opposed to easy work and for independent mastery as opposed to getting good grades between the sixth and the seventh grade—before and after the transition to junior high school.

The possible negative impact of school transition at this period is well illustrated by the work of Simmons and her colleagues who have compared children moving from sixth to seventh grade in a K-8, 9-12 system to children making the same transition in a K-6, 7-9, 10-12 school system. This work unconfounds the conjoint effects of age and transition operating in most developmental studies of this age period. These researchers find clear evidence of school transition effects but the exact nature of these effects and the groups of students most affected varies somewhat across studies. In general, however, girls seem more at risk for negative consequences of the junior high school transition than boys. For example, in Simmons and Blyth (1987), girls moving into a traditional junior high school show a more marked decline in their self-esteem than girls who remain in the same school building; no comparable school transition effect was found for boys' self-esteem.

These studies, and others like them, suggest that something unique may be going on during early adolescence and that it may interact with the nature of school transitions in affecting the motivation of early adolescents. Several investigators have suggested just such a link between these motivational declines and the junior high school transition (Blyth et al., 1983; Eccles et al., 1984; Eccles & Midgley, 1989; Simmons & Blyth, 1987). Simmons and her colleagues proposed the first such hypothesis. Given the sex difference in the transition effect, they focused on the timing issue. Drawing on cumulative stress theory, they argued that the timing of the transition to junior high school should result in more disruption to individuals already undergoing the stress associated with pubertal development than would a similar transition a few years later "after the individual has developed a more mature sense of who he or she is" (Blyth et al., 1983, p. 106).

If the timing of the transition is the critical factor, then when is the timing good or bad and for whom? Investigators who have sought to

replicate and extend Simmons' work have compared the effects of
school transitions at different grade levels. The results of these studies
are largely inconsistent and inconclusive. Thornburg and Jones (1982)
compared students who moved up a grade level within the same
school to students who entered a new school structure. Students who
moved to a new school at sixth grade had lower self-esteem than sixth
grade students who did not make a school transition, while at seventh
grade there were no significant differences in self-esteem for groups
that did or did not make a school transition. They concluded that
school transitions occurring at lower grade levels are more likely to
affect early adolescent self-esteem adversely than school transitions
at higher grade levels. Nottelmann (1987) conducted a longitudinal
study comparing the effects on self-esteem of movement from grades
5 to 6, and grades 6 to 7 in both transition and nontransition groups.
She predicted that there would be less disturbance following the
earlier school transition because the children would not be experiencing the simultaneous stress of physical development and movement
to a new school environment. Not only was this hypothesis not
substantiated, but in contrast to the Simmons and Blyth findings,
Nottelmann found that self-esteem was higher in transition groups
than in nontransition groups. Petersen, Ebata, and Graber (1987) came
up with the remarkable finding that children who make two consecutive school transitions experience greater long-term gains in self-
image than children who make a single transition from fifth to sixth
or sixth to seventh.

Why are these findings so inconsistent? Are some other variables
contributing to the effects that are attributed to time of transition? We
believe that these studies are inconsistent because they do not take
into account what is going on in the classroom and in the school before
and after the transition. Perhaps the children in one study are moving
into a less facilitative environment than children in another study.
How did the junior high school environment in the Simmons and
Blyth study, for example, compare to the middle and junior high
school environment in the Nottelmann study? When children moved
from elementary school to middle school or junior high school in the
Nottelmann study, did they experience similar types of environmental changes? Was there something about the junior high school classroom environment in the Simmons and Blyth study that was
particularly detrimental to pubertal girls? Perhaps there was an increase in competition or ability assessment that contributed to the

effects and perhaps this was not the case in the Nottelmann study. Why did the children in the Petersen et al. study who made two transitions within a relatively short period of time end up with a more positive self-image than children who did not? Did they move into innovative programs?

We believe that the *nature* of the transition, as well as the timing must be considered. This means being attentive to changes in both the school and classroom environment. In addition, we believe that the kinds of changes that children normatively experience during the transition to junior high school must be viewed from at least two perspectives: the standard environmental influences approach and a developmental variant on the person-environment fit paradigm, or as we have called it, the *stage/environment fit* approach (see Eccles & Midgley, 1989). Let us discuss each of these in turn.

General Environmental Influences

Work in a variety of areas has documented the impact of various classroom and school environmental characteristics on motivation. For example, the big-school/small-schools literature has demonstrated the motivational advantages of small schools especially for marginal students (Barker & Gump, 1964). Similarly, the teacher efficacy literature has documented the positive student motivational consequences of high teacher efficacy (Brookover, Beady, Flood, Schweitzer, & Wisenbaker, 1979). Finally, organizational psychology has demonstrated the importance of participatory work structures on worker motivation (Lawler, 1976). The list of such influences could, of course, go on for several pages. The point is that there may be systematic differences between typical elementary classrooms and schools, and typical junior high classrooms and schools, and that these differences may account for some of the motivational changes we see in early adolescents as they make the transition into junior high school or middle school. If so, then some of the motivational problems we see at early adolescence may be a consequence of the type of school environment changes we force them to adapt to rather than characteristics of the developmental period per se. Higgins and Parsons (1983) made a similar argument, suggesting that some of the changes we attribute to stagelike developmental processes may, instead, reflect systematic changes in the social environments and social cultures we provide for our children as they grow up.

Stage-Environment Fit

A more thought provoking analysis of the possible environmental causes of the motivational changes associated with the junior high school transition draws on the idea of person-environment fit. Such a perspective leads one to expect negative motivational consequences for individuals when they are in an environment that does not fit well with their needs (Hunt, 1975; Lewin, 1935). At the most basic level, this perspective suggests that we look at the fit between the needs of early adolescents and the opportunities afforded them in the traditional junior high school environment. A poor fit would help explain the declines in motivation associated with the transition to junior high school.

An even more interesting way to use the person-environment fit perspective is to put it into a developmental framework. Hunt (1975) argued for the importance of adopting a developmental perspective on person-environment fit in the classroom. To quote him: "Maintaining a developmental perspective becomes very important in implementing person-environment matching because a teacher should not only take account of a student's contemporaneous needs by providing whatever structure he presently requires, but also view his present need for structure on a developmental continuum along which growth toward independence and less need for structure is the long-term objective" (Hunt, 1975, p. 221). He was suggesting that teachers should provide the optimal level of structure for children's current levels of maturity, while at the same time providing a sufficiently challenging environment to pull the children along a developmental path toward higher levels of cognitive and social maturity.

But what we find especially intriguing about this suggestion is its application to an analysis of the motivational declines associated with the junior high school transition. If we accept the notion that different types of educational environments may be needed for different age groups in order to meet developmental needs and to foster continued developmental growth, then it is also possible that some types of changes in educational environments may be especially inappropriate at certain stages of development, for example, the early adolescent period. That is, they may be "developmentally regressive." Exposure to such changes at this age could lead to a particularly poor person-environment fit, and this lack of fit could account for some of the declines in motivation we see at this developmental period. Specifically, there may be a mismatch between the developing needs of the early adolescent and the opportunities afforded them by the junior high school environment.

In essence, it is the fit between the developmental needs of the adolescent and the educational environment that is important. Imagine two trajectories: one a developmental trajectory of early adolescent growth, the other a trajectory of environmental change across the school years. We believe there will be positive motivational consequences when these two trajectories are in synchrony with one another; that is, when the environment is both responsive to the changing needs of the individual and offers the kinds of stimulation that will propel continued positive growth. In other words, transition to a facilitative and developmentally appropriate environment, even at this vulnerable age, should have a positive impact on children's perceptions of themselves and their educational environment. In contrast, negative motivational consequences will result if the two trajectories are out of synchrony. In this case, transition into a developmentally inappropriate educational environment should result in the types of motivational declines that have been identified as occurring with the transition into junior high school. This should be particularly true if the environment is developmentally regressive; that is, if it affords the children fewer opportunities for continued growth than previous environments.

This analysis immediately raises a set of researchable theoretical and descriptive questions. First, what are the developmental needs of the early adolescent? Second, what kind of educational environment would be developmentally appropriate in terms of both meeting these needs and stimulating further development? Third, what are the most common changes in the academic environment before and after the transition to middle or junior high school. Finally, and most importantly, are these changes compatible with the physiological, cognitive, and psychological changes early adolescents are experiencing? Or is there a developmental mismatch between maturing early adolescents and the classroom environments they experience before and after the transition to junior high school—a mismatch that results in a deterioration in academic motivation and performance for some children?

We believe that there are developmentally inappropriate changes in a cluster of classroom organizational, instructional, and climate variables, including task structure, task complexity, grouping practices, evaluation techniques, motivational strategies, locus of responsibility for learning, and quality of teacher-student and student-student relationships. These changes contribute to the negative

change in students' motivation and achievement-related beliefs assumed to coincide with the transition into junior high school. Unfortunately, we have been unable to locate very much well-controlled
research with which to test these hypotheses.

Remarkably few empirical studies have focused on differences in
the classroom or school environment across grades or school levels.
Most descriptions have focused on school-level characteristics such
as school size, degree of departmentalization, extent of bureaucrati-
zation, and so forth. Although differences in these characteristics can
have important effects on teacher beliefs and practices, which, in turn,
can have an effect on student alienation and motivation, these
linkages have rarely been assessed.

Most attempts to assess the classroom environment have included
only one grade level and have related differences in the environment
to student outcomes, particularly scores on achievement tests. Little
research has focused on systematic differences in the classroom environment from elementary to junior high school. Thus, we have had
to piece together information from a variety of sources, looking for
converging evidence for the types of negative environmental changes
we predicted (see Eccles & Midgley, 1989). Five patterns have
emerged. First, junior high school classrooms, as compared to elementary school classrooms, are characterized by a greater emphasis on
teacher control and discipline, a less personal and positive teacher-
student relationship, and fewer opportunities for student decision
making, choice, and self-management. Second, the shift to junior high
school is associated with an increase in practices such as whole-class
task organization, between classroom ability grouping, and public
evaluation of the correctness of work, each of which may encourage
the use of social comparison and ability self-assessment. Third, there
is evidence that classwork during the first year of junior high school
requires lower level cognitive skills than classwork at the elementary
level. Fourth, junior high school teachers feel less effective as teachers,
especially for low ability students. Finally, junior high school teachers
appear to use a higher standard in judging students' competence and
in grading their performance than do elementary school teachers (see
Eccles & Midgley, 1989, for details on these studies and references).

We believe that these types of school environmental changes are
particularly harmful at early adolescence, given what is known about
psychological development during this stage of life. Evidence from a
variety of sources suggests that early adolescent development is

characterized by increases in the following: desire for autonomy, peer orientation, self-focus and self-consciousness, salience of identity issues, concern over heterosexual relationships, and capacity for abstract cognitive activity (see Simmons & Blyth, 1987). Simmons and Blyth (1987) have argued that adolescents need a reasonably safe, as well as an intellectually challenging, environment to adapt to these shifts—an environment that provides a "zone of comfort" as well as challenging new opportunities for growth. In light of these needs, the environmental changes often associated with transition to junior high school seem especially harmful in that they emphasize competition, social comparison, and ability self-assessment at a time of heightened self-focus; they decrease decision making and choice at a time when the desire for control is growing; they emphasize lower level cognitive strategies at a time when the ability to use higher level strategies is increasing; and they disrupt social networks at a time when adolescents are especially concerned with peer relationships and may be in special need of close adult relationships outside the home. We believe the nature of these environmental changes coupled with the normal course of individual development results in a developmental mismatch so that the "fit" between the early adolescent and the classroom environment is particularly poor, increasing the risk of negative motivational outcomes, especially for adolescents who are having difficulty succeeding in school academically.

To test these predictions, we have conducted a large-scale two-year, four-wave longitudinal study of the impact of changes in the school and classroom environment on early adolescents' achievement-related beliefs, motives, values, and behaviors. The sample was drawn from 12 school districts located in middle income communities in southeastern Michigan. Because we had found the motivational declines to be most marked in mathematics (Eccles et al., 1983), we focused on this subject area. Mathematics teachers and their students were recruited. A total of 2,501 early adolescents participated at all four waves of the study. Many of these adolescents went from sixth to seventh grade and experienced the junior high school transition during the course of the study. The results reported here focus on this subset of the sample. Questionnaires were administered during the regular period for mathematics instruction for two consecutive days each wave (fall and spring of 1983/84 and fall and spring of 1984/85). In addition, a subset of math classrooms was observed by trained field staff for five consecutive days during late October or November each year.

ENVIRONMENTAL CHANGES BETWEEN
SIXTH AND SEVENTH GRADE

Our first goal was to assess differences in the beliefs and behaviors of the teachers the early adolescents had for mathematics before and after the junior high school transition. Several characteristics of the junior high school make it probable that junior high school teachers will hold different beliefs than elementary teachers. Junior high schools are typically larger, less personal, and more formal than elementary schools. Junior high school teachers are often subject matter specialists, and they typically instruct a much larger number of students than do elementary teachers in self-contained classrooms, making it less likely they will come to know their students well, to feel that they are trustworthy, and to grant them autonomy. Junior high school teachers may feel that it is difficult to affect the achievement of a large number of adolescents, especially as they see each of them for a relatively small proportion of the school day, making it difficult for the teachers to sustain feelings of efficacy. Junior high school is often seen as a time to get serious about instruction and performance evaluation. Assigning early adolescents to classes on the basis of their ability, particularly in mathematics, becomes much more frequent (Oakes, 1981). Once students have been assigned to classrooms on the basis of their ability, mobility to another ability level is infrequent (Metz, 1978; Oakes, 1981). This practice, coupled with increasing pressure to grade children on relative performance rather than on improvement or mastery, may engender a belief in teachers that differences in student ability are stable and teacher influences on student achievement are relatively minor. Finally, cultural stereotypes about early adolescence may flourish in schools that serve only this age group. There is evidence that early adolescence is viewed by society as a particularly difficult and unproductive stage of life (Holmbeck & Hill, 1986; Offer, Ostrov, & Howard, 1981). These societal views are not likely to engender feelings of efficacy or trust in those who work with early adolescents.

We compared the beliefs of the teachers our adolescents had for mathematics before and after the transition (see Midgley, Feldlaufer, & Eccles, 1988b, for a full description of this study). The sample included 107 sixth grade elementary teachers and 64 seventh grade junior high teachers. There are fewer seventh than sixth grade teachers because, at the junior high school level, each teacher instructs several sections of math. As predicted, the seventh grade teachers believed students needed to be disciplined and controlled more than the sixth grade teachers did, using a scale with items such as "it is often necessary to remind students that their status in school differs from that of teachers" and "students should not be permitted to contradict the statements of teachers in class." Similarly, the seventh grade teachers rated students as less trustworthy than did the sixth grade teachers on a scale containing items such as "most students will waste free time if they're not given something to do" and "students can (not) be trusted to correct their own tests." Finally, the seventh grade teachers felt significantly less efficacious than did the sixth grade teachers on a scale including items such as "I am certain I am making a difference in the lives of my students" and "there is really very little I can do to ensure that most of my students achieve at a high level."

Similar patterns emerged for students' and observers' perceptions of the quality of student-teacher relationships before and after the transition (see Feldlaufer, Midgley, & Eccles, 1988, for a complete description). Seventh grade post-transition math teachers were seen as less supportive, friendly, and fair than sixth grade pretransition teachers by both observers and students. In addition, students, teachers, and observers reported an increase, after the transition, in between-classroom ability grouping, whole-class instruction, and social comparison of grades, all of which have been suggested to promote a focus on ability self-perceptions more than a focus on mastering the task (Rosenholtz & Simpson, 1984).

IMPACT OF ENVIRONMENTAL CHANGES ON EARLY ADOLESCENTS' MOTIVATION

Teacher Efficacy

We are now looking at the impact of differences in teacher beliefs and practices before and after the transition on early adolescents' motives, values, beliefs, and behaviors. In a longitudinal study of 1,329 early adolescents and the teachers they had for mathematics before and after the transition to junior high school, we examined the relation between changes in adolescents' self- and task-related beliefs in mathematics and their teachers' sense of efficacy (see Midgley, Feldlaufer, & Eccles, 1989, for a full description of this study). Although the relation between teacher efficacy and student beliefs and attitudes is yet to be firmly established, Brookover et al., (1979) using schools as the unit of analysis, found negative correlations between teachers' sense of academic futility and students' self-concept of ability and self-reliance. Given these associations, differences in teachers' sense of efficacy before and after the transition to junior high school could contribute to the decline in early adolescents' beliefs about their academic competency and potential.

To assess the impact of change in teacher efficacy on adolescents' beliefs, we divided our adolescent sample into four groups based on median splits of their math teachers' ratings of their personal teaching efficacy. The largest group (559 out of the 1,329 included in these analyses) moved from a high efficacy sixth grade math teacher to a low efficacy seventh grade math teacher. Another 474 adolescents had low efficacy teachers both years, 117 moved from low to high efficacy teachers, and 179 had high efficacy teachers both years. Thus, fully 78% of our sample of children moved to a low teacher efficacy math classroom in the seventh grade. The potential impact of such a shift on the motivation and self-perceptions of early adolescents, especially those having difficulty mastering the academic material is frightening. We know, in particular, that low teacher expectations for students undermine the motivation and performance for low achieving students (Eccles & Wigfield, 1985). Moving from a high to a low efficacious teacher may produce a similar effect.

As predicted, the adolescents who had moved from high efficacy to low efficacy teachers during the transition (the most common pattern) ended their first year in junior high school with lower expectancies for themselves in math, lower perceptions of their performance in math, and higher perceptions of the difficulty of math than the adolescents who had experienced no change in teacher efficacy or who had moved from low to high efficacy teachers. Also as predicted, teacher efficacy beliefs had a stronger impact on the low-achieving adolescents' beliefs than on the high-achieving adolescents' beliefs. The results for the low-achieving adolescents are illustrated in Figure 6.1. By the end of the junior high school year, the confidence that those low-achieving adolescents who had moved from high to low efficacy teachers had in their ability to master mathematics had declined dramatically. We may see here the beginning of the downward spiral in school motivation that eventually leads to school drop out among so many low-achieving adolescents. It is important to note, however, that this same decline was not characteristic of the low-achieving adolescents who had moved to high efficacy seventh grade math teachers, suggesting that the decline is not a general feature of

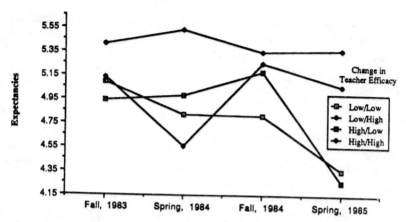

Figure 6.1 Expectancies in Math and Change in Teacher Efficacy for Low-Achieving Students

early adolescent development but rather a consequence of the fact that so many early adolescents experience a debilitating shift in their classroom environments as they make the junior high school transition.

Teacher-Student Relationships

As reported earlier, we found that student-teacher relationships deteriorate after the transition to junior high school. Research on the effects of classroom climate indicates that the quality of student-teacher relationships is associated with students' academic motivation and attitudes toward school (e.g., Fraser & Fisher, 1982; Moos, 1979; Trickett & Moos, 1974). Consequently, there is reason to believe that transition into a less supportive classroom will impact negatively on early adolescents' interest in the subject matter being taught in that classroom.

In a sample of 1,301 students, we looked at the effect of differences in perceived teacher support before and after the transition to junior high school on the value early adolescents attach to mathematics (see Midgley, Feldlaufer, & Eccles, 1988a, for a full description of this study). We found, as predicted, that when our early adolescents moved from elementary teachers they perceived to be low in support to junior high school teachers they perceived to be high in support, the value they attached to math was enhanced; in contrast, early adolescents who moved from teachers they perceived to be high in support to teachers they perceived to be low in support lowered the value they attached to math. Again we found evidence that low-achieving students are particularly at risk when they move to less facilitative classroom environments after the transition.

Both of these studies show that the declines often reported in studies of early adolescents' motivational orientation to school subjects is not inevitable. Instead, these declines are associated with specific types of changes in the nature of the classroom environment experienced by many early adolescents as they make the junior high school transition. The studies also show that a transition into more facilitative types of classrooms can induce positive changes in early adolescents' motivation and self-perceptions. Unfortunately, for all adolescents, but especially for low-achieving adolescents, our findings also indicate that most adolescents experience a negative change in their classroom experiences as they make the junior high school transition. Neither of these studies, however, directly tests our stage-environment fit hypothesis.

STAGE-ENVIRONMENT FIT

We have just completed several sets of analyses that test our developmental approach to person-environment fit more explicitly (see Midgley & Feldlaufer, 1987, and MacIver & Reuman, 1988, for a full description of these studies). In a sample of 2,210 students and their teachers in 117 pretransition and 137 post-transition classrooms, Midgley and Feldlaufer (1987) assessed student and teacher perceptions of actual and preferred decision-making opportunities in the classroom. Yoked pairs of items (Lee, Statuto, & Kedar-Voivodas, 1983) were used to assess actual and preferred decision-making opportunities in five areas in which students might be allowed to help make classroom policy. For example:

For students: Do you help decide what math you work on during class?
Should you have a say about this?
For teachers: Do your students have a say about what math they work on during class?
Do you think students *should* have a say in this?

As expected, early adolescents expressed a desire for more input into decision making after they moved to the junior high school. Unfortunately, both adolescents and teachers reported that students actually had fewer decision-making opportunities after the transition than before; thus, there was a growing lack of congruence between early adolescents' desires and the opportunities afforded by the environment as they moved into junior high school.

Does this increasing mismatch affect early adolescents' motivation? There are several ways to approach this question. If the stage-environment fit perspective outlined earlier is correct, then the early adolescents experiencing one particular type of increasing incongruence should be most likely to evidence declines in motivational variables. Specifically, given the general developmental progression toward increased desire for independence and autonomy during the early adolescent period, those early adolescents who experience a decrease in their opportunities for participation in classroom decision making, coupled with an increasing desire for such opportunities, should evidence the greatest declines in their motivation. In support of this prediction, those adolescents who perceived their seventh grade math classrooms as putting greater constraints on their preferred level of participation in classroom decision making than their sixth grade math classrooms showed larger and more consistent declines in their interest in math than their peers as they made the junior high school transition (MacIver & Reuman, 1988). That is, it was the adolescents who experienced an increase in their unmet desire for input in classroom decision making as they moved from sixth to seventh grade who showed the largest declines in their interest in math as they made this school transition. These are the students who are experiencing the type of developmental mismatch we outlined in our discussion of stage-environment fit.

SUMMARY AND DISCUSSION

Children's orientation toward school achievement and confidence in their own ability to master schoolwork declines as they move from childhood into adolescence. Furthermore, these declines appear to be especially marked as early adolescents enter and experience the junior high school environment. Some would argue that organismic changes, such as pubertal development and the onset of formal operational thought, are responsible for these shifts; that early adolescence, because it is a time of such profound biological and psychological change, puts the developing individual at risk for negative outcomes. Although one can not deny that these are important influences and that early adolescence may well be a particularly interesting transitional period, especially in this culture, we have presented a more social contextual view on the nature of this transition. We have proposed that the transitional status of early adolescence is best understood by focusing on the interaction between organismic maturation and systematic changes in the social environment early adolescents are exposed to. We have used this perspective to analyze the declines in academic motivation and self-perceptions generally associated with the junior high school transition. Specifically, we have suggested that there are systematic differences between sixth grade elementary and seventh grade junior high school classrooms and that these differences help explain the developmental declines in academic motivation and self-perception often reported as characteristic of the early adolescent period. The evidence presented suggests that the declines in motivation are less a consequence of the developmental stage than of a mismatch between the early adolescents' needs and the opportunities afforded them in the junior high school environment. Clearly much more work needs to be done to provide solid evidence in support of this hypothesis.

The theory and evidence presented in this chapter raise several interesting issues. First, is early adolescence a transitional period? The answer to this question depends on one's definition of transitional. Higgins and Parsons (1983) argued that the morphological changes associated with puberty and societal beliefs about adolescent development lead adults and peers to structure the social environments of early adolescents differently than the social environments of either older or younger people, making early adolescence a time of transition between different social cultures. Whether it is also transitional in the organismic, structural sense is a difficult question to answer. Given that developing individuals in this culture experience fairly widespread, systematic changes in their social environments as they pass into and through early adolescence, it is difficult to see whether the psychological changes associated with this developmental period are attributable to social environmental shifts, to maturational processes, or to some interaction between these two influences. Studies such as the ones reported here suggest that the direction of change during this developmental period is greatly influenced by the nature of the shifts in the early adolescents' social environment. Environmental changes that are responsive to the individual's growing desire to be mature should pull the individual toward maturity and positive outcomes. Developmentally regressive environmental changes and environmental changes that decrease the fit between the individual's needs and the opportunities afforded by the environment should lead to negative consequences. It is also possible that early adolescence is a time of increased plasticity and openness (Lerner, 1982: Lipsitz, 1981). If this is true then social environmental influences ought to have an especially marked impact at this developmental period (and early adolescence ought to be a time when children are especially vulnerable to both positive and negative influences). We know of no empirical studies that adequately test this hypothesis.

Second, if developmentally appropriate educational environments have more positive consequences for early adolescents then why are junior high school environments so developmentally inappropriate? Why, for example, do seventh grade teachers have such a negative view of their students and of their own efficacy? Are there other belief systems and social structures that underlie these perceptions and the other nonadaptive characteristics of the junior high school environment? We have become very interested in adults' stereotypes about adolescence. Seventh grade junior high school teachers believe that early adolescence is a difficult time of life for children and their teachers, and those with the most teaching experience endorse this belief most strongly (Miller, Eccles, Flanagan, Midgley, Feldlaufer, & Goldsmith, in press). Are these stereotypes responsible to the other negative attitudes junior high school teachers have? Where do these stereotypes come from? Does the fact that we ghettoize early adolescents into junior high schools and middle schools exacerbate these stereotypes? Is there something about the structure of the junior high school that creates an environment in which early adolescents are more likely to act in accord with the stereotypes than they would if they were in other more facilitative environments (Carnegie Council on Adolescent Development, 1989)? Are there other macrostructural features of our culture that have impact on both the nature of the educational environments provided for early adolescents and the beliefs that adults in this culture have regarding early adolescents in general and specific subgroups of early adolescents in particular? Questions such as these require that we take a broader look at the factors that influence the types of environments we provide for early adolescents as well as at the impact of these environments on early adolescents.

Third, how might the stage-environment fit idea be useful in other areas of early adolescent development? Not surprisingly, we see many possible applications of this perspective. For example, it seems likely that a poor person-environment fit within school might encourage some students to seek a better fit outside of school. Because of their increasing independence and mobility, early adolescents should be more likely to take advantage of this option than children, often at the expense of their school involvement and academic achievement. The evidence of increased rates of truancy during the early adolescent years (Simmons & Blyth, 1987) supports this suggestion.

Similarly, one could look at transitions in family relationships during the early adolescent period in terms of the stage-environment fit perspective. Just as we have suggested for the school environment, optimal development during the early adolescent period ought to be affected by the match between the changing needs of the early adolescent and the opportunities afforded within the family to meet these needs. Montemayor (1986), Steinberg (1989), and others have suggested that early adolescence is characterized by a temporary increase in family frictions. But even this temporary increase is not characteristic of all families. It seems that friction is most likely to result in those families in which the parents are not as responsive to their adolescent's changing needs as they should be, resulting in a temporary mismatch between the needs of the early adolescent and the family environment.

Is early adolescence a distinct developmental, transitional period? We believe it is a period characterized by many transitions—physiological, psychological, and environmental. Only by understanding the complex interactions among these many transitions will we come to understand the special and unique nature of early adolescence.

REFERENCES

Barker, R., & Gump, P. (1964). *Big school, small school: High school size and student behavior.* Stanford, CA: Stanford University Press.

Blyth, D. A., Simmons, R. G., & Carlton-Ford, S. (1983). The adjustment of early adolescents to school transitions. *Journal of Early Adolescence, 3,* 105-120.

Blos, P. (1965). The initial stage of male adolescence. *The Psychoanalytic Study of the Child, 20,* 145-164.

Brookover, W., Beady, C., Flood, P., Schweitzer, J. & Wisenbaker, J. (1979). *School social systems and student achievement: Schools can make a difference.* NY: Praeger.

Carnegie Council on Adolescent Development (1989). *Turning points: Preparing American youth for the 21st century.* New York: Carnegie Corporation.

Eccles, J., Adler, T. F., Futterman, R., Goff, S. B., Kaczala, C. M., Meece, J. L., & Midgley, C. (1983). Expectancies, values, and academic behaviors. In J. T. Spence (Ed.), *Achievement and achievement motivation.* San Francisco, CA: W. H. Freeman.

Eccles, J. S., & Midgley, C. (1989). Stage/environment fit: Developmentally appropriate classrooms for early adolescents. In R. E. Ames & C. Ames (Eds.), *Research on motivation in education* Vol. 3. NY: Academic Press.

Eccles, J., Midgley, C., & Adler, T. (1984). Grade-related changes in the school environment: Effects on achievement motivation. In J. G. Nicholls (Ed.), *The development of achievement motivation* (pp. 283-331). Greenwich, CT: JAI Press.

Eccles, J., & Wigfield, A. (1985). Teacher expectations and student motivation. In J. Dusek (Ed.), *Teacher expectancies* (pp. 185-217). Hillsdale, NJ: Erlbaum.

Epstein, J. L. & McPartland, J. M. (1976). The concept and measurement of the quality of school life. *American Educational Research Journal, 13*, 15-30.

Feldlaufer, H., Midgley, C., & Eccles, J. S. (1988). Student, teacher, and observer perceptions of the classroom environment before and after the transition to junior high school. *Journal of Early Adolescence, 8*, 133-156.

Fraser, B. J., & Fisher, D. L. (1982). Predicting students' outcomes from their perceptions of classroom psychosocial environment. *American Educational Research Journal, 19*, 498-518.

Hamburg, B. A. (1974). Early adolescence: A specific and stressful stage of the life cycle. In G. V. Coelho, B. A. Hamburg, & J. E. Adams (Eds.), *Coping and adaptation.* New York: Basic Books.

Harter, S. (1981). A new self-report scale of intrinsic versus extrinsic orientation in the classroom: Motivational and informational components. *Developmental Psychology, 17*, 300-312.

Harter, S. (1982). The Perceived Competence Scale for Children. *Child Development, 53*, 87-97.

Higgins, E. T. & Parsons, J. E. (1983). Social cognition and the social life of the child: Stages as subcultures. In E. T. Higgins, D. W. Ruble, & W. W. Hartup (Eds.). *Social cognition and social behavior: Developmental issues.* New York: Cambridge University Press.

Hill, K. T. (1980). Motivation, evaluation, and educational test policy. In L. J. Fyans (Ed.), *Achievement motivation: Recent trends in theory and research.* New York: Plenum Press.

Holmbeck, G. N., & Hill, J. P. (1986, March). *Beliefs in storm and stress notions of adolescence: Prevalence and developmental antecedents.* Paper presented at the biennial meeting of the Society for Research on Adolescence, Madison, WI.

Hunt, D. E. (1975). Person-environment interaction: A challenge found wanting before it was tried. *Review of Educational Research, 45*, 209-230.

Lawler, E. E. (1976). Control systems in organizations. In M. D. Dunnette (Ed.), Handbook of industrial and organizational psychology. Chicago: Rand McNally.

Lee, P., Statuto, C., & Kedar-Voivodas, G. (1983). Elementary school children's perceptions of their actual and ideal school experience: A developmental study. *Journal of Educational Psychology, 75*, 838-847.

Lerner, R. M. (1982). Children and adolescents as producers of their own development. *Developmental Review, 2*, 342-370.

Lewin, K. (1935). *A dynamic theory of personality.* New York: McGraw-Hill.

Lipsitz, J. (1981). Educating the early adolescent: Why four model schools are effective in reaching a difficult age group. *American Education*, 13-17.

MacIver, D., & Reuman, D. A. (1988, April). *Decision-making in the classroom and early adolescents' valuing of mathematics.* Paper presented at the annual meeting of the American Educational Research Association, New Orleans.

Metz, M. H. (1978). *Classrooms and corridors: The crisis of authority in desegregated secondary schools.* Berkeley, CA: University of California Press.

Midgley, C., & Feldlaufer, H. (1987). Students' and teachers' decision-making fit before and after the transition to junior high school. *Journal of Early Adolescence, 7*, 225-241.

Midgley, C., Feldlaufer, H., & Eccles, J. (1988a). Student/teacher relations and attitudes towards mathematics before and after the transition to junior high school. *Child Development, 60*, 375-395.

Midgley, C., Feldlaufer, H., & Eccles, J. S. (1988b). The transition to junior high school: Beliefs of pre- and post-transition teachers. *Journal of Youth and Adolescence, 17*, 543-562.

Midgley, C., Feldlaufer, H., & Eccles, J. (1989). Change in teacher efficacy and student self- and task-related beliefs during the transition to junior high school. *Journal of Educational Psychology, 81*.

Miller, C. L., Eccles, J. E., Flanagan, C., Midgley, C., Feldlaufer, H., & Goldsmith, R. (in press). *Parents' and teachers' beliefs about adolescence: Effects of sex and experience. Journal of Youth and Adolescence.*

Montemayor, R. (1986). Family variation in parent-adolescent storm and stress. *Journal of Adolescent Research, 1*, 15-31.

Moos, R. H. (1979). *Evaluating educational environments.* San Francisco, CA: Jossey-Bass.

Nicholls, J. G. (1980). *Striving to develop and demonstrate ability: An intentional theory of achievement motivation.* Paper presented at Conference on Attributional Approaches to Human Motivation, Center for Interdisciplinary Studies, University of Bielefeld, West Germany, June, 1980.

Nottelmann, E. D. (1987). Competence and self-esteem during the transition from childhood to adolescence. *Developmental Psychology, 23*, 441-450.

Oakes, J. (1981). Tracking policies and practices: School by school summaries. *A study of schooling: Technical report no. 25.* Los Angeles, CA: University of California Graduate School of Education.

Offer, D., Ostrov, E., & Howard, K. I. (1981). The mental health professional's concept of the normal adolescent. *Archives of General Psychiatry, 38*, 149-153.

Office of Educational Research and Improvement (1988). *Youth Indicators 1988.* Washington, DC: Government Printing Office.

Parsons, J. E. (1982). *The development of expectancies, attribution, and persistence.* Unpublished manuscript, Ann Arbor: University of Michigan.

Parsons, J. E., & Ruble, D. N. (1977). The development of achievement-related expectancies. *Child Development, 48*, 1975-1979.

Petersen, A., Ebata, A., & Graber, J. (1987, April). *Responses to developmental and family changes in early adolescence.* Paper presented at the annual meeting of the American Educational Research Association, Washington, DC.

Rholes, W. S., Blackwell, J., Jordan, C. & Walters, C. (1980). A developmental study of learned helplessness. *Developmental Psychology, 16*, 616-624.

Rosenbaum, J. E. (1976). *Making inequality: The hidden curriculum of high school tracking.* New York: John Wiley.

Rosenholtz, S. J., & Simpson, C. (1984). The formation of ability conceptions: Developmental trend or social construction? *Review of Educational Research, 54*, 301-325.

Silberman, C. E. (1970). *Crisis in the classroom.* New York: Random House.

Simmons, R. G., & Blyth, D. A. (1987). *Moving into adolescence: The impact of pubertal change and school context.* Hawthorn, NY: Aldine de Gruylter.

Simmons, R. G., Blyth, D. A., Van Cleave, E. F., & Bush, D. (1979). Entry into early adolescence: The impact of school structure, puberty, and early dating on self-esteem. *American Sociological Review, 44*, 948-967.

Steinberg, L. (1989). Pubertal maturation and parent-adolescent distance: An evolutionary perspective. In G. R. Adams, R. Montemayor, & T. P. Gullotta (Eds.), *Biology of adolescent behavior and development.* Newbury Park, CA: Sage.

Thornburg, H. D., & Jones, R. M. (1982). Social characteristics of early adolescents: Age versus grade. *Journal of Early Adolescence, 2*, 229-239.

Trickett, E. J., & Moos, R. H. (1974). Personal correlates of contrasting environments: Student satisfactions in high school classrooms. *American Journal of Community Psychology, 2*, 1-12.

7. The Socialization Context of Gender Role Development in Early Adolescence

Aletha C. Huston
University of Kansas

Mildred M. Alvarez
Cornell University

As children undergo the many physical and social changes of early adolescence, they must come to terms with new definitions of their roles as females or males. Sex-role development or sex-typing is the "process whereby children come to acquire the behaviors, attitudes, interests, emotional reactions, and motives that are culturally defined as appropriate for members of their sex" (Perry & Bussey, 1984, p. 262). Sex-typing is multidimensional in nature, encompassing a diversity of content areas (e.g., interests and activities) and constructs (e.g., knowledge about gender expectations) (Huston, 1983). Early adolescence is the time when young people develop the adult physical, sexual attributes of their gender, and family, friends, and social institutions may demand increasing conformity to societal rules and adult roles.

The physical and biological changes occurring during the early adolescent years are usually accompanied by a host of contextual transitions (e.g., elementary to junior high school), which serve to mark this age period as unique. Moreover, physical changes usually result in changes in the role expectations of significant others. In this chapter, we review some of the theories proposing developmental changes in gender roles during adolescence; then we review literature on the sources of socialization thought to contribute to the development of gender roles—specifically, family, school, peers, and television.

AUTHORS' NOTE: *The authors wish to thank several anonymous reviewers and David R. Rolandelli for their constructive comments and suggestions on an earlier draft of this chapter.*

THEORIES OF ADOLESCENT SEX-ROLE DEVELOPMENT

Theorists acknowledge that children in every society learn social expectations for males and females, develop basic gender identity, and adopt sex-typed preferences and behavior during the first five years of life. In fact, the empirical data indicate that preschool children often adopt rather rigid standards of sex-role conformity. Hence, the development of sex-typing during the later years must be conceptualized as a change (or lack thereof) in well-ingrained beliefs and attitudes.

Psychological stage theories. Some theories identify individual psychological changes associated with development as important determinants of developmental transitions. Block (1984) proposed a sequence of sex-role stages based on ego development. She suggested that middle childhood was a period of bifurcation of sex roles—girls and boys were concerned with conformity to social definitions of their gender roles and learned to suppress personality components that were associated with the other gender. In particular, girls suppressed their agentic, individualistic, and aggressive tendencies; boys suppressed their communal, expressive, and tender tendencies.

This period of conformity to externally imposed roles was followed by a "conscientious" period in which role values were internalized (Block, 1984). While exact ages were not attached to these stages, it appears most children in early adolescence would be expected to be in the transition from conformity to conscientiousness. This theory then might predict increasing internalization of sex-typed attributes.

In a highly influential work, Kohlberg (1966) proposed that sex-typing was based on cognitive development. He articulated the transition from preoperational to concrete operational functioning as a time when children in middle childhood become more flexible in their thinking about gender because they understand gender constancy, the fact that gender does not change with superficial changes in appearance or behavior, and because of the flexibility of concrete operational thought. Hence, although knowledge and acceptance of socially prescribed gender roles might increase with age, children in middle childhood at least have the potential for increasing sex-role flexibility as well. An expansion of the theory to adolescence proposed an alternating pattern of rigidity and flexibility as new levels of abstraction in the definitions of sex roles are incorporated into the person's understanding (Ullian, 1976). Overall, then, early adolescence can be a period of increasing flexibility in sex-role definitions.

Secular change and developmental change. Life-span developmental theory extends the notion of developmental change to include secular or historical change as well as ontogenetic sources of development (Goulet & Baltes, 1970). Women's adult roles have altered markedly in the past generation or two. Children in early adolescence in 1990 experience a very different image of the adult female role than did those in 1960. Although the theory has not been directly applied to sex-role development, secular change may be an important source of developmental change in this domain.

Gender intensification. One frequent hypothesis about the transition from childhood to adolescence is that gender-related development is intensified in early adolescence. Freudian psychoanalytic theory proposed a period of latency in middle childhood followed by the genital stage in which oedipal conflicts were reactivated. Successful resolution of this stage resulted in adult sex roles and sexual preferences.

Other theorists have proposed that social pressures for sex-appropriate behavior are relatively benign during middle childhood, particularly for girls. With the onset of puberty, however, both psychological and social forces act to increase awareness of gender roles and efforts to adhere to them. For example, Douvan and Adelson (1966) proposed that girls in middle childhood had the latitude to be tomboys, but at adolescence, they exhibited a "flight into femininity" that entailed not only adoption of adult feminine norms, but a narrowing of interests and aspirations. As a result, girls' school and career motivation declines in early adolescence as the demands for feminine noncompetitiveness and subservience to men become internalized (Huston-Stein & Welch, 1979).

A more recent and elaborated version of the gender intensification hypothesis was provided by Hill and Lynch (1983). They examined evidence from measures of personality (e.g., self-esteem), friendship patterns, and the like to determine if sex differences increase in adolescence. Hill and Lynch concluded that there was some support for the notion that gender roles become increasingly differentiated during this period. Gender intensification in early adolescence may be precipitated by the physical changes of puberty, but Hill and Lynch (1983) propose that social variables are primary. That is, the physical changes themselves, with resulting hormonal changes, may lead directly to behaviors associated with adult and peer gender expectations. These changing expectations of socialization agents can have wide-ranging effects during the transition to adolescence.

In summary, one can reasonably postulate several sources of developmental change in early adolescence: physical-hormonal changes, socialization pressures, individual ego and cognitive development, and secular historical influences. Although all of these components probably play a role in adolescent sex-role development, physical and psychological changes occur in a social context. Therefore, our purpose in this chapter is to consider socialization influences in depth, examining the gender intensification hypothesis wherever possible. We examine four major socialization contexts: family, peers, school, and television.

FAMILY INFLUENCES

Relationship with family members. During the transition from childhood to early adolescence, parents allow boys more independence than girls, and "chaperonage" associated with awareness of girls' sexual vulnerability may increase (Block, 1984). Families with young adolescent daughters report more intense conflict about such matters as sex, choice of friends, and curfews than families with young adolescent sons (Papini & Sebby, 1988). Moreover, family adjustment to puberty has been shown to involve a change in the parent-adolescent relationship; and pubertal maturation has been shown to increase parent-adolescent distance (Steinberg, 1981; 1988). Steinberg (1988) found that pubertal maturation increases girls' reports of father-daughter conflicts about such matters as curfews. Similarly, boys' reports of family relations suggest that pubertal maturation led to distance between the adolescent male and parents (e.g., increased number of arguments with mother). Moreover, sons reported increases in emotional and behavioral autonomy. Steinberg also examined the impact of family relations on pubertal maturation. His findings suggest that distance in the mother-child relationship may accelerate pubertal maturation in girls, while mother-child closeness may slow the process. No effect of family relationship on pubertal development was found for boys. Steinberg suggests there may be an evolutionary basis for individuals to physically distance themselves, shortly after puberty. He points out that most adolescents' economic dependence on their families makes physical separation unrealistic, perhaps resulting in psychological distance (e.g., increased conflict and autonomy) during this age period. So while biological and hormonal changes result in needs for greater autonomy during the early adolescent years, secular changes have postponed the end of adolescence and of dependence (cf. Hamburg & Takanishi, 1989).

Evidence is less clear about the effect of siblings on sex-typing during early adolescence. A recent study on the influence of siblings on girls' sex-role attitudes suggested that junior high girls without brothers or with only one brother have more "liberal" attitudes toward women's rights and roles than girls with more than one brother (Hertsgaard & Light, 1984). An examination of birth order and number of sisters indicated no differences. However, for younger children the effect of birth order may be important in that for cross-sex siblings, sex-typing of activities tends to be influenced by the gender of the older child (Stoneman, Brody, & MacKinnon, 1986). More research is needed to examine the influence of siblings (older, younger, same- and opposite-sex) in the development of gender roles in early adolescence.

Parental expectations and encouragement. Differential parent socialization is well documented in the area of children's achievement activities and career preparation. In particular, the early adolescent years are important in the development of gender-differentiated expectations in mathematics and science, and parents contribute to those expectations.

Boys and girls perceive different levels of parent encouragement and expectations for accomplishment in math and science (Marini, 1978). Eccles, Adler, and Kaczala (1982) demonstrated that parents typically believe mathematics is more important for their son's futures than for their daughters', and their beliefs influence the value early adolescents placed on math achievement. Gender differences in attainment value in combination with the transition to junior high (allowing for greater independence in course choices) may influence boys to take more advanced elective math courses than girls; hence, males are more apt to be prepared for careers in science, engineering, or other areas requiring advanced mathematics. Parents also expect better math performance from sons than from daughters. Moreover, children's own concepts about their math ability are more closely related to parental beliefs than to their level of performance in math (Eccles, 1983).

Maternal employment. One of the major secular trends in the last 40 years has been the increase in labor force participation by mothers. Most early adolescents today have a mother who is employed at least part time. Although maternal employment is not specific to early adolescence, it does influence sex-role development, and its influences probably depend on the age of the child involved. Children in early adolescence may be especially attuned to understanding adult roles; hence, their mother's role choices may be salient influences on their concepts and attitudes about women's roles.

Maternal employment appears to affect sex-typed concepts and behavior through at least three different processes: (a) modeling, (b) changes in household activities and roles for all family members, and (c) changes in maternal power within the family. Data suggest that children of employed mothers have less stereotyped concepts of female roles (and sometimes male roles as well) than children of full-time homemakers. They also have more positive attitudes about nontraditional roles for women. Daughters of employed mothers have higher educational and occupational aspirations than daughters of homemakers. Such differences occur throughout childhood and especially adolescence (Chandler, Sawicki, & Stryffeler, 1981; Hoffman, 1989; Huston, 1983; Robb & Raven, 1982; Rollins & White, 1982). Thus, it appears that employed mothers often serve as models who combine the traditional feminine home roles with less traditional activities away from home.

Adolescents of both genders report less traditional sex-role attitudes and more egalitarian views regarding responsibility for household tasks when the mother is employed outside the home than when she is not (Robb & Raven, 1982). When mothers are employed, fathers and children of both genders spend more time doing household chores than when mothers are not employed. However, the type of housework girls do often involves a greater daily time commitment (e.g., doing dishes) than that engaged in by boys (e.g., doing yard work), and many household tasks are sex-typed (Cogle, Tasker, & Morton, 1982).

In adolescence, there are shifts in parental power relative to their children, and these shifts may be different for the two parents. For example, Steinberg and Hill (1978) found that as boys passed through puberty, they became more powerful in the triad (e.g., boys interrupted more), and their mothers became less powerful (Steinberg & Hill, 1978). However, maternal employment often increases mothers' power because of their role in providing family income. One investigation demonstrated that girls who perceived their mothers as the more dominant parent expressed preferences for neutral or predominantly masculine jobs, whereas girls who perceived their fathers as the more dominant parent displayed a preference for feminine jobs (Lavine, 1982).

Socializing influence of fathers. Ironically, the influences of fathers are often investigated by studying their absence. In Hetherington's (1972) studies of early adolescent females, interaction with males was the one domain of girls' sex-typing that was affected by father absence. The effects of father absence were significant, but they also depended on whether the absence was because of divorce or death. Daughters of divorced parents seemed very interested in masculine attention, whereas daughters of widows appeared to be shy and uncomfortable around males. As heterosexual interactions are an important aspect of sex-role development during early adolescence, fathers may play a particularly important role for their daughters during this period.

With respect to males, Lynn (1966) suggested that limited sex-role information was imparted to sons by their fathers, attributable in part to their general unavailability in the child-rearing process, leading adolescent males to rely increasingly on social definitions of the male role. The greater value placed by society on the masculine rather than feminine role, would indicate that boys would identify more strongly with the stereotyped male role and girls' preference for the feminine role would weaken with age (Lynn, 1966; Teti & Lamb, 1986). When fathers do interact with their children, they are more likely to convey sex-appropriate behavior than are mothers (see Perry & Bussey, 1984). Perry and Bussey (1984) suggest that perhaps men are more concerned than women in perpetuating appropriate sex roles because of the pressures to conform to the culturally prescribed male sex role that they themselves have experienced.

Summary. Family socialization may contribute to gender intensification in early adolescence, while at the same time encourage divergence from socially stereotypic roles. On the one hand, the nature of family relations during the early adolescent years indicate a distancing between parent and child associated with changes in pubertal maturation as well as an increase in restrictions (e.g., curfew) in the case of females. Moreover, parents differential expectations and encouragement may influence girls to perceive themselves as less capable than males in certain areas (e.g., math). Coupled with a transition to junior high, where students have more independence in choosing course offerings, girls' lowered expectations may be reflected in their choice not to take challenging courses. On the other hand, secular changes in maternal employment have changed the role models available to many children, resulting in less stereotyped beliefs about men's and women's activities. Maternal employment also leads to more household responsibilities for adolescents—though these are often sex-typed—and to greater maternal power, which may in turn reduce stereotypic role acceptance by developing children.

Early adolescent males may rely increasingly on the socially valued definitions of the masculine role. Similarly, girls also become increasingly aware that society values masculine over feminine roles. At the same time, the traditional masculine role valued by society often demands that girls adhere to the traditional feminine role. Consequently, during the early adolescent years it may be that girls adopt more traditional feminine behaviors regardless of their increased misgivings about the value of the feminine role. Finally, fathers may play a significant role in teaching their daughters about adultlike interactions with males during a period when such interactions are of intense concern to young people.

PEER INFLUENCES ON EARLY ADOLESCENT GENDER ROLES

Attitudes about peers' sex-role characteristics. Partially conflicting predictions can be derived from cognitive developmental theory and gender intensification theory about the attitudes of adolescents toward their peers (and others). The former predicts increasing flexibility of sex-role concepts in early adolescence, but the latter suggests a narrowing of the range of acceptable attributes for girls and boys. Paradoxically, both appear to occur.

From kindergarten through eighth grade, children increasingly come to think of sex-role prescriptions as social conventions. For example, older children more often say yes to questions such as, "Do you think there might be another country where people do (a sex-role transgression, e.g., men do most of the cooking?)" (Carter & Patterson, 1982; Stoddart & Turiel, 1985). Over the elementary years, children are also increasingly likely to say that both sexes can perform sex-typed tasks and activities (Huston, 1983). Hence, sex-role concepts appear to become less absolute and more flexible.

Attitudes about sex-role transgressions, however, appear to become more tolerant in middle childhood and less tolerant again in early adolescence. Stoddart & Turiel (1985) found that kindergarteners and eighth graders ranked scenes of sex-role transgressions by children as more wrong than did third and fifth graders. Kindergarteners justified their judgments on the basis of preserving physical characteristics;

eighth graders judged deviance from sex-role conformity as psychologically abnormal. Kindergarten and eighth grade children were also more likely than third and fifth graders to state that the character in the scene should not engage in the act and that they would not want to attend a school allowing the acts.

Gender-related attitudes also change over time. An eleven-year survey of fifth, eighth, and eleventh grade students showed that they became more egalitarian with regard to family issues (e.g., husband and wife sharing decision making), but more traditional on cross-gender issues (e.g., letting boys play with dolls) and cross-sex social interactions (e.g., social courtesies such as opening doors for females) (Thompson, 1988).

Peer support. With age, peers become increasingly important sources of support, approval and disapproval, and social influence, even though parents continue to play an important part. For example, in a sample of adolescents in grades 7 through 10, peers were the largest category of persons listed as significant others. However, parents were listed at all grade levels, indicating that most adolescents rely on both peers and adults as sources of support and socialization (Blyth, Hill, and Thiel, 1982). Parents and peers may be important for different domains of one's life. For example, when asked to whom they would turn for help and support, Black adolescents named parents when the problem was material (e.g., the need for money) and peers when the problem was emotional (e.g., a fight with a friend) (Coates, 1987).

Support from peers probably becomes increasingly important to both genders during early adolescence, but girls appear to place more importance on intimacy with friends than boys do. For example, Blyth and Foster-Clark (1987) found that girls reported higher levels of intimacy (e.g., understanding, advice-seeking) with same-sex friends than boys did. In another investigation (Bukowski & Kramer, 1986) 10- and 13-year-olds believed intimacy characterized girls' friendships more than boys' friendships.

Peer acceptance. Peers may socialize sex-typed behavior partly by accepting or rejecting others on the basis of their sex-typed attributes. Early adolescents interact primarily with peers of their own gender, but cross-gender interactions also increase (Maccoby & Jacklin, in press). In one investigation, students reported that friendships between males had lasted longer than either female-female friendships or male-female friendships (Montemayor & Van Komen, 1985). Cross-gender friendships may be more important to girls than to boys during this period. In a survey of seventh through tenth graders, girls named boys as "significant others" more often than boys named girls (Blyth et al., 1982).

On the whole, members of both genders who have "androgynous sex-role identities" and boys with high levels of masculinity are most widely accepted as friends and companions (Massad, 1981). Androgynous adolescents also report feeling less lonely than other groups (Avery, 1982). Adolescents with cross-gender characteristics are apt to be rejected by peers.

However, the reasons for these patterns may have little to do with sex-typing. *Androgyny* consists of feminine and masculine sex-stereotyped personality attributes that are generally socially desirable. Masculine attributes such as leadership ability, dominance, and confidence are especially likely to be associated with self-esteem and assertiveness for both sexes (Huston, 1983). Therefore, peer acceptance may be based on an adolescent's socially desirable characteristics, regardless of gender. This hypothesis was supported in an investigation of children's and adolescents' perceptions of girls and boys displaying "sex-appropriate" and "sex-inappropriate" personality traits in a series of vignettes. Certain behaviors resulted in high approval (e.g., steadiness, timidity, and politeness) regardless of gender or consistency with gender roles. In a sample ranging from third to twelfth grades, only the late adolescents displayed concern with conformity to gender roles, (i.e., a boy who acted like a boy was liked more than a girl who acted like a boy) (Sigelman, Carr, & Begley, 1986). It seems likely that clear deviance from sex-typed norms leads to low peer acceptance, but within a broad range of normal behavior, it is not clear that conformity to sex-typed personality attributes is a major predictor of peer acceptance.

Dating and sexuality. Early pubertal maturation, frequent dating, and going steady are some factors associated with early initiation of sexual activity (Sonenstein, 1986) and can intensify role expectations. Sexual maturity often results in different messages for males and females. Males are often encouraged to engage in sexual activity, whereas females are encouraged to focus on relationships and romantic love (Sonenstein, 1986). Data regarding young adolescent men and women's first sexual relationship provides some support. Seventy-one percent of 15- to 17-year-old females, while only 47% of like-aged males, report being engaged or going steady at the time of first intercourse (Zelnick & Shah, 1983, cited in Sonenstein, 1986).

During the early adolescent years, changing role expectations as well as biological, hormonal changes affect the likelihood of dating (Gargiulo, Attie, Brooks-Gunn, & Warren, 1987). Gargiulo and her colleagues cite evidence indicating "linear and direct effects of androgen on sexual behavior in adolescent boys" (p. 731). Corresponding data for females are not available. In a study of 12- to 15-year-old female students, Gargiulo and her associates compared student ballet dancers' and nondancers' dating behaviors. Within the nondance group, premenarcheal girls dated as much as postmenarcheal girls at each grade level, suggesting that peer effects may be more important than pubertal status for this group. Postmenarcheal dancers engaged in more dating than premenarcheal dancers. As an explanation of the findings for the dance group, the authors note the importance, not just of maturational timing, but of the perception and value of such timing depending on one's referent group or social context. For an aspiring dancer, late maturation may be more highly valued than early maturation. That is, premenarcheal dancers may postpone dating because of greater investment in their dancing careers. Therefore, while it may be important for researchers to match subjects on pubertal status rather than age (Hill & Lynch, 1983), the timing of puberty in its social context should also be considered.

Summary. Although children's concepts of sex-typed behavior become more flexible and relativistic as they move from early childhood to early adolescence, their attitudes do not follow the same pattern. In middle childhood, children accept deviations from sex-typed norms, but as they move into early and late adolescence, they become less tolerant of such deviations. Similarly, during middle childhood, most children spend their time in highly sex-segregated peer groups (Maccoby & Jacklin, in press). However, in early adolescence, pressures for dating and sexual attractiveness are intensified, and may result in greater cross-sex interaction, perhaps increasing concern about conforming to cultural ideals of femininity and masculinity. Peers become central sources of support and influence during early adolescence. Intimacy with friends of both genders appears to be somewhat more important to girls than to boys, but other forms of peer approval and support may be central for boys. Peer social acceptance is greatest for those with androgynous and masculine personality attributes, probably because these represent socially desirable attributes in general. Deviation from sex-typed norms can produce peer rejection, but to a certain extent, gender-appropriateness may be less crucial than other aspects of an adolescent's behavior. Finally, assessing how the adolescent perceives pubertal maturation (e.g., is it valued or accepted?) during this age period may be at least as important as matching subjects on actual level of physical maturation.

SCHOOL INFLUENCES

School-related subjects. Although children in middle childhood have sex stereotypes for many domains of achievement, such beliefs become more pronounced in early adolescence. Elementary school children often view math as equally appropriate for girls and boys; during adolescence, they increasingly consider math a "masculine" domain (Huston, 1983; Stein & Smithells, 1969). In a survey of children and adolescents, science was perceived as slightly more appropriate for males than females; writing was viewed as more appropriate for females. In the elementary and middle school years, boys viewed math as more appropriate to males than females, but girls considered it neutral. High school students of both genders viewed math as slightly more appropriate for males (Wilder, Mackie, & Cooper, 1985). Girls have less positive attitudes toward math and science in the middle school years than boys and these attitudes continue into high school (Tittle, 1986).

Computer skills are also stereotyped as masculine, and males report liking computers more than girls at all age levels (Wilder et al., 1985) In a survey of computer camps, workshops, and summer classes, boys outnumbered girls by 3 to 1, a difference which increased with age (Hess & Miura, 1985). The differences between males' and females' participation and interest in computers increase with both age and experience. Among seventh and eighth graders with less than a year of experience with computers, females reported less anxiety and greater liking of computers than males. For those with more than a year of experience, males reported liking to work with computers more than females (Loyd, Loyd, & Gressard, 1987).

One reason computers become relatively less attractive to females than to males as they get older is that computer software and games are often designed with male themes (e.g., battles and violence). Huff and Cooper (1987) asked educators to design software for seventh-grade "boys," "girls," or "students" that would help teach the correct use of commas. The designs were rated on several qualities that defined a "game versus learning tool" dimension. "Games" required eye-hand coordination and competition, whereas "learning tools" required longer sessions, had color and sound effects (melodies), and had preset difficulty levels. Programs designed for boys and students were game-oriented, whereas programs designed for girls were more often learning tools.

School structure. Although sex-stereotyped achievement patterns emerge or become intensified in early adolescence, it is not entirely clear what contribution school structure makes to the process. Most children experience a change from an elementary school with self-contained classrooms to a middle school or junior high with different teachers for each subject sometime between the ages of 10 and 14.

There is speculation that "junior high school serves as a transition period to a more masculine environment" (LaTorre, Yu, Fortin, & Marrache, 1983, p. 1133). In the preschool and middle childhood years, girls consistently prefer tasks in which adults provide models, suggestions, and feedback about performance. Boys more often choose tasks and activities in which adults are not involved (Carpenter, 1983; Huston, Carpenter, Atwater, & Johnson, 1986). Junior high provides a more impersonal environment, which may fit the average boy's learning style better than the average girl's preferred style. As a result, boys have more opportunities to learn how to accomplish tasks without adult help and support; they may be better prepared for a learning environment requiring independence (Tittle, 1986). Moreover, some have suggested that the transition itself to the more impersonal junior high school, rather than biological or maturational changes, may result in negative consequences especially for girls, for whom self-esteem and leadership skills apparently decline upon entry to junior high (Jackson & Hornbeck, 1989).

Some theorists argue that independent learning styles are particularly important for achievement in advanced math and science. Fennema and Peterson (1985) proposed that boys may have more opportunities to practice "autonomous learning behaviors" (e.g., working independently and persistently on high-level tasks) that contribute to math skills. Dweck (1986) proposed that bright girls prefer familiarity (i.e., tasks they are good at and know they can do well), whereas bright boys prefer challenges. She points out that verbal skills build on one another using a familiar base, even at the more complex levels. On the other hand, mathematics, especially starting at the junior high and high school levels, begins to focus on new skills and often entirely new conceptual frameworks (e.g., geometry). Hence, math and verbal skills fit sex-typed learning and motivational styles, which may be heightened during the early adolescent years.

Summary. During early adolescence, children come to view math, science, and computer skills as male domains, and boys generally have more positive attitudes and more confidence about their abilities in these areas than girls do. Also, boys practice such skills more than girls do.

The transition from elementary to junior high school, which occurs in early adolescence, may have important influences on gender differences in school attitudes and performance. The more independent, masculine learning environment of the junior high appears better suited to the learning style of the average boy than to that of the average girl. In middle childhood, girls seek adult-structured learning activities more than boys do. Boys appear to have more experience with autonomous and challenging learning activities.

TELEVISION

Television has been recognized as an important socializing influence throughout childhood and adolescence. Early adolescents spend 3 to 4 hours a day watching television (Liebert & Sprafkin, 1988), and they use television as a source of information about appropriate social behavior. Music videos have become a popular source of entertainment for this age group, and many feature films, available in theaters or on videotape, are specially designed for a teenage audience.

Adolescence as a sensitive period. Children are exposed to television from infancy onward, but the lessons and messages that they take from it depend on their level of cognitive understanding and their motivations and interests (Huston & Wright, 1983). Several developmental changes suggest that early adolescence may be a period of heightened sensitivity to television messages about adult gender roles. During the period from about age 6 to 11, children increasingly view programs designed for adults (or general audiences). By the end of this age period, they are able to comprehend plot narratives and character motives in a reasonably adult manner (Collins, 1982). They are also moving away from family toward peers as sources of sex-role information; television supplies a wealth of appealing models who are young, glamorous, and successful (Durkin, 1985b). The increasing concern about gender-appropriate behavior, especially heterosexual relationships, during early adolescence may lead young people to be especially sensitive to social information about gender roles and to the innumerable messages about female-male relationships on television. It has been suggested that television portrayals of adolescents may account for some of the behavior of early adolescents who are pressured to date before puberty (Matteson, 1975).

Television content. The world of television is highly gender-stereotyped and conveys clear messages about the relative power and importance of women and men (Durkin, 1985a; Huston, 1983). Males are over-represented and females are under-represented; on virtually every type of programming males outnumber females by 2 or 3 to 1 (Mackey & Hess, 1982; Williams, Baron, Phillips, Travis, & Jackson, 1986). In advertisements, males and females appear equally often, but the "voice-over" is male about 90% of the time. Authority figures, therefore, are largely male except in advertisements for feminine products such as cleaning materials or feminine hygiene (Bretl & Cantor, 1988; Livingstone & Green, 1986).

Men and women typically engage in sex-typed occupational and family roles, and interests on television. In the late 1970s, female characters appeared more often than males in the context of home, romance, and physical appearance, and males more frequently than females in the context of work, car, and sports. Women characters were more often portrayed without reference to an occupation in both programs and commercials (Bretl & Cantor, 1988; Williams et al., 1986). In the mid-1980s, there were some changes in the occupations portrayed by women. When major female characters had an occupation outside the home, it was almost as likely to be nontraditional (e.g., attorney, police officer) as to be traditional (e.g., nurse, secretary). Men continued to be shown almost entirely in traditional male occupations (Williams et al., 1986).

Typically, women on television are young adults in their 20s; most men are young or middle-aged adults. Women were shown as sex objects (i.e., shown in scant clothing or engaged in sexually provocative behavior) in 35% of the commercial television programs in a 1985 sample (Williams et al., 1986). Such portrayals are even more common on music videos. Women are portrayed as happy and as demonstrating emotions more often than men (Harris & Voorhees, 1981). Male characters are more often aggressive, dominant, competent, autonomous, and active, while female characters are passive and deferent (Huston, 1983; Williams et al., 1986).

Effects of television portrayals. Correlational studies relating television viewing to some index of sex typing have produced mixed results, with most reporting only moderate associations between overall viewing and gender-related attitudes or beliefs (Durkin, 1985b; Huston, 1983). Causal direction is obviously ambiguous in such studies in any case.

Two longitudinal studies of early adolescents, however, indicate that television viewing influences gender-role attitudes and beliefs. Both studies are based on the assumption that television conveys a uniform set of sexist messages; hence, the more a person is exposed, the more stereotyped messages are likely to be received. In a two-year panel study of sixth through tenth graders, Morgan (1982) examined the association between television viewing and attitudes toward women in the workplace. For girls, the amount of television viewed predicted sexism scores a year later; conversely, boys' sexist attitudes predicted the amount of television viewed a year later. Using a similar design, Morgan (1987) assessed attitudes toward, and completion of, household chores, and amount of nightly television exposure for eighth graders. For both boys and girls, heavy television viewing predicted an increased tendency to endorse traditional sex-role divisions of labor with respect to household chores. Although television viewing did not predict the sex-typing of chores actually done, heavy viewers did show increases in the congruence between their attitudes and their behaviors. Taken together, these studies suggest that exposure to highly stereotyped messages on television, increases adolescents' sex-stereotyped beliefs and attitudes.

As noted earlier, the one change in sex-role portrayals in the mid-1980s was an increase in women working in traditionally male occupations. The possible effects of these portrayals were evaluated by questioning 10- to 12-year-olds about traditionally masculine and feminine occupations of two types: those often shown on television and those children encounter frequently in real life. Girls expressed the most positive attitudes toward feminine television occupations (e.g., model) followed by masculine television occupations (e.g., private detective); real-life feminine occupations (e.g., dental hygienist) and real-life masculine occupations (e.g., dentist) in that order (Wroblewski & Huston, 1987).

Interventions to change sex stereotypes. Just as television can convey sex stereotypes, it can also transmit nonstereotyped messages. Experimental studies have shown short-term effects in which children express less stereotyped beliefs or attitudes after seeing a nontraditional portrayal (Calvert & Huston, 1987; Durkin, 1985c). One investigation, however, found developmental differences in children's responses to counterstereotyped portrayals of women. Third-grade boys and girls and eighth-grade girls expressed less traditional attitudes toward women after exposure to advertisements showing women in nontraditional activities, but eighth-grade boys expressed more traditional attitudes (Pingree, 1978). Gender intensification during this age period may lead boys to react negatively to portrayals that violate their sex-role norms.

One major effort to change sex stereotypes with television was the *Freestyle* television series (Williams, LaRose, & Frost, 1981). It was designed to counteract the effects of sex and ethnic stereotypes on the career interests of 9- to 12-year-olds. The series was fairly successful in countering sex-stereotyped attitudes and beliefs among children of this age in several areas, but its only behavioral effect was that girls who saw the series said they would participate in athletics and engage in mechanical activities more than a control group (Johnston & Ettema, 1982).

Individual differences: Sex-typing affects what is learned from television. Several theorists have proposed that gender intensification in early adolescence may lead children to be sensitized to messages about sex typing. Throughout childhood and adolescence, individuals who are more strongly sex-typed are more likely to perceive and recall information that is consistent with sex stereotypes (cf. Calvert & Huston, 1987).

Counterstereotyped portrayals may be most effective for children who can identify with the nonstereotyped models. In one study, children were classified as androgynous, masculine, or feminine on the basis of their personality attributes and activity interests. They then watched a *Freestyle* episode portraying a girl and a boy in nontraditional activities and were asked whether they would like to do things like each character. Androgynous children of both genders identified with the nontraditional female character; sex-typed children more often identified with the same-sex character (Eisenstock, 1984).

Gender and sex-typing guide children's program choices. Boys watch more cartoons, action adventure, and sports than girls (Huston, Wright, Rice, Kerkman, & St. Peters, 1987), and boys are more attentive to programs with high levels of animation and violence (Alvarez, Huston, Wright, & Kerkman, 1988). Elementary-school-age girls with

nontraditional play and activity preferences watch more violent television and more television with nontraditional female characters than
girls with traditional preferences (Eron, Huesmann, Brice, Fischer, &
Mermelstein, 1983; Miller & Reeves, 1976).

Summary. Most television presents highly stereotyped images of
adult men and women and both longitudinal and experimental studies support the hypothesis that televised sex roles influence children's
sex stereotypes and attitudes. The evidence for effects on behavior is
weaker than that for attitudes. Counterstereotyped portrayals can
influence children in early adolescence. With gender intensification,
children may be increasingly sensitized to sex-typed portrayals and
may be particularly responsive to them. Adolescents who are highly
sex-typed are apt to choose television messages that are consistent
with their sex-role orientation.

CONCLUSION

We have focused this chapter on the socialization effects of family,
peers, school, and television on gender-role development in early
adolescence. In varying ways, each of these socialization influences
conveys some common norms or expectations about gender held by
the culture for social behaviors, occupations, interests, emotional
expression, and so on. Gender-related expectations contribute to the
differential socialization of males and females such that a subtle
message is conveyed that males are more valuable, competent, and
powerful than females.

The process of sex-typing begins in early childhood, but early
adolescence is a period of consolidation and intensification of gender-
related behaviors and attitudes. Although cognitive developmental
changes lead children to conceptualize sex roles in relativistic, flexible
ways as they grow older, social and institutional influences lead to
greater conformity to sex-typed norms as children enter adolescence.
Perhaps the need for clarity of roles during the early adolescent years
results in greater reliance on stereotypes (Nash & Feldman, 1981).

The many physical and biological changes occurring during the
early adolescent years may further intensify role expectations. For
girls, menarche is a sharp and concrete event announcing puberty
(Greif & Ulman, 1982). Boys' pubertal development is perhaps more
gradual and more difficult to document than girls' development.
Moreover, the timing and "developmental readiness" (Simmons,

Burgeson, Carlton-Ford, & Blyth, 1987) of the individual are important factors in one's adjustment to such changes; the fewer concurrent changes to contend with upon entry to early adolescence (e.g., changes in school, dating behavior, family disruption), the more likely the adolescent will be to cope with the changes (Simmons et al.). The differences in the nature of pubertal development between male and female adolescents, and the adjustment to these changes, may have consequences for the quality of social interactions with family and peers. For example, with physical maturation, males may experience greater autonomy from parents, whereas females may experience an increase in parental supervision.

As children move through early adolescence, parental influence diminishes somewhat, and peer influence increases. However, different sources of socialization may be important for different domains. Much of the literature on parent and school influences concerns sex-typed achievement values and expectations. Parents and schools may be particularly important for socializing adolescents' expectancies of success and values concerning achievement. The early adolescent years may be important in the development of gender-differentiated expectations in math, science, and computer skills. In combination with the transition to a more impersonal junior high school environment, girls' self-perceptions of decreased ability in these subject areas could influence them to decide on nonchallenging courses possibly narrowing later career options. Occupational aspirations and expectations, which may guide the value students place on different domains of school achievement, are influenced by television portrayals as well.

Peers and television are particularly important in socializing sex-typed social behavior and emotional expression. Peers convey clear attitudes about appropriate and inappropriate social behavior. Entertainment television is full of messages about social relationships, friendship, enmity, emotional expression, and sexuality. The young adults on television and same-age peers may seem to an early adolescent to be more appropriate models and sources of standards for social interaction than parents and older adults. Moreover, sexual maturation may be a cue to adopt perceived adolescent roles learned before adolescence from such sources as television and movies, thereby making it difficult to differentiate transitions attributable to physical and biological causes from changes attributable to cultural and group expectations (Matteson, 1975). There is a need for more short-term longitudinal studies that would help clarify the sources of transitions and that would document age-related gender differential socialization (Hill & Lynch, 1983); cross-sectional studies may risk assessing historical or secular effects rather than age-related differences (Emmerich & Shepard, 1982).

The development of sex-typing in early adolescence is not a fixed process; nonstereotyped attitudes and behaviors can be acquired as well as those fitting social stereotypes. Secular changes in family roles, television content, and the like lead to changes in the norms conveyed to new generations of adolescents. Early adolescents are often intensely concerned with "sex-appropriate" attributes, but what they absorb about femininity and masculinity can vary widely, depending on the ideas conveyed by various socialization agents during the particular slice of historical time when they pass through this period.

REFERENCES

Alvarez, M., Huston, A. C., Wright, J. C., & Kerkman, D. (1988). Gender differences in visual attention to television form and content. *Journal of Applied Developmental Psychology, 9*, 459-475.

Avery, A. W. (1982). Escaping loneliness in adolescence: the case for androgyny. *Journal of Youth and Adolescence, 11*, 451-459.

Block, J. H. (1984). *Sex role identity and ego development.* San Francisco: Jossey-Bass.

Blyth, D. A., Hill, J. P., & Thiel, K. S. (1982). Early adolescents' significant others: Grade and gender differences in perceived relationships with familial and nonfamilial adults and young people. *Journal of Youth and Adolescence, 11*, 425-450.

Blyth, D. A., & Foster-Clark, F. S. (1987). Gender differences in perceived intimacy with different members of adolescents' social networks. *Sex Roles, 17*, 689-718.

Bretl, D. J., & Cantor, J. (1988). The portrayal of men and women in U.S. television commercials: A recent content analysis trends over 15 years. *Sex Roles, 18*, 595-609.

Bukowski, W. M., & Kramer, T. L. (1986). Judgments of the features of friendship among early adolescent boys and girls. *Journal of Early Adolescence, 6*, 331-338.

Calvert, S. L., & Huston, A. C. (1987). Television and children's gender schemata. In L. Liben and M. L. Signorella (Eds.), *Children's gender schemata: Origins and implications.* In the quarterly series, *New directions for child development.* San Francisco: Jossey-Bass.

Carpenter, C. J. (1983). Activity structure and play: Implications for socialization. In M. B. Liss (Ed.), *Social and cognitive skills: Sex roles and children's play.* New York: Academic Press.

Carter, D. B., & Patterson, C. J. (1982). Sex roles as social conventions: The development of children's conceptions of sex-role stereotypes. *Developmental Psychology, 18*, 812-824.

Chandler, T. A., Sawicki, R. F., & Stryffeler, J. M. (1981). Relationship between adolescent sexual stereotypes and working mothers. *Journal of Early Adolescence, 1*, 72-83.

Coates, D. L. (1987). Gender differences in the structure and support characteristics of black adolescents' social networks. *Sex Roles, 17,* 667-687.

Cogle, F. L., Tasker, G. E., & Morton, D. G. (1982). Adolescent time use in household work. *Adolescence, 17,* 451-455.

Collins, A. (1982). Cognitive processing in television viewing. In D. Pearl, L. Bouthilet, & J. Lazar (Eds.), *Television and behavior: Ten years of scientific progress and implications for the eighties: Vol. 2, Technical reviews* (pp. 9-23). Washington, DC: National Institute of Mental Health.

Douvan, E. & Adelson, J. (1966). *The adolescent experience.* New York: John Wiley.

Durkin, K. (1985a). Television and sex-role acquisition 1: Content. *British Journal of Social Psychology, 24,* 101-113.

Durkin, K. (1985b). Television and sex-role acquisition 2: Effects. *British Journal of Social Psychology, 24,* 191-210.

Durkin, K. (1985c). Television and sex-role acquisition 3: Counter-stereotyping. *British Journal of Social Psychology, 24,* 211-222.

Dweck, C. S. (1986). Motivational process affecting learning. *American Psychologist, 41,* 1040-1048.

Eccles, J. P. (1983). Expectancies, values, and academic behaviors. In J. T. Spence (Ed.), *Achievement and achievement motives: Psychological and sociological approaches* (pp. 75-146). San Francisco: W. H. Freeman.

Eccles, J. P., Adler, T., Kaczala, C. (1982). Socialization of achievement attitudes and beliefs: Parental influences. *Child Development, 53,* 310-321.

Eisenstock, B. (1984). Sex-role differences in children's identification with counterstereotypical televised portrayals. *Sex Roles, 10,* 417-430.

Emmerich, W., & Shepard, K. (1982). Development of sex-differentiated preferences during late childhood and adolescence. *Developmental Psychology, 18,* 406-417.

Eron, L. D., Huesmann, L. R., Brice, P., Fischer, P., & Mermelstein, R. (1983). Age trends in the development of aggression, sex typing, and related television habits. *Developmental Psychology, 19,* 71-77.

Fennema, E., & Peterson, P. (1985). Autonomous learning behavior: A possible explanation of gender-related differences in mathematics. In L. C. Wilkinson & C. B. Marrett (Eds.), *Gender influences in classroom interaction* (pp. 17-36). New York: Academic Press.

Gargiulo, J., Attie, I., Brooks-Gunn, J., & Warren, M. (1987). Girls' dating behavior as a function of social context and maturation. *Developmental Psychology, 23,* 730-737.

Greif, E. B, & Ulman, K. (1982). The psychological impact of menarche on early adolescent females: A review of the literature. *Child Development, 53,* 1413-1430.

Goulet, L. R., & Baltes, P. B. (Eds.), (1970). *Life span developmental psychology: Research and theory.* New York: Academic Press.

Hamburg, D., & Takanishi, R. (1989). Preparing for life: The critical transition of adolescence. *American Psychologist, 44,* 825-827.

Harris, M. B., & Voorhees, S. D. (1981). Sex-role stereotypes and televised models of emotion. *Psychological Reports, 48,* 826.

Hess, R. D., & Miura, I. T. (1985). Gender differences in enrollment in computer camps and classes. *Sex Roles, 13,* 193-203.

Hertsgaard, D., & Light, H. (1984). Junior high girls' attitudes toward the rights and roles of women. *Adolescence, 19,* 847-853.

Hetherington, E. M. (1972). Effects of father absence on personality development in adolescent daughters. *Developmental Psychology, 7,* 313-326.

Hill, J. P., & Lynch, M. E. (1983). The intensification of gender-related role expectations during early adolescence. In J. Brooks-Gunn & A. C. Petersen (Eds.), *Girls at puberty: Biological and psychological perspectives.* New York: Plenum.

Hoffman, L. W. (1989). Effects of maternal employment in the two-parent family: A review of recent research. *American Psychologist, 44,* 283-292.

Huff, C., & Cooper, J. (1987). Sex bias in educational software: The effects of designers' stereotypes on the software they design. *Journal of Applied Social Psychology, 17,* 519-532.

Huston, A. C. (1983). Sex-typing. In E. M. Hetherington (Ed.), P. H. Mussen (Series Ed.), *Handbook of Child Psychology, Vol. 4. Socialization, Personality, and Social Development* (pp. 387-468). New York: John Wiley.

Huston, A. C., Carpenter, J. C., Atwater, J. B., & Johnson, L. M. (1986). Gender, adult structuring of activities, and social behavior in middle childhood. *Child Development, 57,* 1200-1209.

Huston, A. C., & Wright, J. C. (1983). Children's processing of television: The informative functions of formal features. In J. Bryant & D. R. Anderson (Eds.), *Children's understanding of television: Research on attention and comprehension.* New York: Academic Press.

Huston, A. C., Wright, J. C., Rice, M., Kerkman, D., & St. Peters, M. (1987). *The development of television viewing patterns in early childhood: A longitudinal investigation.* Paper presented at the Society for Research in Child Development, Baltimore.

Huston-Stein, A., & Welch, R. L. (1979). Sex role development and the adolescent. In J. Adams (Ed.), *Understanding adolescence* (4th ed.). Boston: Allyn & Bacon.

Jackson, A., & Hornbeck, D. (1989). Educating young adolescents: Why we must restructure middle grade schools. *American Psychologist, 44,* 831-836.

Johnston, J., & Ettema, J. S. (1982). *Positive images: Breaking stereotypes with children's television.* Beverly Hills, CA: Sage.

Kohlberg, L. (1966). A cognitive-developmental analysis of children's sex role concepts and attitudes. In E. E. Maccoby (Ed.), *The development of sex differences* (pp. 82-172). Stanford: Stanford University Press.

LaTorre, Yu, Fortin, & Marrache (1983). Gender-role adoption and sex as academic and psychological risk factors. *Sex Roles, 9,* 1127-1136.

Lavine, L. O. (1982). Parental power as a potential influence on girls' career choice. *Child Development, 53,* 658-663.

Liebert, R. M., & Sprafkin, J. (1988). *The early window: Effects of television on children and youth* (3rd ed.). New York: Pergamon.

Livingstone, S., & Green, G. (1986). Television advertisements and the portrayal of gender. *British Journal of Social Psychology, 25,* 149-154.

Loyd, B. H., Loyd, D. E., & Gressard, C. P. (1987). Gender and computer attitudes of middle school students. *Journal of Early Adolescence, 7,* 13-19.

Lynn, D. B. (1966). The process of learning parental and sex-role identification. *Journal of Marriage and the Family Review, 28,* 466-470.

Maccoby, E. E., & Jacklin, C. N. (in press). Gender segregation in childhood. In H. Reese (Ed.), *Advances in child behavior and development.* New York: Academic Press.

Mackey, W. D., & Hess, D. J. (1982). Attention structure and stereotype of gender on television: An empirical analysis. *Genetic psychology monographs, 106,* 199-215.

Marini, M. M. (1978). Sex differences in the determination of adolescent aspirations: A review of research. *Sex Roles, 4,* 723-753.

Massad, C. M. (1981). Sex role identity and adjustment during adolescence. *Child Development, 52,* 1290-1298.

Matteson, D. R. (1975). *Adolescence today: Sex roles and the search for identity.* Homewood, IL: Dorsey Press.

Miller, M. M., & Reeves, B. B. (1976). Children's occupational sex role stereotypes: The linkage between television content and perception. *Journal of Broadcasting, 20,* 35-50.

Montemayor, R., & Van Komen, R. (1985). The development of sex differences in friendship patterns and peer group structure during adolescence. *Journal of Early Adolescence, 5,* 285-294.

Morgan, M. (1982). Television and adolescents' sex role stereotypes: A longitudinal study. *Journal of Personality and Social Psychology, 43,* 947-955.

Morgan, M. (1987). Television, sex-role attitudes, and sex-role behavior. *Journal of Early Adolescence, 7,* 269-282.

Nash, S., & Feldman, S. (1981). Sex-role and sex-related attributions: Constancy and change across the family life cycle. In M. E. Lamb & A. L. Brown (Eds.), *Advances in developmental psychology* (Vol. 1). Hillsdale, NJ: Erlbaum.

Papini, D., & Sebby, R. (1988). Variations in conflictual family issues by adolescent pubertal status, gender, and family member. *Journal of Early Adolescence, 8,* 1-15.

Perry, D., & Bussey, K. (1984). *Social development.* Englewood Cliffs, NJ: Prentice-Hall.

Pingree, S. (1978). The effects of nonsexist television commercials and perceptions of reality on children's attitudes about women. *Psychology of Women Quarterly, 2,* 262-276.

Robb, B., & Raven, M. (1982). Working mothers and children's perceptions. *Research in Education,* No. 27, 75-83.

Rollins, J., & White, P. N. (1982). The relationship between mothers' and daughters' sex role attitudes and self-concepts in three types of family environment. *Sex Roles, 8,* 1141-1155.

Sigelman, C. K., Carr, M. B., & Begley, N. L. (1986). Developmental changes in the influence of sex-role stereotypes on person perception. *Child Study Journal, 16,* 191-205.

Simmons, R., Burgeson, R., Carlton-Ford, S., & Blyth, D. (1987). The impact of cumulative change in early adolescence. *Child Development, 58,* 1220-1234.

Sonenstein, F. (1986). Risking paternity: Sex and contraception among adolescent males. In A. B. Elster & M. E. Lamb (Eds.), *Adolescent fatherhood.* Hillsdale, NJ: Erlbaum. (Pp. 31-54).

Stein, A. H., & Smithells, J. (1969). Age and sex differences in children's sex role standards about achievement. *Developmental Psychology, 1,* 252-259.

Steinberg, L. D. (1981). Transformations in family relations at puberty. *Developmental Psychology, 17,* 833-840.

Steinberg, L. D. (1988). Reciprocal relation between parent-child distance and pubertal maturation. *Developmental Psychology, 24,* 122-128.

Steinberg, L. D., & Hill, J. P. (1978). Patterns of family interactions as a function of age, the onset of puberty, and formal thinking. *Developmental Psychology, 14,* 683-684.

Stoddart, T., & Turiel, E. (1985). Children's concepts of cross-gender activities. *Child Development, 56,* 1241-1252.

Stoneman, Z., Brody, G., & MacKinnon, C. (1986). Same-sex and cross-sex siblings: Activity choices, roles, behavior, and gender stereotypes. *Sex Roles, 15,* 495-511.

Teti, D. M., & Lamb, M. E. (1986). Sex-role learning and adolescent fatherhood. In A. B. Elster & M. E. Lamb (Eds.), *Adolescent fatherhood* (pp. 19-30). Hillsdale, NJ: Erlbaum.

Thompson, S. K. (1988, March). *Adolescents' attitudes about sex role egalitarianism: 1976-1987.* Paper presented at the Southwestern Society for Research in Human Development, New Orleans.

Tittle, C. K. (1986). Gender research in education. *American Psychologist, 41,* 1161-1168.

Ullian, D. Z. (1976). The development of conceptions of masculinity and femininity. In B. Lloyd & J. Archer (Eds.), *Exploring sex differences* (pp. 25-48). London: Academic Press.

Wilder, G., Mackie, D., & Cooper, J. (1985). Gender and computers: Two surveys of computer-related attitudes. *Sex Roles, 13,* 215-228.

Williams, F., LaRose, R., & Frost, F. (1981). *Children, television, and sex-role stereotyping.* New York: Praeger.

Williams, T. M., Baron, D., Phillips, S., Travis, L., & Jackson, D. (1986, August). *The portrayal of sex roles on Canadian and U.S. television.* Paper presented at the conference of the International Association for Mass Communication Research, New Delhi, India.

Wroblewski, R., & Huston, A. C. (1987). Televised occupational stereotypes and their effects on early adolescents: Are they changing? *Journal of Early Adolescence, 7,* 283-297.

PART III

SOCIAL COGNITIVE DEVELOPMENT

8. Continuity and Discontinuity in Adolescent Social Cognitive Development

Daniel K. Lapsley
University of Notre Dame

In general terms, social cognitive development is the study of how children reason about their social world, and how patterns of social reasoning undergo sequential variation during the course of ontogenesis. The purpose of this chapter is to explore whether or not the literature on social cognitive development supports the claim that early adolescence is a unique transition in ontogenesis. Is early adolescence of singular importance, for example, for certain kinds of development in social cognition? A strong claim for developmental uniqueness would be supported by observing patterns of social reasoning that are qualitatively distinct and discontinuous with childhood patterns of social cognition and with patterns that are unique to both late adolescence and early adulthood. Hence, the observance of unique discontinuities in social cognition in early adolescence would constitute strong support for the putative uniqueness of this developmental transition.

It should be noted, of course, that asking if early adolescence is a unique transition in ontogenesis is not the same thing as asking if there is continuity or discontinuity in (for example) social cognitive development. There may, in fact, be sharp discontinuities evident in a range of social cognitive developmental domains, but none of which are observed during the period of early adolescence. If these discontinuities are not observed in early adolescence or, alternatively, if childhood patterns of social cognition persist into adolescence, or if patterns of social cognitive reasoning emerge in early adolescence but persist into early adulthood, then one would not be inclined to attribute developmental uniqueness to the early adolescence transition.

The ability to adduce continuity and discontinuity in developmental data is made problematic by a host of complicating factors. It is

AUTHOR'S NOTE: *This chapter benefited from the many helpful comments that were provided by Robert Enright, Ray Montemayor and his doctoral students, and an anonymous reviewer. I retain, of course, all responsibility for its shortcomings.*

well known, for example, that different metatheoretical allegiances will yield different understandings of the rhythm of development (Reese & Overton, 1970). A further complication is that continuity and discontinuity may be characteristic of both quantitative and qualitative change. As Werner (1957; also, Overton & Reese, 1981) points out, novelty may become evident gradually (qualitative continuity), while continuity may become evident rapidly (quantitative discontinuity). This suggests that an inspection of data may not provide compelling grounds for inferring continuity or discontinuity (Overton & Reese, 1981). Further difficulties are encountered when one attempts to chart the developmental trajectories of patterns of individual differences and developmental functions. Continuity in developmental functions, that is, in the relationship between prior and later organizations of behavior, as observed in group data, does not necessarily imply continuity of individual differences (Cairns & Hood, 1983). Indeed, as McCall (1983, p. 66) points out, "developmental change can occur within the context of a developmental function independent of change across age in the individual differences in performance for a given variable. This means that evidence for stability does not necessarily imply continuity, and evidence for continuity does not necessarily imply stability." Even evidence for stagelike progressions in various ability domains does not constitute unambiguous evidence for discontinuity (Lewis & Starr, 1979). As Overton and Reese (1981) point out, stage theories are an assertion of discontinuity, and not a demonstration of it. Indeed, developmental discontinuities may well evaporate upon closer inspection with finer grains of analysis (Case, 1985; Siegler, 1986).

Although discerning developmental continuity and discontinuity is certainly no easy matter, it is not an intractable problem, at least for the task at hand, and can be approached by making a number of methodological assumptions. I will assume, for example, that researchers in social cognitive development share a commitment to organismic assumptions about development. This includes the understanding that stages are structured into coherent organizations and implicate qualitative change, abruptness, and concurrence of acquisition (Flavell, 1971). In addition, as a methodological heuristic, I will simply assume that the various social cognitive stage sequences do, in fact, describe developmental discontinuities. It will then be a relatively straightforward matter, for the task at hand, to determine if these discontinuities are pronounced during the period of early adolescence.

My review of the social cognitive developmental literature cannot hope to be exhaustive. Several reviews of this sprawling literature have appeared over the years (e.g., Chandler, 1977; Enright & Lapsley, 1980; Ford, 1979; Shantz, 1975, 1983), and one is duly impressed by the diversity and range of social cognitive developmental topics reviewed therein. One striking impression of this literature is that numerous features of social cognition reach impressive developmental heights by middle to late childhood. Of concern here will be four domains that would seem to hold much promise for locating the early adolescence transition. These domains include adolescent egocentrism, skeptical doubt, interpersonal understanding, and moral development. In the next section I will deal with the claim that at least some of these domains (e.g., adolescent egocentrism, skeptical doubt) emerge in early adolescence because of the emergence of formal operations. I will then review the empirical evidence on their emergence during this transition and next consider the domains of interpersonal understanding and moral development.

THE COGNITIVE-DEVELOPMENTAL HYPOTHESIS
OF ADOLESCENCE

In Piagetian theory (Inhelder & Piaget, 1958; Piaget, 1972) the capacity for formal thought is a characteristic of adolescent reasoning. The ability to reason about the possible, impossible, and hypothetical, as opposed to the real, and the ability to reflect on one's own thoughts, are said to be the hallmarks of formal operations. These features of formal operations are thought to underly the many typically observed behaviors of adolescents, for example, the emphasis on internal life, the preoccupation with life plans, and an orientation toward the future and toward ideology (Inhelder & Piaget, 1958).

One can think of formal thought as undergoing two phases of development. In the first phase the press toward hypothetical thinking results in an unconstrained surge of possibilities, which submerges reality (Broughton, 1983). This excess of assimilation subjectivizes reality, overwhelming the real and actual with the ideal and possible. The intellectual balance is restored by accommodatory compensations by middle adolescence. Here the adolescent can now test out the products of his or her reasoning against experience, and, in the process, move reasoning away from the hegemony of the self, away from the domination of the "adolescent ego." One may hence view the assimilatory emphasis of formal thought as marking the transition into adolescence, and the accommodatory activity of formal thought as marking the consolidation of formal operations. In early writings there is some indication that the onset and consolidation of formal thought is completed by early adolescence (age 12 to 15), although a later account (Piaget, 1972) suggests that that formal thought is not achieved until late adolescence (age 15 to 20). In this latter account, the compensatory decentering is effected as one moves into the role structure of society, as one takes on an occupation and becomes an adult. Hence, the onset of adolescence is marked by cognitive factors—by subjectivizing reality in a flush of egocentric thinking, while the transition out of adolescence is marked by noncognitive, societal factors (Broughton, 1983; Lapsley, 1985). Thus conceived, formal operations ranges across the span of adolescence to the threshold of adulthood, rather than being an achievement of early to middle adolescence.

The cognitive developmental hypothesis, then, suggests that the onset of formal operations yields a characteristic pattern of social reasoning that results from an overemphasis on the assimilatory (subject) pole of subject-object reasoning. Young adolescents, as opposed to children and older adolescents, subjectivize reality, and the causes can be traced to the assimilatory workings of formal thought. This key insight has been extended in Elkind's (1967, 1985) well-known theory of adolescent egocentrism. Formal thought has also been invoked to explain the emergence of "epistemological relativity and loneliness" (Chandler, 1975), skeptical doubt, and "Cartesian anxiety" (Chandler, 1987). Further, formal thought is also said to underlie other social cognitive developmental domains, such as certain attribution processes (e.g., Allen, Walker, Schroeder, & Johnson, 1987), interpersonal understanding (Selman, 1980), and moral development (Kuhn, Langer, Kohlberg, & Haan, 1977).

In Chandler's (1987) theory, for example, adolescence is to be distinguished from childhood by the fact that young adolescents come to doubt that there could be any good grounds for belief entitlement. Children and preadolescents, on the other hand, tend to believe that objectively true knowledge exists, that facts are an attribute of the environment and can be used as a standard for evaluating different perspectives, and that persons of good will and who are free of prejudice and who possess the right information will come to agree on the interpretation of facts. The shift in adolescence to formal operational thought brings with it a shift toward skeptical doubt, epistemological confusion, and a collapse of absolute conviction (although mature role-taking competence is also invoked). Knowledge is seen to be a manufactured mental product that is person-relative. This pervasive subjectivity undermines any belief in objective knowledge. As a consequence adolescents are gripped with "Cartesian anxiety" or a sense of "epistemological loneliness" (Chandler, 1975), all of which reflects their thoroughgoing skepticism and epistemological relativism. Chandler (1975, 1987) suggests that this way of thinking about belief entitlement accounts for some commonly observed behaviors of the adolescent period. Adolescents who are awash in skeptical doubt and who suffer from the ensuing "vertigo of relativity" are seen to respond with characteristic maneuvers, such as clique formation, intellectualization, intolerance, stereotypy (Chandler, 1975), and also by what Chandler (1987) terms impulsivism (acting without thought), intuitionism (doing what feels good), conformism (doing the done thing), and indifferentism (acting on whim).

One way, then, to distinguish adolescence from childhood is to watch for the emergence of relativism and skeptical doubt. One way to distinguish adolescence from adulthood is to discern the transcendence of skeptical doubt by "post-skeptical rationalism" (Chandler, 1987). The paralysis of radical skepticism is overcome by a new phase of thinking that recognizes that shared experience provides sufficient grounds for a measure of intersubjectivity; that argumentation and social discourse allows us to keep obtainable truth in sight, although we recognize that what we do know is fallible.

Elkind's (1967) theory of adolescent egocentrism is perhaps the better known example of the cognitive developmental hypothesis of adolescence. According to Elkind (1967) any emergent structure-information involves an initial overemphasis on assimilatory cognitive activity. This results in a differentiation failure, or egocentrism. Each of Piaget's major stages can thus be described in terms of a characteristic differentiation failure, with adolescent egocentrism being the strain that is associated with formal operations. One "gets out of" the various egocentrisms, except for adolescent egocentrism, by the emergence of the next stage in the sequence. However, this transition mechanism obviously cannot work for adolescent egocentrism because there is no next stage to act as liberator (Lapsley & Murphy, 1985). Instead, adolescent egocentrism is transcended by involvement in social roles and intimate social relationships, a maneuver that recalls Piaget's two-phase account of formal operations.

The differentiation failure of formal operations has been described by Elkind (1967, p. 1029) in the following way:

> [F]ormal operational thought not only enables the adolescent to conceptualize his thoughts, it also permits him to conceptualize the thought of other people. It is this capacity to take account of other people's thought, however, which is the crux of adolescent egocentrism. This egocentrism emerges because, while the adolescent can now cognize the thoughts of others, he fails to differentiate between the objects toward which the thoughts of others are directed and those which are the focus of his own concern.

This differentiation failure of formal operations yields two complementary ideations, the imaginary audience and the personal fable. The imaginary audience describes the adolescent's tendency to anticipate the reactions of others to the self in real or imagined situations. The adolescent believes, as a result, that he or she will be the object of attention and concern, that others are preoccupied with the adolescent's appearance and behavior (Lapsley, in press). The personal fable reflects the concomitant belief in one's personal uniqueness, invulnerability, and omnipotence. A variety of typically observed adolescent behaviors have been linked to the twin operations of these complementary ideations, including heightened self-consciousness, idealism, show-off and risk-taking behaviors, and a concern with shame and shyness (Elkind, 1967, 1985; Lapsley & Rice, 1988; Lapsley, in press).

Hence, along with generic skeptical doubt, the ideations associated with adolescent egocentrism are another candidate for demarcating early adolescence from childhood and from late adolescence and adulthood. These constructs do indeed constitute reasonable demarcation criteria if one assumes (1) that formal operations is singularly characteristic of early adolescence, and (2) that formal operations does, in fact, generate these patterns of social cognition. Unfortunately, there are theoretical and empirical reasons to doubt both assumptions.

To be used as demarcation criteria, these constructs must deal with the fact that formal operations does not seem to be a normative feature of even adult cognition. This incidence problem suggests that formal thought is itself a poor candidate for signaling the onset of adolescence. Indeed, Kohlberg and Gilligan (1971, p. 1065) noted that almost

50% of American adults never reach adolescence in the cognitive sense and, consequently, "we cannot equate a cognitive stage with a definite age period." And there are conceptual grounds as well for doubting the role of formal thought for signaling the advent of adolescence. In an underappreciated paper, Blasi and Hoeffel (1974, p. 351) argue that the twin pillars of formal thought, the ability to think about the possible and about one's own thoughts (reflective thinking), are not up to the task of describing typical adolescent patterns of social reasoning. They point out that there is a fundamental asymmetry between the physical possibility that is endemic to perfectly compensated closed systems (e.g., INRC-lattice structure of formal operations), and psychological and subjective possibility. This asymmetry can be illustrated by comparing the understanding of possibility that devolves from formal and concrete operations. Blasi and Hoeffel (1974) draw the following distinctions: Formal possibility is abstract and theoretical, viewing the real as a special case of the possible. Subjective possibility is concrete, seeing the possible as an extension of the real. Formal operations approaches problems deductively by seeking the underlying causal structure and then deducing the specific case. Concrete operations is inductive and consists of making extrapolations from relevant prior experience. Formal thought is adaptive if the causal structure is known and the rules of deduction are correctly followed. Concrete operations is adaptive if one has a rich and varied social history from which to make the relevant inductions. The upshot of this analysis is to suggest that the kinds of "possibilities" that are the concern of typical adolescents (e.g., ideological orientation, life plans, social and political commitments) are precisely the kind for which formal operations cannot be of much help. The possibilities that spring from social life require not an understanding of perfect compensations in closed physical systems, but something else, something about motivation, imagination, alienation, desire, will, creativity, and the like (Blasi & Hoeffel, 1974; Broughton, 1977). For this a rich and varied social life seems sufficient. Hence, according to Blasi and Hoeffel (1974):

"The understanding of possibility into which adolescents grow seems to be related, in general, to their own personal, social, and civic life—precisely the areas in which the understanding of perfectly compensated systems would not be possible" (p. 354) . . . [C]oncrete operational thinking may be perfectly adequate in order to function as a typical Western adolescent, namely in order to think 'hypothetically' about the future, to organize a plan, and even to compare ideologies, choose one, and to become politically and socially committed."

The second pillar of formal thought, reflective thinking, is also ill-suited to account for adolescent ideation and behavior (Blasi & Hoeffel, 1974; Broughton, 1977). The problems that are of concern to various social cognitive developmental theories are, in one way or another, problems of self- or interpersonal understanding (e.g., adolescent egocentrism, see Lapsley & Murphy, 1985). But a number of commentators (e.g., Broughton, 1977; Blasi & Hoeffel, 1974; Blasi, 1983) have shown that "thinking about thoughts" is not the same thing as "thinking about the *self*," although Piaget probably had the latter in mind when he suggested that formal operations is the source of adolescent personality.

It seems clear, then, that formal operationally based theories of social cognitive development cannot serve as demarcation criteria for early adolescence. The warrant for this claim devolves not only from the incidence data for formal operations, but also from the conceptual analyses advanced by Blasi and Hoeffel (1974) and others (Broughton, 1977; Lapsley, 1985; Lapsley & Murphy, 1985; Vikan, 1983) that show that many typically observed adolescent behaviors can be explained without recourse to formal thought. Yet there is empirical data that can be brought to bear as well.

Research on adolescent egocentrism has undergone three phases (Lapsley, in press). The first phase was concerned with the operationalization of the imaginary audience and personal fable, and with the charting of age, sex, and other correlates of the constructs (Elkind & Bowen, 1979; Enright, Lapsley, & Shukla, 1979; Enright, Shukla, & Lapsley, 1980; Adams & Jones, 1981; Lechner & Rosenthal, 1983). During the second phase, there was a concern for testing the crucial assumption of the theory, namely, that the tendency to engage in imaginary audience and personal fable ideations is somehow related to formal operational thought. The third phase, currently in progress, attempts to provide alternative theoretical contexts for understanding the imaginary audience and personal fable (Lapsley & Rice, 1988; Lapsley, Jackson, Rice, & Shadid, 1988). Of concern here are the results of the second phase of research, which are not supportive of the putative relation between formal thought and "adolescent egocentrism" (Lapsley, in press). Gray and Hudson (1984; also, Goossens, 1984), for example, found that imaginary audience and personal fable scores were highest in subjects who were in concrete operations. Similarly, Riley, Adams, and Nielson (1984) found that the onset of formal operations diminishes imaginary audience ideation. Finally, in two studies, Lapsley, Milstead, Quintana, Flannery, and Buss (1986) found uniformly null relations between formal thought and measures of imaginary audience and personal fable. It certainly seems to be the case that "the developmental pattern of egocentrism . . . does not appear to be consistently linked to theoretical based patterns in formal operations of cognitive development" (Riley et al., 1984, p. 402).

Although this conclusion seems reasonable, it must be tempered by two considerations. First, the psychometric properties of the extant measures of adolescent egocentrism are not well-researched. More extensive measures of the imaginary audience and personal fable are in development (Lapsley, FitzGerald, Rice, & Jackson, 1989), and these may provide a more veridical assessment of their relationship to formal operations. In addition, previous research has not distinguished between "early formal" and formal operations proper in their assessment of this construct. It may be that the former provides the grounding of imaginary audience and personal fable ideations, although this possibility has yet to be explored.

Whether these methodological variations will eventually establish the empirical linkage between "adolescent egocentrism" and formal operations cannot, of course, be known in advance. And whether the linkage is established or not is independent of our interest in using this data for locating the early adolescence transition. A recent paper (Allen, Walker, Schroeder, & Johnson, 1987) is illustrative. Across two studies using college-age subjects, these authors found that only formal operators could make valid causal attributions to explain the performance of another on an achievement test. Although these findings demonstrate a linkage between formal thought and social cognition, they illustrate other issues as well. First, these data, because they were generated from young adults, cannot be used to say anything about how formal operationally based patterns of social cognition distinguishes early adolescence from childhood or from late adolescence. In addition, about 75% of the college subjects in the first study were either in concrete operations, or were in transition to formal thought, while approximately 50% of the subjects were formal operational in Study 2. Hence, it is reasonable to suppose that in early adolescence most children are concrete operational, and will remain so for the duration of adolescence and early adulthood (Keating & Clark, 1980). Those social cognitive developmental constructs that are said to devolve from formal thought cannot, then, be used to highlight the developmental uniqueness of early adolescence without incoherence.

The empirical status of skeptical doubt is more difficult to evaluate. This writer, perhaps because of long memories of his own adolescence, is convinced that young adolescents reason about belief entitlement much the way Chandler (1987) describes it. Convincing empirical evidence, however, does not seem to be available as yet, and, as noted above, there are good grounds for believing that formal operations may not have much to do with its appearance in early adolescence. However, if research were to show that generic skeptical doubt is indeed ushered in by formal operations, then it is difficult to know what cognitive mechanism might be responsible for the transcendence of skeptical doubt. There is evidence to suggest that relativism may persist well into early adulthood (Perry, 1970), making it a problem not just for adolescents. One tentative conclusion seems reasonable at this point, namely, that while the emergence of skeptical doubt may indeed demarcate adolescence from childhood, it does not indicate that early adolescence is distinct from late adolescence or early adulthood.

One option that must be considered is that young adolescents do engage in certain characteristic patterns of social cognition, and that they do so independently of developments in formal thought. This option de-couples the putative linkage between formal thought and social cognition (leaving open the possibility that there might be other ways to conceptualize the relation between cognition and social cognition; see, e.g., Blasi, 1983) and suggests that the various social cognitive developmental sequences could serve as suitable demarcation criteria for distinguishing the early adolescence transition, even though formal operations does not. In the next section the evidence regarding adolescent egocentrism will be considered anew. Then the data on interpersonal understanding and moral development will be considered.

ADOLESCENT EGOCENTRISM

The first two phases of research on adolescent egocentrism have reached inconsistent findings regarding the developmental trajectories of the imaginary audience and personal fable constructs. These inconsistencies are found regardless of which of the two extant measures of adolescent egocentrism are used, the Imaginary Audience Scale (Elkind & Bowen, 1979) or the Adolescent Egocentrism Scale (Enright et al., 1979; 1980). The Imaginary Audience Scale (Elkind & Bowen, 1979) attempts to assess the extent to which adolescents are willing to reveal abiding and transient aspects of the self to others. The "imaginary audience" is inferred when adolescents appear to be self-conscious about such revelations. Elkind and Bowen (1979) found that eighth graders were more concerned about the imaginary audience than were younger children or older adolescents. Lechner and Rosenthal (1983) also reported peak imaginary audience behavior in eighth grade. Finally, Lapsley et al. (1986, Study 2) found that seventh- and ninth-grade subjects had higher imaginary audience scores than did college freshmen, and that ninth graders had higher scores than did eleventh graders. However, at least three studies failed to report any significant grade effects at all using this scale (Gray & Hudson, 1984; Goossens, 1984; Peterson, 1982), and one study (Adams & Jones, 1981) actually found a linear increase from 11-13 years to 17-18 years of age.

Research using the Adolescent Egocentrism Scale (AES) has also yielded inconsistent findings on age effects. The AES is comprised of three subscales that directly assess imaginary audience, personal fable ideation, and also self-focused concerns. In the first study using this measure, Enright, Lapsley & Shukla (1979) found that imaginary audience and personal fable scores declined significantly from sixth grade to college, although self-focused concerns increased during this period. Sixth and eighth graders had higher scores on imaginary audience and personal fable than did college subjects. However, no grade differences were evident for the personal fable. In a second study (Enright, Shukla, & Lapsley, 1980), sixth graders had higher imaginary audience scores than did eighth, tenth, and twelfth graders, and higher personal fable scores for all grades except tenth grade. Mixed results were also reported by Lapsley et al. (1985). In one study (Study 2) ninth graders had higher scores on the imaginary audience and personal fable than did seventh and eleventh graders and college subjects. However, no age effects at all were reported for these constructs in the first study. Finally, in a recent study, Lapsley, Jackson, Rice, and Shadid (1988) found peak imaginary audience scores in *fifth* graders, and also that fifth, seventh, and eleventh graders had higher personal fable scores than did college subjects.

Clearly, the onset and decline of adolescent egocentrism, when it is observed at all, shows considerable sample specific variability. Although imaginary audience and personal fable ideation is more often observed than not, the variability of onset and decline makes these constructs only uncertain or probablistic indicators of early adolescence. This is perhaps to be expected, given the cross-sectional nature of all of the investigations in this area. The best that one can say at this juncture is that imaginary audience and personal fable ideations *probably* emerges in early adolescence, but not always, and *probably* declines by late adolescence, although the factors that govern probable appearance, onset, and decline have yet to be specified. This also points out that an alternative theoretical context must be developed to anchor the operation of these constructs, now that considerable doubt has been cast on the foundational role of formal operations. There have been recent attempts to link the emergence of imaginary audience and personal fable ideations to stages of interpersonal understanding (Lapsley & Murphy, 1985; Lapsley, 1985) and to the separation-individuation process of adolescent ego development (Lapsley & Rice, 1988; Lapsley et al., 1989). For example, one theory (Lapsley & Murphy, 1985) suggests that the onset and decline of imaginary audience and personal fable ideations is linked to the emergence of Levels 3 and 4, respectively, in the sequence describing interpersonal understanding (Selman, 1980). But, as we shall see in the following section, this theoretical grounding of the IA and PF constructs still fails to locate the early adolescence transition.

INTERPERSONAL UNDERSTANDING AND MORAL DEVELOPMENT

The stage sequences that describe role-taking, interpersonal understanding, and moral development are perhaps the best known social cognitive developmental sequences and would, hence, be good candidates to serve as demarcation criteria for early adolescence. Let us first consider the domain of interpersonal understanding. In Selman's (1980) theory interpersonal understanding is seen to range across four domains. It involves conceptions of: (1) *individuals and persons* (subjectivity, self-reflection, personality and personality change); (2) *close friendship* (formation, intimacy, trust, jealousy, conflict resolution, termination); (3) *peer group organization* (group formation, cohesion, conformity, rules and norms, decision-making, leadership, termination); and (4) *parent-child relations* (formation, love and cooperation, demands, punishment, conflict). Reasoning in each domain can be described in terms of a stage sequence that ranges from early child-hood to late adolescence and early adulthood. The sequences adhere to structural developmental stage criteria, such as qualitative change, invariant sequence, structured wholeness, hierarchical integration, and the like. And what motivates change from stage to stage in the various domains are advances in perspective-taking development, which can be described in terms of its own sequence of development. In general, early adolescence (about ages 10 to 15) is marked by the emergence of Level 3 role-taking (Damon & Hart, 1982), which gen-erates parallel (Level 3) developments in each of the four domains of interpersonal understanding.

Strong empirical support for the sequentiality of perspective-taking development has been amply demonstrated for early (Selman, 1971) and middle childhood (Selman & Byrne, 1974) and for adolescence and early adulthood (Byrne, 1973). However, can one use this se-quence to locate the early adolescence transition? Selman and Byrne (1974), in a study of 4-, 6-, 8-, and 10-year-olds, reported that 60% of 10-year-olds were at Level 2, with the remaining 40% evenly divided between Levels 1 and 3. So, at the threshold of early adolescence, 80% of 10-year-olds are likely to be no higher than Level 2 in social per-spective-taking. In a study of adolescents and young adults Byrne (1973) found that only 6 out of 28 subjects age 10 to 13 were at Level 3 or higher, with about 78% of the early adolescence sample being no higher than Level 2. In this sample, Level 3 was not firmly in evidence until middle adolescence (age 16), although it is absent in the sample by adulthood. Hence, given the persistence of middle-childhood patterns of social perspective-taking (e.g., Level 2) into adolescence, and the appearance of Level 3 in middle adolescence, one can con-clude that early adolescence is not strongly indicated by develop-ments in social perspective-taking. Indeed, Selman (1980, Table 8.5) indicates that the range in age in interpersonal understanding for Level 2 is from age 6 (years): 9 (months)—15 (years): 10 (months), while the range for Level 3 is from 11:3—adulthood (+20). The con-siderable overlap during early adolescence of Levels 2 and 3, and the persistence of Level 3 to adulthood further suggests that early adoles-cence cannot be distinguished from childhood or from late adoles-cence and adulthood by appeals to interpersonal understanding. Indeed, given this variability, Level 3 could mark either the beginning *or* the end of adolescence. It should be recalled that our working assumption is that the stage sequences that are under consideration do, in fact, describe discontinuities and qualitative change. For example, we have just concluded that, although perspective-taking and interpersonal understanding do show stagelike developments, no cleanly demarcated shift in stage use is evident in these domains during the period of early adolescence. There have been some recent suggestions, however, that advances in perspective-taking reflect quantitative, and not qualitative change (Turiel, 1983), and is perhaps tied to quantitative increments in mental capacity (Lapsley & Quintana, 1989; Higgins, 1981). This issue, however, need not detain us here.

The topic of moral development is fully addressed in the chapter by Eisenberg (this volume), so only a number of general comments will be offered here. It has been noted thus far that the domain of interpersonal understanding, and the social cognitive abilities putatively linked with formal operations, are not suitable for denoting the singular developmental importance of early adolescence. A similar claim will be pressed with regard to moral development.

It was once commonplace to suppose that adolescence was marked by the emergence of post-conventional forms of moral reasoning (e.g., Kohlberg & Gilligan, 1971). A typical formulation asserted that formal thought (later downsized to the transitional "beginning" or "early" formal operations) was a necessary but not sufficient prerequisite for principled reasoning. This would lead us to expect that some formal operators would be conventional in their moral deliberations, given the developmental lag between the logical and moral domains. This view was revised when empirical realities forced a change in the scoring of moral stages (Colby, 1978). Revisions of the scoring manual resulted in the finding that what was previously seen as principled reasoning was, in actuality, a sophisticated form of conventional reasoning (Murphy & Gilligan, 1980). The necessary-but-not-sufficient formula would then lead us to expect that some formal operators (the incidence problem notwithstanding) could also be preconventional in their moral reasoning (Broughton, 1983). This revised formulation suggested that the dawn of adolescence was to be associated not with principled thinking after all but with the advent of conventional moral reasoning. But the incidence problem of formal operations sufficiently complicates the notion of a necessary-but-not-sufficient relation between the logical and moral domains. The fact that formal thought may not be evident at all in many adults and that concrete operations may persist well into adulthood suggests that adolescence is marked not only by "formal" and "concrete" types of logical reasoners, but by "conventional" and "preconventional" (moral) types as well (Broughton, 1983). This is seen most readily in Kohlberg's longitudinal data (Colby & Kohlberg, 1987, Table 3.12). In one assessment over 80% of the 13- to 14-year-olds and over 30% of the 16- to 18-year-olds were no better than Stages 2/3. Hence the vast majority of early adolescents were still preconventional (or in transition) in their moral thinking, as were a sizeable number of middle adolescents. Almost half of the late adolescents were scored at Stage 3, the first moral conventional stage. This stage was not firmly in evidence before age 16-18, and it persisted well into early adulthood.

These data show how difficult it is to locate early adolescence with the facts of moral development. Childhood patterns of preconventional moral thinking are seen to persist (in pure or transitional forms) into middle adolescence, while conventional thought is seen to persist well into early adulthood. Although this state of affairs does not call into question the stagelike character of moral development (see, e.g., Flavell, 1971, and Davison, King, Kitchener, & Parker, 1980 on the complexities of stage development), it does undermine any appeal to moral development to support the significance of the early adolescence transition. Hence, as was the case with Level 3 in the interpersonal understanding sequence, the emergence of conventional moral reasoning could be said to signal either the beginning *or* the end of adolescence (Broughton, 1983). Indeed, Broughton's (1983, p. 225) conclusion is apt: "Moral stages no longer hold any potential for characterizing or explaining adolescence in any straightforward way."

CONCLUDING COMMENTS

I have examined four domains of adolescent social cognitive development, namely, skeptical doubt, adolescent egocentrism, interpersonal understanding, and moral development. I have argued that none of these domains seems to be a reliable indicator of the early adolescence transition. Hence, although one might expect early adolescence to be period of singular developmental significance, its psychological importance cannot be easily discerned by examining the pattern of developmental changes in the social cognitive constructs reviewed here. To be sure, there are important developments in social cognition during adolescence, but they simply cannot be counted on to occur during early adolescence. In a sense, this should not surprise, because there is no necessary isomorphism between age and stage in structural developmental theory. But more fundamentally, "The view that important transitions in children's thinking are limited to certain transition periods is . . . almost certainly wrong. Children's thinking is continually changing, and most changes seem to be gradual rather than sudden" (Siegler, 1986, p. 11). Consequently, any search for the developmental primacy of certain transitions is bound to disappoint. A shift in focus toward investigating the relationship among developmental processes and constructs would be better suited for explicating the developmental importance of adolescence.

An example from the adolescent egocentrism literature is illustrative. Much of the work in this area has been concerned with charting age-related patterns of onset and decline of imaginary audience and personal fable ideations. The general expectation is that these ideations should predominate in early adolescence, then attenuate thereafter. As I noted earlier, however, there is wide, sample-specific variability in the observed onset and decline of imaginary audience and personal fable ideations. Indeed, as we saw earlier, when one compares "grade effects" across the numerous studies in this literature, one observes what looks like enigmatic age patterns. The absence of longitudinal studies surely has contributed to the apparent confusion. But research in this area has also been handicapped by the ill-founded expectation that early adolescence is the sole breeding ground of "adolescent egocentrism," and the resulting belief that the search for the imaginary audience and personal fable must therefore be restricted to this developmental transition. Recent research has undermined this expectation. According to the "new look" (see Lapsley & Rice, 1988) the imaginary audience and personal fable are constructs that integrate social cognitive accounts of adolescent self-understanding (e.g., Selman, 1980) with neopsychoanalyatic accounts of adolescent ego development, understood in terms of the separation-individuation process (e.g., Blos, 1962; Josselson, 1980).

One task of adolescent separation-individuation is to maintain a hold on object relations in the face of the decathexis of the object world, and to reestablish firm ego boundaries. According to Blos (1962, p. 98) the former is accomplished by "object relational ideation," the latter by the "willful creation of ego states of a poignant internal perception of the self." Object relational ideations are private fantasies, trial actions, "visions of the self" (Josselson, 1980, p. 199) that prepare the adolescent for the affective experience of interpersonal interaction—and, in our view, what have been called "imaginary audience" ideations in social cognitive theory (Lapsley & Rice, 1988). The creation of "poignant internal perceptions of the self" by a "self-observing ego" serves to establish firm ego boundaries. "Self-induced ego states of affective and sensory intensity allow the ego to experience a feeling of self and thus protect the integrity of its boundaries and its cohesion" (Blos, 1962, p. 92). This often results, according to Blos (1962), in a heightened sense of personal uniqueness, a surge of personal agency, and a sense of invulnerability—or what social cognitive theory has called "personal fable" ideations.

This theory, then, implicates the imaginary audience and personal fable in the separation-individuation project of adolescent ego development. But we have also argued that the ability to engage these ideations may depend on the social cognitive abilities afforded by Level 3 in Selman's (1980) interpersonal understanding sequence (Lapsley & Rice, 1988). As we saw earlier, however, the emergence of Level 3 could range anywhere from late childhood to middle adolescence. Consequently, there is little reason to anchor the imaginary audience and personal fable ideations, or the separation-individuation process generally, to the early adolescence transition. These ideations will emerge whenever Level 3 emerges, and this may show considerable interindividual variability. The specific developmental hypothesis of this model is that the onset of these ideations is to be linked to the emergence of Level 3, and their attenuation to the emergence of Level 4, but the test of this hypothesis is independent of any consideration of age, per se, or any concern for any particular developmental transition period (e.g., early adolescence). Indeed, some research suggests that psychological separation is a task not entirely completed by the last years of college (Lapsley, Rice, & Shadid, 1989).

Research on the new look has only recently begun, but the results thus far are encouraging. In one study we were able to show, among other things, that high self-monitors (the operationalization of the "self-observing ego") had significantly higher imaginary audience and personal fable scores than did low self-monitors (Lapsley, Jackson, Rice & Shadid, 1988). In a second study, we demonstrated a pervasive relationship between imaginary audience and personal fable ideation and separation-individuation, as measured by the Separation Individuation Test of Adolescence (Lapsley, FitzGerald, Rice, & Jackson, 1989). For example, the imaginary audience was positively related to object relational concerns such as engulfment, symbiosis, succorance, enmeshment, and separation anxiety. The personal fable was positively related to dependency need denial and to self-centeredness and negatively related to separation anxiety and engulfment. This pattern of results suggest that imaginary audience and personal fable ideations may serve different functions during separation-individuation. The imaginary audience, as an expression of object relational ideation and the concomitant desire to maintain a hold on object ties, is constructed because of the separation anxiety engendered by the "loss" of the introjected parents. The personal fable, on the other hand, serves to deny dependency needs and separation anxiety through agentic self-centeredness. Hence, the imaginary audience may express the anxiety associated with object relations, while the personal fable constitutes a defense against it. It is interesting to note that the imaginary audience and personal fable may capture on the intrapsychic level the themes of connectedness (imaginary audience) and assertion (personal fable) that others have used to describe the individuation process (e.g., Grotevant & Cooper, 1985). According to Josselson (1988), for example, the goal of separation-individuation is rapprochement, or the sense of individuation in the context of on-going relationships. It may be the case that the concern with connectedness and relationships is bound up with imaginary audience ideations, while individuation, the other side of the separation-individuation coin, is powered by personal fable constructions.

This research assumes that separation-individuation is the principal developmental task of adolescence. Indeed, this project, in our view, is what makes adolescence psychologically distinctive. In addition, this research illustrates the shift in focus from a concern with the early adolescence transition to the relation among theoretically derived constructs. This kind of research strategy would seem to be a more promising way to highlight the developmental importance of adolescence.

A number of caveats are in order about our conclusion that the early adolescence transition is not indicated by advances in social cognitive development. Attempts to locate the early adolescence transition requires one to specify the heuristic or demarcation criteria by which one approaches the developmental data. Conceivably, different criteria will yield different understandings of the developmental primacy of this transition. The demarcation criteria used here may be quite stringent such that less stringent criteria would more readily reveal the singular importance of the early adolescent transition. My interest, however, was in the possibility of making strong claims about early adolescence, and this required the criteria used here. In addition, as was intimated earlier, certain methodological advances, when applied to this literature, may inevitably support the significance of this transition. For example, longitudinal studies of sufficient contextual complexity, the development of rigorous measurements, and the like, would be welcome additions to much of this literature, and may reveal early adolescence to be a significant event in the lifecourse. As it currently stands however, the literature on social cognitive development does not encourage this conclusion.

REFERENCES

Adams, G. R., & Jones, R. (1981). Imaginary audience behavior: A validation study. *Journal of Early Adolescence, 1*, 1-10.

Allen, J. L., Walker, L. D., Schroeder, D. A., & Johnson, D. E. (1987). Attributions and attribution-behavior relations: The effect of level of cognitive development. *Journal of Personality and Social Psychology, 52*, 1099-1109.

Blasi, A. (1983). The self and cognition: The roles of the self in the acquisition of knowledge, and the role of cognition in the acquisition of the self. In B. Lee and G. Noam (Eds.), *Developmental approaches to the self* (pp. 189-213). New York: Plenum.

Blasi, A., & Hoeffel, E. C. (1974). Adolescence and formal operations. *Human Development, 17*, 344-363.

Blos, P. (1962). *On adolescence.* New York: Free Press.

Broughton, J. (1977). "Beyond formal operations": Theoretical thought in adolescence. *Teachers College Record, 79*, 87-96.

Broughton, J. (1983). The cognitive-developmental theory of adolescent self and identity. In B. Lee & G. Noam (Eds.), *Developmental approaches to the self* (pp. 215-266). New York: Plenum.

Byrne, D. (1973). *The development of role-taking in adolescence.* Unpublished doctoral dissertation, Harvard Graduate School of Education.

Cairns, R. B., & Hood, K. E. (1983). Continuity in social development: A comparative perspective on individual differences prediction. *Life-span development and behavior, 5*, 301-358.

Case, R. (1985). *Intellectual development: Birth to adulthood.* Orlando, FL: Academic Press.

Chandler, M. (1975). Relativism and the problem of epistemological loneliness. *Human Development, 18*, 171-180.

Chandler, M. J. (1977). Social cognition: A selective review of current research. In W. Overton & J. Gallagher (Eds.), *Knowledge and development* (pp. 93-147).

Chandler, M. (1987). The othello effect: Essay on the emergence and eclipse of skeptical doubt. *Human Development, 30*, 137-159.

Colby, A. (1978). Evolution of a moral-developmental theory. In W. Damon (Ed.), *New directions for child development.* Vol. 2. San Francisco: Jossey-Bass.

Colby, A., & Kohlberg, L., and collaborators (1987). *The measurement of moral judgment: Theoretical foundations and research validation. Vol. 1.* Cambridge: Cambridge University Press.

Damon, W., & Hart, D. (1982). The development of self-understanding from infancy through adolescence. *Child Development, 53*, 841-864.

Davison, M. L., King, P. M., Kitchener, K. S., & Parker, C. A. (1980). The stage sequence concept in cognitive and social development. *Developmental Psychology, 16,* 121-132.

Elkind, D. (1967). Egocentrism in adolescence. *Child Development, 38,* 1025-1034.

Elkind, D. (1985). Egocentrism redux. *Developmental Review, 5,* 218-226.

Elkind, D., & Bowen, R. (1979). Imaginary audience behavior in children and adolescents. *Developmental Psychology, 15,* 33-44.

Enright, R., & Lapsley, D. (1980). Social role-taking: A review of the construct, measures, and measurement prospectives. *Review of Educational Research, 56,* 647-674.

Enright, R. D., Lapsley, D. K., & Shukla, D. (1979). Adolescent egocentrism in early and late adolescence. *Adolescence, 14,* 687-695.

Enright, R., Shukla, D., & Lapsley, D. (1980). Adolescent egocentrism-sociocentrism and self-consciousness. *Journal of Youth and Adolescence, 9,* 101-116.

Flavell, J. (1971). Stage related properties of cognitive development. *Cognitive Psychology, 2,* 421-453.

Ford, M. (1979). The construct validity of egocentrism. *Psychological Bulletin, 86,* 1169-1188.

Goossens, L. (1984). Imaginary audience behavior as a function of age, sex, and formal operations. *International Journal of Behavioral Development, 1,* 77-93.

Gray, W., & Hudson, L. (1984). Formal operations and the imaginary audience. *Developmental Psychology, 20,* 619-627.

Grotevant, H., & Cooper, C. (1985). Patterns of interaction in family relationships and development of identity exploration in adolescence. *Child Development, 56,* 405-428.

Higgins, E. T. (1981). Role-taking and social judgment: Alternative developmental perspectives and processes. In J. Flavell & L. Ross (Eds.), *Social cognitive development: Frontiers and possible futures* (pp. 119-153). Cambridge, England: Cambridge University Press.

Inhelder, B., & Piaget, J. (1958). *The growth of logical thinking from childhood to adolescence.* New York: Basic Books.

Josselson, R. (1980). Ego development in adolescence. In J. Adelson (Ed.), *Handbook of adolescent psychology* (pp. 188-210). New York: John Wiley.

Josselson, R. (1988). The embedded self: I and thou revisited. In D. Lapsley and F. C. Power (Eds.), *Self, ego, and identity: Integrative approaches.* (pp. 91-108) New York: Springer.

Keating, D. P., & Clark, L. V. (1980). Development of physical and social reasoning in adolescence. *Developmental Psychology, 16,* 23-30.

Kohlberg, L., & Gilligan, C. (1971). The adolescent as a philosopher. The discovery of the self in a postconventional world. *Daedalus, 110,* 1051-1086.

Kuhn, D., Langer, J., Kohlberg, L., & Haan, N. (1977). The development of formal operations in logical and moral judgment. *Genetic Psychology Monograph, 89,* 97-188.

Lapsley, D. (1985). Elkind on egocentrism. *Developmental Review, 5,* 227-236.

Lapsley, D. (in press). The adolescent egocentrism theory and the "new look" at the imaginary audience and personal fable. In R. M. Lerner, A. C. Petersen, & J. Brooks-Gunn (Eds.), *The encyclopedia of adolescence.* New York: Garland.

Lapsley, D., FitzGerald, D., Rice, K., & Jackson, S. (1989). Separation-individuation and the "new look" at the imaginary audience and personal fable: A test of an integrative model. *Journal of Adolescent Research, 4,* 483-505.

Lapsley, D., Jackson, S., Rice, K., & Shadid, G. (1988). Self-monitoring and the "new look" at the imaginary audience and personal fable: An ego-developmental analysis. *Journal of Adolescent Research, 3,* 17-31.

Lapsley, D. K., Milstead, M., Quintana, S., Flannery, D., & Buss, R. (1986). Adolescent egocentrism and formal operations: Tests of a theoretical assumption. *Developmental Psychology, 22,* 800-807.

Lapsley, D., & Murphy, M. (1985). Another look at the theoretical assumptions of adolescent egocentrism. *Developmental Review, 5,* 201-217.

Lapsley, D., & Quintana, S. (1989). Mental capacity and role-taking: A structural equations approach. *Merrill-Palmer Quarterly, 35,* 143-164.

Lapsley, D., & Rice, K. (1988). The "new look" at the imaginary audience and personal fable: Towards an integrative model of adolescent ego development. In D. K. Lapsley & F. C. Power (Eds.), *Self, ego and identity: Integrative approaches* (pp. 109-129). New York: Springer.

Lapsley, D., Rice, K., & Shadid, G. (1989). Psychological separation and adjustment to college. *Journal of Counseling Psychology, 36,* 286-294.

Lechner, C., & Rosenthal, D. (1983). Adolescents, self-consciousness and the imaginary audience. *Genetic Psychology Monographs, 110,* 289-305.

Lewis, M., & Starr, M. D. (1979). Developmental continuity. In J. Osofsky (Ed.), *Handbook of infant development* (pp. 653-765). New York: John Wiley.

McCall, R. B. (1983). Exploring developmental transitions in mental performance. In K. Fischer (Ed.), *New directions for child development.* No. 21. (pp. 65-80). San Francisco: Jossey-Bass.

Murphy, M., & Gilligan, C. (1980). Moral development in late adolescence and adulthood: A critique and reconstruction of Kohlberg's theory. *Human Development, 23,* 77-104.

Overton, W., & Reese, H. (1981). Conceptual prerequisites for an understanding of stability-change and continuity-discontinuity. *International Journal of Behavioral Development, 4,* 99-123.

Perry, W. G. (1970). *Forms of intellectual and ethical development in the college years.* New York: Academic Press.

Peterson, C. (1982). The imaginary audience and age, cognition, and dating. *Journal of Genetic Psychology, 140,* 317-318.

Piaget, J. (1972). Intellectual evolution from adolescence to adulthood. *Human Development, 15,* 1-12.

Reese, H. W., & Overton, W. F. (1970). Models of development and theories of development. In L. R. Goulet & P. B. Baltes (Eds.), *Lifespan developmental psychology* (pp. 115-145). New York: Academic Press.

Riley, T., Adams, G., & Nielson, E. (1984). Adolescent egocentrism: The association among imaginary audience behavior, cognitive development, and parental support and negation. *Journal of Youth and Adolescence, 13,* 401-417.

Selman, R. (1971). Taking another's perspective: Role-taking development in early childhood. *Child Development, 42,* 1721-1734.

Selman, R. (1980). *The growth of interpersonal understanding.* New York: Academic Press.

Selman, R., & Byrne, D. (1974). A structural developmental analysis of levels of role-taking in middle childhood. *Child Development, 45,* 803-806.

Shantz, C. U. (1975). The development of social cognition. In E. M. Hetherington (Ed.), *Review of child development research.* Vol. 5. Chicago: University of Chicago Press.

Shantz, C. (1983). Social cognition. In P. Mussen (General Ed.), *Carmichael's manual of child psychology* (4th ed.): Vol. 3. *Cognitive development* (J. Flavell & E. Markman, Eds., pp. 495-555). New York: John Wiley.

Siegler, R. (1986). *Children's thinking.* Englewood Cliffs, NJ: Prentice-Hall.

Turiel, E. (1978). Social regulations and domains of social concepts. In W. Damon (Ed.), *New Directions for Child Development* Vol. 1 (pp. 45-74). San Francisco: Jossey-Bass.

Turiel, E. (1983). Domains and categories in social-cognitive development. In W. Overton (Ed.), *The relationship between social and cognitive development* (pp. 53-90). Hillsdale, NJ: Erlbaum.

Vikan, A. (1983). Piagetian inconsistencies: A note on the formal operational interpretation of adolescent psychological development. *Scandinavian Journal of Psychology, 24,* 339-342.

Werner, H. (1957). The concept of development from a comparative and organismic point of view. In D. Harris (Ed.), *The concept of development* (pp. 125-148). Minneapolis: University of Minnesota Press.

9. Processes Underlying Adolescent Self-Concept Formation

Susan Harter
University of Denver

INTRODUCTION

The issue of whether ontogenetic change is best characterized as continuous or discontinuous has long occupied stage for developmentalists. In recent years, it has become of paramount concern to those interested in the development of the self. The cognitive revolution was in part responsible. Whereas the 1950s and 1960s witnessed an interest in the self as a personality dimension, in the 1970s and 1980s the spotlight shifted to the self as a cognitive construction. Thus, the focus became how the concept of self was constructed over the course of development through the complex interaction of an individual's changing cognitive capacities and socialization experiences. The period of adolescence represents a particularly fascinating transitional period, given the emergence of newfound cognitive capabilities as well as changing societal expectations that, in concert, profoundly shape and potentially alter the very nature of the self-concept. It is within this context that one can ask whether self-development is best characterized as continuous or discontinuous. Is the adolescent self qualitatively different from the self-concept of childhood or does it reflect a more continuous process through which information about personal attributes and propensities is accumulated?

In this chapter, changes in the content of self-description between childhood and adolescence will be addressed, and these differences will be linked to cognitive-developmental changes that may, in part, be responsible. Wherever possible, there will be an attempt to move beyond the broad stages identified by Piaget to specify more particular cognitive processes that may be involved. While there exists some controversy over the role that cognitive development plays in impacting perceptions about self and others, it will be argued that changes in certain cognitive processes are intimately related to changes in the nature of the self. To the extent that these processes are discontinuous across the transition to adolescence, one would expect qualitative differences in the self-concept as a person enters adolescence. Similarly, if an individual can identify relatively universal changes in societal expectations or in the social environment upon entering adolescence, one would also anticipate qualitative shifts in the self-concept.

After examining changes in the content of self-descriptions between childhood and adolescence, issues involving the differentiation of the self into multiple roles during adolescence will be discussed. The construction of actual and ideal selves, as well as true and false selves, will also be addressed. Special attention will be given to the challenge of integrating diverse self-attributes and multiple selves into a unified self-theory, as well as to fluctuations within the adolescent self. Many of these same processes create discontinuities in the self over time as the adolescent struggles, on a larger scale, to fashion his or her identity. Moreover, they contribute to the adolescent's preoccupation with understanding the self. "In Search of Self" defines a major drama that takes center stage during adolescence, with a complicated cast of characters that do not always speak with a single voice.

In the last section, attention will focus on the more evaluative processes that have impact on adolescent self-esteem. Two determinants of self-esteem, competence in domains deemed important, from James, and the incorporation of the attitudes of others toward the self, from Cooley, will be explored. Changes in self-esteem will be discussed within this context. In addition, emphasis will be placed on the *functional* role of self-esteem, including its role in mediating depressive and suicidal reactions. Finally, implications for continuities and discontinuities in self-development will be summarized.

CHANGES IN THE CONTENT OF SELF-DESCRIPTIONS BETWEEN CHILDHOOD AND ADOLESCENCE

There is now considerable evidence (Damon & Hart, 1982; Harter, 1983; Rosenberg, 1979, 1986) that the content of the self-concept shifts from self-descriptions of the individual's behavioral and social exterior to his or her psychological interior. The young child employs self-descriptors that are overt, in the form of behaviors, achievements, preferences, possessions, physical attributes, and membership categories readily observable by others. For this reason, Rosenberg metaphorically likens the young child to a demographer and radical behaviorist.

During middle childhood, one sees a shift from self-attributes that are observable to those that are more conceptual or traitlike (Rosenberg, 1979; Montemayor & Eisen, 1977). The earliest trait descriptions focus on qualities of character or ability (honest, smart) emotional characteristics (happy, cheerful), and emotional control (don't have a temper). With increasing age, there is a greater emphasis on *interpersonal* traits, for example, friendly, outgoing, shy, sociable, popular. Thus, Rosenberg likens older children to trait theorists because they appear to emphasize personality constructs in their self-descriptions.

With adolescence comes the emergence of descriptions of a person's *psychological interior*, his or her emotions, attitudes, beliefs, wishes, motives. At this stage, the self-reflective gaze is turned inward toward those internal, private attributes of the self. Rosenberg, therefore, likens the adolescent to the Freudian clinician in that he or she is probing the inner, abstract world of thoughts and feelings, both real and hypothetical. Thus, there would appear to be critical qualitative changes in the nature of the self-concept as the individual makes the transition to adolescence.

Damon and Hart (1988) have recently suggested a refinement that adds another developmental trajectory to the content of self-descriptions across childhood and adolescence. They identify four developmental levels and suggest that at *each* of these levels, one may find behavioral, social, and psychological descriptions of the self, although they will be qualitatively different at each level. At Level 1, the self is understood only as separate categorical or taxonomic identification, for example, young children will describe typical behaviors or momentary moods, feelings, preferences, or aversions. At Level 2, middle to late childhood, the self is defined comparatively, in relation to others or normative standards, for example, cognitive abilities relative to those of peers. At Level 3, early adolescence, for example, attributes or social skills that influence interactions with others or the individual's social appeal are prominent. At level 4, late adolescence, the self is described according to systematic beliefs, personal philosophy, and life plans, including dimensions of personal choice, inner thought processes, and moral standards.

These developmental trajectories represent the acquisition of qualitatively different forms of self-description as a person moves through childhood and adolescence. Although these newly acquired self-descriptors may become the most salient, earlier forms do not necessarily drop out of the self-descriptive repertoire. That is, the developmental shifts represent an acquisition sequence rather than an acquisition-deletion sequence (where earlier forms of self-understanding are no longer observed). Thus, during adolescence, many self-statements may well focus on social attributes, personal choice, and moral issues. However, self-descriptions will also continue to reflect the use of developmentally prior categories.

COGNITIVE-DEVELOPMENTAL PROCESSES ASSOCIATED WITH CONTENT SHIFTS IN SELF-DESCRIPTION

Developmental differences in the content of the self-concept are intimately related to the emergence of cognitive abilities across childhood and adolescence (see Harter, 1983, Montemayor & Eisen, 1977; Rosenberg, 1979, 1986). These changes can be directly related to the shifts identified by Piaget (1960, 1963), as well as by neo-Piagetians (Fischer, 1980), shifts that represent the emergence of new cognitive structures for processing information about the self. During the preoperational period, the young child can only describe observable characteristics, giving specific examples or single representations (Fischer, 1980), rather than generalizations about the self. Thus, the young child will provide a disjointed array of descriptors, making reference to behavioral skills (I can run fast), physical characteristics (I have blond hair), preferences (I like pizza), and possessions (I have a cat) that will lack coherence or organization.

The emergence of *concrete operational* thought in middle childhood makes the construction of *trait* labels possible. Trait labels such as helpful, friendly, smart, popular, or good-looking represent the newfound ability to classify specific attributes into categories, to form higher-order generalizations or representational sets (Fischer, 1980). Thus, specific behaviors such as mastery of several school subjects (e.g., science, social studies, language arts) can be integrated into the concept of *smartness*. The ability to be helpful, to listen, and to share possessions may lead a person to conceptualize the self as *friendly*. Such trait labels represent a qualitative conceptual advance over the previous period as the older child becomes capable of integrating behavioral attributes into higher-order concepts about the self.

There are further qualitative shifts during adolescence in the emergence of *abstract concepts* or single abstractions (Fischer, 1980) that come to define the self during the period of *formal operations*. As noted earlier, the adolescent often focuses on self-descriptions of his or her psychological interior, couched in the language of abstractions (e.g., sensitive, moody, self-conscious, affectionate, obnoxious, tolerant, introverted). These abstractions represent a cognitive advance over the preadolescent, who could only combine particular behaviors into trait labels. The adolescent can now integrate trait labels themselves into higher-order abstractions, for example, "cheerful" and "depressed" can be integrated into the abstraction "moody."

The ability to construct abstractions typically results in unobservable and often hypothetical self-descriptions that require more inference about one's latent characteristics. Paradoxically, perhaps, this newfound ability to conceptualize the self more abstractly represents a double-edged sword. Although abstractions are clearly more advanced cognitive structures, they become further removed from concrete behaviors, thereby ushering in greater potential for distortion. Thus, the self-concept becomes more difficult to verify and, as a result, potentially less realistic. Moreover, as Fischer's theory reveals, although the young adolescent now possesses the ability to differentiate the self into numerous abstractions, he or she does not yet have the skills to *integrate* these abstract self-descriptions into a coherent and consistent self-theory. As a result, certain abstractions (e.g., considerate versus obnoxious, easy-going versus self-conscious) may appear contradictory, and the adolescent will become confused over how he or she can be both, a topic to which we shall return.

Social Comparison, Perspective-Taking, and Self-Awareness

A variety of social-cognitive processes are also relevant to the changing nature of the self-concept. The first of these involves the ability to bring social comparison information to bear on self-evaluation. It is not until middle childhood that comparisons with others are invoked as a barometer of the skills and attributes of the self (Boggiano & Ruble, 1979; Damon & Hart, 1988; Masters, 1971; Nicholls, 1978; Ruble & Rholes, 1981; Ruble, Parsons, & Ross, 1976; Ruble, Boggiano, Feldman, & Loebl, 1980; Suls & Sanders, 1982). From a cognitive-developmental perspective, the use of social comparison information toward this end requires that the child have the ability to relate one concept to another, across many domains (e.g., conservation, multiplication of classes), a skill not present in the repertoire of the young child. Similarly, the young child cannot simultaneously compare his own and another's characteristics in order to detect similarities or differences that have implications for his own skill level. Ruble and her colleagues place the advent of the ability to make such comparative judgments at about age 8 or 9, consistent with Damon and Hart's analysis.

Although the ability to utilize social comparison is associated with a cognitive-developmental advance, it also ushers in new vulnerabilities. (Maccoby, 1983). With the emergence of the ability to rank order the performance of every pupil in the class, all but the most competent children will necessarily fall short of excellence. Thus, the very ability to compare the self to others makes a child's self-concept vulnerable. Peer popularity, appearance, scholastic competence are all domains in which children become increasingly invested as they move into middle and later childhood (Harter, 1987). As our own findings attest, judging oneself less adequate than others in domains deemed important takes its toll on a child's global self-esteem, another theme to which we will return.

There has been relatively little attention paid to social comparison processes in adolescence. Ruble and her colleagues infer that the *use* of social comparison increases as a child moves into adolescence. However, the *admission* that an adolescent is relying on this source of information declines, because it is viewed as socially undesirable, endangering his or her peer relationships. The reliance on social comparison information in adolescence may also lead to confusion about self-attributes, to the extent that the range of possible social reference groups proliferates. Does he compare himself to his classmates in general? To his friends? To his own gender? To those children who are the most popular? Good-looking? Intelligent? Athletic? The very ability to simultaneously consider all of these social comparison groups leads to perplexities for the adolescent, a liability that will persist until he or she is able to identify appropriate reference groups that will remain relatively stable.

Developmental differences in perspective taking and self-awareness are also implicated in the qualitative self-concept changes observed. Across the periods of childhood and adolescence, there is increasing reliance on the opinions that significant others hold toward the self. Historical scholars of the self (Cooley, 1902; Mead, 1934) first directed attention to the importance of the regard in which others hold the self, attitudes that are internalized in constructing the self-concept. For Cooley, the self was primarily a social construction through which the reflected appraisals of others came to define what he metaphorically labeled the "looking glass self." Mead extended this analysis, pointing out that an important task of childhood was to coordinate the collective opinions of others into a "generalized other," an inferred judgment that comes to represent the self.

Contemporary theorists have developed these themes, specifying the processes through which individuals come to adopt the opinions of significant others (Harter, 1986a; Leahy & Shirk, 1985; Rosenberg, 1979, 1986; Selman, 1980). At Selman's Level 1, the young child's egocentrism precludes his or her understanding that others are even observing the self. At Level 2 (ages 7-12), the child comes to appreciate the fact that others are observing and evaluating the self. However, the limitations of this period is that the child cannot critically observe the self directly. Nevertheless, this intermediate level in which the child comes to realize that others are appraising the self sets the stage for the incorporation of these attitudes in the form of the looking glass self. At Level 3 (ages 10-15), the adolescent comes to *internalize* the standards by which significant others are judging the self. He or she can now directly observe and evaluate self, remaining sensitive to, yet taking over, many of the evaluative functions performed by others.

Although the ability to incorporate the opinions of others in forming the self-concept constitutes another cognitive-developmental advance, it introduces another potential vulnerability in that the adolescent must now cope with the realization that others may have negative attitudes about the adolescent's self (Maccoby, 1983; Leahy, 1985). Thus, this ability represents a liability for those children who cannot garner the positive regard of significant others. The period of early to middle adolescence may be particularly stressful and confusing, given a preoccupation with the opinions of a network of significant others that is typically expanding into subgroups whose opinions of the self may not be compatible, for example, parents, close friends, teachers, classmates, job, supervisors, and romantic partners (Rosenberg, 1986). The need to differentiate the self into the different social roles children must play as they move into adolescence will next be examined.

THE DIFFERENTIATION OF THE SELF
INTO MULTIPLE DOMAINS AND ROLES

A cardinal principle of developmental theory is that there is increasing differentiation with age (Werner, 1957), a principle that also applies to the self (see Harter, 1983; 1989; Montemayor & Eisen, 1977;

Lively & Bromley, 1973; Mullener & Laird, 1971; Secord & Peevers, 1974; Rosenberg, 1986). Between childhood and adolescence, there are a number of manifestations of increasing differentiation within the self-concept. Not only are more categories of self-description added to a person's repertoire, but the range of trait labels and abstractions becomes expanded and differentiated. For example, one is not merely nice or mean, but each of these general traits can be further differentiated. Thus, the adolescent can distinguish between numerous dimensions of niceness (e.g., generous, sociable, sensitive, cheerful, empathic, supportive), as well as of meanness (e.g., selfish, unfriendly, insensitive, bad-tempered, egocentric, unsupportive).

Differentiation is also revealed by the number of domain-specific self-evaluations required on multidimensional instruments of the adolescent's self-concept, as revealed in factor-analytic studies (Harter, 1988; Marsh, 1986). For example, on our Self-Perception Profile for Adolescents (Harter, 1988), nine domains are discriminable: scholastic competence, job competence, athletic competence, physical appearance, peer social acceptance, close friendship, romantic appeal, relationship with parents, and behavioral conduct.

Evidence for the increasing differentiation of the self-concept during adolescence can also be found in recent studies documenting how self-descriptions vary across different social roles (see Gecas, 1972; Hart, 1988; Harter, 1986a; Griffin, Chassin, & Young, 1981; Smollar & Youniss, 1985). Different, and often seemingly contradictory attributes are generated for one's self with mother, father, close friend, romantic relationships, classmates, as well as self in the role of student, athlete, and employee. Socialization pressures during adolescence require that a person differentiate the self vis-à-vis such roles, given the different expectations and demands within each role. One's self with parents may be responsible, depressed, sarcastic, whereas one's self with friends may be caring, cheerful, rowdy, and with someone in whom one is romantically interested, the self may be fun-loving, self-conscious, or flirtatious.

Thus, along a number of dimensions, there is increasing differentiation of the self-concept into domains and roles as a child enters adolescence. This particular developmental trajectory would appear to be relatively continuous in nature. However, a related developmental task involves the need to integrate these multiple self-concepts into a unified, consistent theory of self. Adolescence poses unique challenges in this regard, ushering in a discontinuous developmental shift in the nature of self-theory.

THE STRUGGLE TO INTEGRATE DIVERSE SELF-ATTRIBUTES INTO A UNIFIED SELF-THEORY

The adult self literature is replete with formulations emphasizing the need to integrate one's multiple attributes into a theory of self or one's personality that is coherent and unified (Allport, 1955; 1961; Brim, 1976; Epstein, 1973; Horney, 1950; Jung, 1928; Kelly, 1955; Lecky, 1945; Maslow, 1961; Rogers, 1950). Epstein (1973) has cogently argued by analogy that one's theory of self, like any comprehensive scientific theory, must meet certain criteria (e.g., parsimony, usefulness, testability, and *internal consistency*). Therefore, like any formal theory, one's self-theory will be threatened by evidence that is inconsistent with the portrait constructed of the self or by postulates within the theory that appear to be contradictory.

Central to developmental theories is the process not only of differentiation but of hierarchic integration (Werner, 1957), a theme that is paramount within Piagetian (1960, 1963) and neo-Piagetian (e.g., Fischer, 1980) theories as well. Given the role-related differentiation requiring the creation of multiple selves during adolescence, the task of integrating these diverse self-perceptions poses a challenge. Almost a century ago, James (1892) acknowledged these potential contradictions in his reference to the "conflict of the different Me's." "Many a youth who is demure enough before his parents and teachers swaggers like a pirate among his tough young friends," James observed. The developmental task of the adolescent, therefore, is to consolidate these multiple selves into a coherent self-theory.

From a classical Piagetian perspective, there should be little cause for concern. That is, it would appear that at precisely the time that the adolescent is faced with socialization pressures toward the role *differentiation* of the self, there are cognitive advances in the emergence of formal operational skills that allow for *integration*, toward the formation of an internally consistent, coherent theory of the self. However, the more recent neo-Piagetian approaches alert us to the fact that the formal operational abilities described by Piaget are actually preceded by qualitatively different substages that represent precursors to the abilities that define the hallmark of this final period of cognitive development.

What are the data that require such a substage analysis of the evolving self-theory during adolescence? Our own findings (Harter, 1986b; Monsour, 1985; Harter & Bresnick, 1989) reveal a clear three-stage sequence of self-theory development during adolescence (see also Damon & Hart, 1982; Hart, 1988). Our procedure requires that subjects between the ages of 11 and 18 first generate separate lists of self-attributes for several roles (e.g., what they are like with their parents, friends, romantic partners, in their scholastic environment, and on the job). They are next asked to identify pairs of attributes that they feel represent opposites (e.g., cheerful versus depressed, anxious versus laid back, curious versus bored). Of the opposites they identify, they then indicate which are in conflict, or at "war with one another," as well as which can coexist harmoniously, describing why certain pairs cause conflict whereas others do not.

The findings reveal clear developmental differences across ages 11 to 18. The youngest adolescents, ages 11 to 13, detect a few opposing attributes in their self-portraits; however, they rarely report that such opposites cause them conflict. There is a dramatic peak in middle adolescence (ages 14 to 16) in that not only are far more opposites identified, but these opposites generate considerable internal conflict and distress. These adolescents are very troubled over the contradictions within their personality. For example, they cannot reconcile the fact that they are cheerful with their friends or depressed with their parents; that they are rowdy or laid-back with friends, but up-tight and self-conscious on dates; or that they are angry around their dads, but comfortable with their moms. Many of these adolescents expressed confusion over how they could be the same person, yet act so differently with different persons, leading them to ponder which was the "real me." Such conflict diminishes considerably among older adolescents. Although these adolescents still *identified* opposing attributes, there was much less concern, distress, and conflict. Rather, they gave descriptions of how such opposites could harmoniously coexist within their personality.

These findings lead us to ask why the detection and distress over inconsistencies within self-theory should peak in middle adolescence? In interpreting these findings, we turned to Fischer's (1980) theory for a partial answer. Fischer's theory provides an analysis of the substages of formal operational thinking, distinguishing qualitative levels that paralleled our empirical findings. According to Fischer, young adolescents are moving into the earliest phase of formal operations in which they are capable of constructing "single abstractions" about the self. Although they can now construct abstractions such as considerate, obnoxious, self-conscious, laid-back, outgoing, cheerful, depressed, they cannot yet cognitively relate these abstractions about the self to one another. As a result, they tend not to detect, or be concerned about, self-attributes that are potential opposites.

The cognitive skills necessary to compare such abstractions, what Fischer calls "abstract mappings," do not emerge until middle adolescence. With the advent of the ability to relate one abstract attribute to another, a young person can now evaluate the postulates of self-theory from the standpoint of whether they are internally consistent. Unfortunately, although an adolescent can now *detect* inconsistencies within the self-portrait, he or she cannot yet integrate them. Opposites, particularly seemingly contradictory self-attributes, therefore become very salient and psychologically troublesome. Interestingly, our findings reveal that there are more numerous and distressing contradictions *across* rather than within roles, that is, subjects are primarily troubled over the fact that they act in one way in one role but appear to be a different person in another role. The different persona they appear to adopt with mother versus with father produced the most conflict.

Conflict should diminish, according to Fischer, in later adolescence when people become capable of a new cognitive level which he terms "abstract systems." This qualitative shift brings with it the ability to now *integrate* single abstractions into compatible higher-order abstractions about the self. Thus, cheerful and depressive attributes can be combined into the higher-order abstraction of "moody." At an even more advanced level, the individual can resolve seemingly contradictory attributes across roles by asserting that he or she is flexible, adaptive, sensitive to the needs of various others, thereby subsuming these characteristics under more generalized abstractions about the self.

Another strategy employed by older adolescents to reduce the potential conflict between opposing self-attributes is to tout the desirability or normalcy of behaving differently across roles (Harter, 1988b). These older adolescents assert that "it wouldn't be normal to act the same way with everyone, you act one way with your friends and a different way with your parents, that's the way it should be," and "It's good to be able to be different with different people in your life, you'd be pretty strange and also pretty boring if you weren't." In adopting such a stance, older adolescents appear to shift to the model espoused for adults in the social psychological literature (Gergen, 1968; Vallacher, 1980), namely that consistency of the self *within* a role is desirable, but not necessarily consistent *across* roles. In fact,

Vallacher argues that the construction of different selves in different roles represents *differentiation* rather than inconsistency per se. While this may well represent the adult norm, our findings suggest that adolescents do not arrive at this stage without first wrestling with the seeming contradictions that different selves pose, a struggle that can be directly related to qualitatively different substages of cognitive development during adolescence.

THE CONSTRUCTION OF ACTUAL AND IDEAL, AS WELL AS TRUE AND FALSE SELVES

We have seen how the creation of role-related multiple selves poses threats to the development of a unified, coherent self. Another such challenge comes with the adolescent's emerging ability to construct actual versus ideal or imagined selves, as well as true versus false selves. From a cognitive-developmental perspective, these concerns parallel the advent of those formal operational skills that allow one to think about the *hypothetical*, a penchant that is also directed toward the self. As a result, adolescent self-descriptions typically make reference to their future selves (see Secord & Peevers, 1974), including both positive and negative images of what they might become (Markus & Nurius, 1986). The potential to conceptualize these various selves introduces the possibility for a discrepancy between real and ideal selves, although there has been some disagreement in the literature over how such a discrepancy should be interpreted. While Rogers (Rogers & Dymond, 1954) viewed the magnitude of this discrepancy as an index of maladjustment, others (see Glick & Zigler, 1985) have argued that from a cognitive-developmental perspective, such a discrepancy is a sign of maturity.

These positions are not necessarily antithetical, particularly in considering the nature of self-image disparities during adolescence. Interestingly, recent findings reveal that during mid-adolescence the discrepancy between the actual and the ideal self is larger than in either early or late adolescence (Strachen & Jones, 1982). Applying the neo-Piagetian analysis of Fischer (1980), those in middle adolescence are now capable of "abstract mappings," allowing them to compare and detect discrepancies between these different selves. However, they do not yet have the cognitive capacities in the form of "abstract systems" to integrate these disparate selves. Thus, such inconsistencies may well provoke distress, particularly during middle adolescence.

Alternatively, the formation of a positive ideal may provide the motivation to aspire to such an ideal. Markus and Nurius (1986) have recently introduced the concept of "possible selves" suggesting their motivational function. Possible selves represent both the hoped for, as well as dreaded, selves and function as incentives that clarify those selves that are to be approached as well as avoided. From this perspective, it is most desirable for the adolescent to have a balance between the positive, expected selves and the negative, feared selves within a given domain. Positive selves (e.g., well-paying job, loved by family, recognized and admired by peers) can give direction toward desired future states, whereas the negative possible selves (unemployed, lonely, socially ignored) make salient what is to be avoided.

Hypothetical selves can involve not only future goals but desired or feared self-attributes in the present. In fact, adolescents commonly act out these possible selves in the form of role experimentation, donning the attributes of desired and at times, undesirable alternative selves (Erikson, 1959, 1968; Rosenberg, 1986). Such role experimentation may usher in the potential for another source of tension among the individual's multiple selves, namely concern and confusion over his or her true and false selves. Broughton (1978, 1981) describes the adolescent's preoccupation with real and false or phony selves that during middle adolescence are often seen as divided, as does Selman, who notes that the adolescent views the true self as inner thoughts and feelings, distinguishable from outer manifestations of feelings and behavior.

In our own work on self-attributes across multiple roles, we have become sensitized to this issue given the concerns spontaneously expressed by some adolescents over which attributes represent their true self. During middle adolescence in general, and among girls in particular, the identification of seemingly contradictory self-attributes causes subjects to agonize about which is the "real me." Recently, we have begun to pursue the issue of adolescent true and false selves more systematically (Harter & Lee, 1989). Our initial inquiry involved open-ended interviews to determine how young adolescents understood the concept of true self and its opposite. Interestingly, we found that many of our youngest subjects, sixth graders, had little insight into this distinction. By eighth grade, virtually all of our subjects found the distinction quite compelling. The true self was described as "acting naturally," being "who one really is inside," "not putting on a show," "not trying to impress other people." In contrast, the false self was defined as behaving in ways primarily to "please others," to "try to impress others," and to "be something that someone else wants you to be." Thus, adolescents locate their true and false selves within the context of their social interactions with others. True selves were identified with the more *positive* core attributes that define who one is as a *person* (e.g., sensitive, open, happy, understanding, caring). False selves often represent negative personas who display less desirable attributes (e.g., intolerant, disloyal, phony, obnoxious, insecure), primarily reflecting how one merely *acts*. Adolescents also report liking certain false self-behavior, particularly if it is the service of experimenting with different forms of self-presentation. In general, adolescents are *most* likely to display false self-behaviors with classmates and romantic partners, and *least* likely to show false self-attributes with close friends (as anticipated), with displays of false self-behaviors to parents falling in between.

Why should adolescents feel the need to display false self-attributes, what function do these selves serve? Here the interview findings revealed several motives: (a) significant others encourage or provoke the display of false self-behaviors; (b) one is driven to engage in these behaviors to impress or please others, (c) one is experimenting with the display of attributes and their social impact, particularly with classmates and romantic partners; and (d) one must protect or conceal one's real self out of fear that it would meet with disapproval or not be understood.

There is much to be known, however, about the conditions under which false selves are benevolent, representing the adoption of different behaviors in the service of experimentation, versus the conditions under which false selves are perceived as distress-producing phony, empty facades. Within the clinical literature (Bleiberg, 1984; Winnicott, 1965) "false self" phenomena are related to narcissism during childhood leading to alienation from any sense of a real or validated core self. These formulations emphasize etiological factors that have prevented such children from the normal processes of introjection of, and identification with, parental values. However, these more pathological avenues to the development of a sense of false self may well need to be distinguished from the stage-appropriate concerns of an adolescent who is experimenting with different persona in search of the real self that will serve him well as he enters into young adulthood.

FLUCTUATIONS OR LACK OF STABILITY WITHIN THE ADOLESCENT SELF

We have highlighted the adolescent's active struggle to create multiple selves in different roles, yet at the same time create a unified theory of self. The potential discrepancies between actual and ideal selves, as well as between true and false selves, add to this challenge. Given these numerous, seemingly contradictory selves, it is not surprising that the adolescent self would fluctuate over situations and time. Unlike the previous period of childhood where there was little need or ability to construct multiple selves, adolescence, by definition, will be characterized by instability within the self until a more unified self can be constructed.

In our own work (Harter, 1988b) we have metaphorically described these fluctuations as "lack of conservation of self." In the face of demands and experiences that represent transformations or perturbations, to use Piaget's terminology, the adolescent is frequently catapulted from the short wide beakers of life to the tall, thin beakers! In the face of such transformations, it is difficult for the adolescent to conserve his or her sense of self, to see the self as constant across roles, situations, or time.

Rosenberg (1986) invokes a similar metaphor in describing the adolescent's "barometric self-concept," providing evidence that the self-concept is particularly volatile during adolescence. Whereas our analysis focused on the contribution of cognitive-developmental processes, Rosenberg has provided a complementary portrait that emphasizes the adolescent's social interactions. He observes that the adolescent is tremendously concerned with the impression that he or she is making on others, given the dependence on what others think of the self. However, the difficulty of divining others' impressions leads to ambiguity about their attitudes toward the self, and therefore about what the self is really like. Self-concept volatility will also be fostered by the fact that different people will have different impressions of the self, creating contradictory feedback that must necessarily result in uncertainty about the self.

In addition, the adolescent's attempts at role experimentation are characterized by a preoccupation with self-presentation or impression management. As part of this process, she or he may tentatively adopt, and as readily abandon a variety of persona. To the extent that one observes oneself enacting these varying and often contradictory roles, one comes to experience the self as highly mutable. Finally,

Rosenberg points to the ambiguous status of adolescence withi American society (see also Baumeister & Tice, 1986). Because there ar no clear age markers as to when this period begins or ends, a perso may be treated more like a child by some, more like an adult by other and of uncertain status by yet other people with whom she or h interacts. Given these fluctuations, in the face of the adolescent' dependence upon the opinions of others toward the self, his or he own appraisal of the self will undoubtedly vary.

We have dealt primarily with short-term fluctuations in the adoles cent self, indicating how various cognitive-developmental and soci factors conspire to produce a sense of "self as chameleon" acros different social roles or situations. We next consider those changes i the self over *time* that are dictated by discontinuities defining the ver nature of the adolescent experience.

DISCONTINUITIES IN THE SELF OVER TIME IN THE CONTEXT OF IDENTITY FORMATION

The task of adolescence is not only to define the self in terms o attributes displayed across multiple social roles, but to consider mor general identities that one will adopt within the larger society. Thu the creation of one's self-portrait is shifted to a larger canvas, wher broad psychological brush strokes must come to define occupationa and gender identities, as well as the religious and political identitie that one will assume. The processes of reformulating the multipl selves that will come to wear the mantle of one's chosen identities ha been articulated by several theorists (Blasi, 1988; Damon & Hart, 198 Erikson, 1968; Hauser & Follansbee, 1984; Josselson, 1980). As a com plete discussion of identity formation is beyond the scope of thi chapter, the interested reader is referred to these theorists. Here, w will primarily focus on issues involving continuity and discontinuit

As James first observed, a major challenge involves the preserva tion of one's sense of personal continuity over time, of establishing sense of sameness about oneself, despite the necessary changes tha one must undergo in terms of redefining the self. For Erikson, thi concern became paramount in adolescence, forming the basis for th identity crisis. The continuity of the self becomes threatened in th face of numerous developmental discontinuities, namely marke physical changes, cognitive advances, and shifting societal expecta tions. Erikson succinctly captures this concern in quoting a slogan h once observed: "I ain't what I ought to be, I ain't what I'm going to be, but I ain't what I was?" (1959, p. 19). Thus, while James appreciated the general need to preserve one's continuity over time, the many discontinuous changes during adolescence make such a task rather formidable.

Two additional self-processes have been emphasized in adolescent identity formation, the need for distinctiveness and uniqueness, and the renewed awareness of one's sense of volition or agency. With regard to the former, there is tension between the need for the self to be distinct and unique and the need to construct an identity that will meet with the support of significant others as well as society. Whereas the task of self-development in childhood involved the processes of identification and introjection, a major goal of adolescent identify formation involves differentiation from parents, individuation without becoming disconnected (see Blasi, 1988; Grotevant & Cooper, 1983; Hauser & Follansbee, 1984; Josselson, 1980). The immersion in peer identifications and conformity to stereotypes is considered by these theorists to be a manifestation of the need for temporary alternatives in the face of pressure to abandon parental introjects.

These investigators, in emphasizing the need to both individuate *and* remain connected, have identified patterns of parent-child interactions that foster this goal. Parent styles considered enabling, rather than constraining (Hauser & Follansbee, 1984) and those that allow the adolescent to express points of view that may differ from those of others within a context of mutual respect produce the healthiest patterns of identity formation (see Grotevant & Cooper, 1983).

Theorists have also pointed to the heightened sense of volition or agency, in the very act of reshaping one's identity during adolescence (Blasi, 1988; Damon & Hart, 1988). Blasi describes the sense of agency involved in the adolescent's "management of identity." The individual must orchestrate these changes by actively proving who he is and by shaping himself according to his ego ideal. In a sense this developmental shift to a greater sense of agency and volition would seem well suited to the tasks of the psychological moratorium that has been provided for adolescents in our culture, namely a period in which he or she has the opportunity to experiment with different roles, persona, and identities (Erikson, 1959, 1968).

However, from a broader cultural perspective, there are also forces that make the process of identity formation decidedly difficult. In their historical analysis of adolescence, Baumeister and Tice (1986) observe that the contemporary trend toward requiring the self to actively create itself is a large and somewhat paradoxical demand, necessarily leading to a phase of soul-searching, identity crisis, and struggle for the self. They note that around the end of the nineteenth century, there was a shift in the locus and burden of self-definition. Prior to this era, the adult identity was primarily determined by family, community, and shared cultural values. However, economic and ideological changes have caused a shift from the adoption of preselected occupational and personal identities to the more recent scenario in which the adolescent must fashion an identity out of a myriad of options. The opportunity for modern-day adolescents to choose their occupational identity in the face of liberal educational policies that provide a spectrum of choices, combined with Western society's loss of ideological consensus regarding fundamental religious, moral, and political truths, have all conspired to produce a protracted, adolescent moratorium. As Baumeister and Tice cogently observe, while society was offering adolescents an increasing range of identity options, it was simultaneously depriving them of unequivocal bases for making these decisions. Thus, the adolescent's task becomes considerably more difficult in that he or she must not only define an identity within a given context, but choose and recreate the context as well.

With regard to the crisis involved in making these decisions, Erikson anticipated that the adolescent should first experience identity diffusion, followed by experimentation during the moratorium period, culminating in identity formation that involved choice, commitment, and the consolidation of his or her identity. Thus, the very process of identity formation involves several discontinuous substages. As the work of Marcia (1966, 1980, 1988) reveals, progression along this path can also be halted for those manifesting foreclosure, namely the adoption of identities proscribed by parents (or other authority figures) with a keen sense of commitment, however without ever exploring options or experiencing an identity crisis. While Marcia's earlier work focused on these constructs as individual *statuses,* more recent work has viewed them as normative stagelike processes through which adolescents proceed, although there are alternative pathways manifest by subgroups (Waterman, 1982, 1985). With each such pathway, however, the experience of shifting from status to status represents a discontinuous experience for the adolescent, seriously threatening his or her sense of continuity over time.

ADOLESCENT PREOCCUPATION WITH UNDERSTANDING THE SELF

The unique and changing demands of adolescence requiring the creation and integration of fluctuating multiple selves, the formation of ideal selves toward which they should aspire, and the need to resolve the discontinuity experienced as an individual must forge a new identity clearly provide ample food for adolescent thought, if not a reflective preoccupation with the self. The clinical literature (A. Freud, 1965) bolsters the developmentalist's contention that the period of adolescence brings about a dramatic shift toward introspection, where the self becomes an object of observation and reflection. According to Rosenberg's (1979) findings, the period of childhood unreflective self-acceptance vanishes. "What were formerly unquestioned self-truths now become problematic self-hypotheses and the search for the truth about the self is on" (p. 255).

Erikson (1959, 1968) also describes the tortuous self-consciousness of this period, although from a somewhat different perspective. He observes that adolescents, in their search for a coherent, unified self are often morbidly preoccupied with what they appear to be in the eyes of others and with the question of how to connect earlier cultivated roles and skills with the ideal prototypes of the day. More recent theorizing on adolescent self-reflection (Broughton, 1978, 1981; Lapsley & Rice, 1988; Selman, 1980), has described early adolescence as a period in which there is an awakened concern over convincing the self "that I am," particularly with regard to the *mental* self's existence. There is a developmental shift during later adolescence to issues involving the legitimization of *what* or *who* I am, as the adolescent seeks to establish self-boundaries and more clearly sort out the multiple selves that now provide for a very crowded self-landscape.

The advent of formal operational thought is, in the view of many theorists, a prerequisite for adolescent self-reflection. The very ability to think about one's thinking, to reflect on internal events, does not become fully developed until adolescence. Given that there is also an increasing focus on the self as a repository of mental processes that are capable of directing one's experience, there is both respect and intrigue for the manner in which the self, so defined, operates. The mental machinations of the self, including an appreciation for one's unconscious processes, become yet another impetus toward introspection, reflection, and a preoccupation with the self. As other theorists have pointed out (Elkind, 1967), a major task of early adolescence becomes the conquest of thought, one's own as well as others'.

With the emergence of any cognitive capacities, there is the penchant for exercising these newfound abilities; however, there is also difficulty in controlling and applying them effectively (Fischer, 1980; Harter, 1983). Such a liability can be seen in the adolescent's application of those skills involved in perspective-taking and self-reflective judgment. For example, the adolescent has difficulty differentiating his or her own mental preoccupations from what others are thinking about him or her, leading to a form of adolescent egocentrism that Elkind has labelled the "imaginary audience." Thus, the adolescent falsely assumes that others are equally preoccupied with his or her behavior or appearance.

Interestingly, the inability to control and to effectively apply new cognitive structures can result in both lack of differentiation between self and other, as in the case of the imaginary audience, as well as excessive or unrealistic differentiation between the self and other. The latter penchant can be seen in another form of adolescent egocentrism that Elkind has identified as the "personal fable." In recreating his or her life story, the adolescent protagonist asserts that his thoughts and feelings are uniquely experienced by the self. No one else can possibly experience the ecstasy of his or her rapture nor the intensity of his or her despair.

A cognitive-developmental analysis of both the imaginary audience and the personal fable can be complemented by more psychodynamic interpretations of the transitory phase of adolescent ego development (Blos, 1962; Lapsley & Rice, 1988). Tremendous conflict is produced by the need to relinquish the omnipotent, internalized parent. The love of the omnipotent parent must be replaced by the love of, or narcissistic visions of, the self (Josselson, 1980). From this perspective, the imaginary audience performs a restitutive function, participating in these visions of the self.

Yet at the same time that the adolescent wishes to remain connected to the parent, there is also the push to separate, to differentiate and to establish clear, if not rigid self-boundaries. The construction of a personal fable, in which his or her own experiences are so different as to be totally unique, represents an understandably extreme interpretation in the service of forcing the necessary boundaries between self and other.

From cognitive-developmental as well as psychodynamic perspectives, therefore, one can appreciate those factors that contribute to the adolescent's heightened self-consciousness and intense preoccupation with the self. Thus, there would appear to be considerable discontinuity between the self-processes observed in childhood and those that emerge during adolescence. In the preceding sections, attention has been focused on the processes of self-*construction*. We now turn to self-*evaluation*, in terms of specific personal attributes as well as the individual's overall sense of self-esteem.

THE DETERMINANTS OF ADOLESCENT SELF-ESTEEM

Despite hundreds of studies on adolescent self-esteem (see Offer, Ostrow, & Howard, 1981; Wylie, 1979), this research has not, until recently, provided a cohesive picture. Ambiguous definitions of the construct, inadequate instruments, and lack of theory have plagued self-esteem research. There is now a growing consensus (see Harter, 1986; Rosenberg, 1979; 1986) that self-esteem is poorly captured by measures that combine evaluations across diverse domains into a single summary score (as in the Coopersmith Self-Esteem Inventory, 1967), as this masks the evaluative distinctions that children and adolescents are capable of making. A more fruitful approach is to tap discrete domains of the self-concept separately, as well as to assess global self-esteem directly, through its own independent set of items (Harter, 1982, 1985, 1986; Marsh, 1986; Rosenberg, 1979). Self-esteem, so defined, represents how much a person likes, accepts, and respects himself overall as a person.

The field has also shifted its emphasis from the mere demonstration of the *correlates* of self-esteem to a more thoughtful consideration of the *determinants* of self-esteem, as well as the emotional, motivational, and behavioral systems that it, in turn, mediates. Earlier correlational studies documented modest relationships between self-esteem and achievement, adjustment, negative emotional states such as depression and anxiety and locus of control. However, the theoretical and/or methodological weaknesses of these studies have rendered the findings inconclusive or difficult to interpret.

Two recent programs of research, one by our own group (Harter, 1986b, 1987, 1988a; 1989) and one by Rosenberg (1979, 1986), have been built upon sounder theoretical foundations, employing assessment procedures that meet many of the earlier objections. Each draws upon the theoretical legacies of James (1892) and Cooley (1902), and each taps self-esteem with items that directly inquire about the individual's overall sense of self-acceptance and worth as a person.

For James, global self-esteem reflected the *ratio* of a person's perceptions of competence or success in discrete domains relative to the *importance* of success (pretensions, in his parlance) in these domains. If the individual's perceived successes were at a level equal to or greater than his or her pretensions of success, a high level of global self-esteem would result. Conversely, if his pretensions exceeded his perceived level of success, he would experience low self-esteem. In contrast to this cognitive-evaluative model, Cooley (1902) postulated that the origins of self-esteem lay in an individual's perceptions of what significant others thought of the self. Thus, the self was a social construction in which a person incorporates the attitudes that others hold toward the self, reflected appraisals that for Cooley became the "looking glass self."

There is a growing body of evidence revealing that both formulations are relevant to our understanding of the determinants of adolescent self-esteem. Our own work has put these two formulations to the most direct test. James' theory has been examined by demonstrating that the discrepancy between adolescents' perceptions of competence across domains and the importance they attach to success in those domains are highly and systematically correlated with global self-esteem (Harter, 1986a). The domains we have included are Scholastic Competence, Athletic Competence, Social Acceptance, Physical Appearance, and Behavioral Conduct. Small discrepancies, indicating that an individual is competent in domains deemed important are associated with high levels of self-esteem. Conversely, when the importance of success far outweighs perceived competencies, low self-esteem is experienced. Here we can appreciate the convergence between the Jamesian discrepancy and the discrepancy between the actual and ideal self-concept discussed earlier. There is now a growing body of evidence that such discrepancies clearly exert a powerful influence on self-esteem (see Higgins, 1987; Rosenberg, 1979; Simmons & Blyth, 1987; Tesser & Campbell, 1983).

Findings with adolescents also support Cooley's looking-glass-self model of the determinants of self-esteem. Our own work (Harter, 1986a, 1987), as well as Rosenberg's (1979), has demonstrated that adolescents' perceptions of the attitudes of significant others toward the self profoundly impact their global self-esteem. Thus, the adolescent who feels that he or she is receiving the positive regard of significant others (e.g., parents and peers) will express positive regard for the self in the form of high self-esteem. Conversely, lack of perceived support and regard from significant others will take its toll in the form of low self-esteem.

THE RELATIVE CONTRIBUTION OF SPECIFIC DOMAINS AND SOURCES OF SUPPORT

When one examines the particular domains that contribute most to self-esteem during adolescence, there is considerable consensus that physical appearance heads the list (Adams, 1977; Harter, 1987; 1989; Lerner & Brackney, 1978; Lerner, Orlos, & Knapp, 1976; Simmons & Rosenberg, 1975; Simmons & Blyth, 1987). Our own findings reveal that among adolescents, physical appearance is the domain that consistently correlates the most highly with global self-esteem (r's between .65 and .80), followed by peer social acceptance as the next most predictive domain. Interestingly, the relationship between perceived appearance and self-worth is not confined to adolescence but is extremely robust across the life span, from childhood through middle age and adulthood (Harter, 1989). Thus, there would appear to be a developmental continuity in the relationship that appearance bears to self-worth.

Although physical attractiveness is clearly touted in our society (Elkind, 1984; Hatfield & Sprechner, 1986), we speculate that the effects of perceived appearance on self-esteem does not only reflect societal emphasis on the importance of good looks. Rather, there may also be a more basic relationship between the outer self, reflected in the appearance, and the inner self, namely global feelings of self-esteem. Developmentally, physical capabilities represent the first sense of self to emerge (see Harter, 1983; Lewis & Brooks-Gunn, 1979). Moreover, from an early age the physical or outer self is a salient dimension that provokes evaluative reactions from others (Langlois, 1981; Maccoby & Martin, 1983), reactions that may well be incorporated into the emerging sense of inner self.

Sources of social support. With regard to the relative impact of different sources of social support on global self-worth, we can ask: Mirror, mirror on the wall, whose opinion is the most influential of all? Rosenberg (1979) has suggested a developmental shift in that for young children, perceived parental attitudes toward the self are of almost exclusive significance, whereas among older children and adolescents, peer judgments gain increasing importance. Our own findings also reveal that while peer support becomes more relevant among young adolescents, the effects of classmate support and parent support are not significantly different (Harter, 1987). Among older adolescents, the effect of peer support is greater than parent support.

We have distinguished between two types of peer support, discovering that classmate support has considerably more influence on self-worth than close friend support. Moreover, we have obtained this effect at every developmental level, childhood, adolescence, the college years, and among adults in the world of work and family, a very robust developmental continuity. Thus, acknowledgement of peers from more public domains appears more critical than the personal regard of a close friend with whom one can share the more intimate details of one's life. Given that, by definition, close friends provide support, it may well be that their regard is not perceived as enhancing. Rather, one must turn to somewhat more objective sources of support, to the social mirror, as it were, in order to validate the self.

CHANGES IN GLOBAL SELF-ESTEEM DURING ADOLESCENCE

Self-esteem undergoes change during adolescence. Longitudinal studies reveal gradual, consistent improvements in self-esteem over grades 7 through 12 (Engel, 1959; McCarthy & Hoge, 1982; O'Malley & Bachman, 1983; Rosenberg, 1986; Simmons, Rosenberg, & Rosenberg, 1973). In fact, the cumulative impact is substantial, exceeding a full standard deviation over an 8-year span (O'Malley & Bachman, 1983).

McCarthy and Hoge (1982) offer several reasons for such gains that can be interpreted within the frameworks of James and Cooley. There may be increasing realism about the ideal self presumably, according to a Jamesian analysis, because the discrepancy between the actual and the ideal self-image would be reduced. Increased autonomy and freedom of choice over the adolescent years may also play a role. A Jamesian interpretation would suggest that if the individual has more opportunity to select valued performance domains in which he or she is competent, self-esteem will be increased. Such freedom may also provide the older adolescent with more opportunity to select those peer support groups that will provide the positive regard necessary to maintain or enhance self-esteem. Relatedly, increased role-taking ability may lead the adolescent to behave in more socially acceptable ways that enhance the evaluation of the self by others.

The picture of self-esteem change in early adolescence is less sanguine, however. There, the findings reveal that self-esteem begins to decline at age 11 and reaches its low point between the ages of 12 and 13 (see Rosenberg, 1986). The magnitude of change is, in large part, dependent on two factors, the impact of the school environment as well as pubertal change, factors that have been studied extensively by Simmons and Blyth (1987). Students making the shift to junior high in the seventh grade show greater self-esteem losses than those making the transition a year later, after eighth grade. In addition, students making the earlier shift, particularly girls, do not recover their self-esteem losses during the high school years. Simmons and Blyth suggest a developmental readiness hypothesis, namely that children can be thrust into environments before they are psychologically equipped to handle the social and academic demands of the new school structure.

With regard to the timing of puberty, early maturing girls fare the worst. (Brooks-Gunn & Peterson, 1983; Simmons & Blyth, 1987). They are the most dissatisfied with their body image, particularly their weight and figure, which exerts an influence on their self-esteem. Evidentally, earlier maturing girls tend to be somewhat heavier and thus do not fit the cultural stereotypes of female attractiveness (Peterson & Taylor, 1980). Moreover, according to the developmental readiness hypothesis, early maturing girls are not yet emotionally prepared to deal with the social expectations and greater independence that dating often demands. Simmons and Blyth highlight the cumulative effects of pubertal level and the timing of school transitions. Detrimental effects on self-esteem can occur if change occurs at too young an age, if an individual is off-time in terms of pubertal development, if a school transition places him or her in the lowest ranks of the new environment, and if the change is marked by sharp discontinuity.

A more theoretically driven approach to self-esteem change has characterized our own efforts to determine whether such changes are systematically related to changes in the competence/importance discrepancy construct derived from James, as well as to changes in social support, as predicted by the looking-glass-self theory of Cooley (Harter, 1986a). Our one-year longitudinal findings reveal that changes in self-esteem, as students make the transition from elementary school (sixth grade) to junior high school (seventh grade), is directly predicted by corresponding changes in both the discrepancy score and social support. Students whose self-esteem *increases* between sixth and seventh grades manifest a decrease in the discrepancy between the importance of success and perceived competence; that is, these judgments become more congruent. Students whose self-esteem *decreases* over this transition display an increase in their discrepancy scores such that in seventh grade, there is a much wider gap between the importance of success in particular domains and their perceived competence. Students manifesting no change in self-esteem show no changes in their discrepancy score. With regard to social support, students whose self-esteem increases report greater social support in the new environment, students whose self-esteem decreases report less social support after transition, and students showing no changes in self-esteem report no changes in social support.

This pattern suggests that new school environments provide new social comparison groups and new standards of evaluation that provoke the adolescent to re-evaluate his or her competence as well as the importance of success in various domains. Moreover, such transitions can lead to alterations in the social network that, in turn, will lead to new opportunities and/or challenges for obtaining social support. Each of these potential changes can have an effect on the individual's self-esteem. This framework strongly suggests that we not consider self-esteem to be an immutable trait but rather seek to illuminate the processes responsible for its potential change. Only by understanding these processes can we seek strategies to maintain or enhance self-esteem. Strategies implied by this research include valuing the individual's areas of competence and discounting domains in which he or she is not competent (see Harter, 1986a), selecting social comparison groups that are more similar to the self (see Tesser & Campbell, 1980, 1983), as well as interacting with peers who can provide support and affirmation that can be internalized in the form of positive regard for the self.

THE FUNCTIONAL ROLE OF SELF-ESTEEM

The preceding sections have focused primarily on the developmental, environmental related psychological factors that affect self-esteem. However, a second critical issue involves the extent to which the self, so constructed, performs a *functional* role in impacting the adolescent's behavior. It is commonly assumed that a positive sense of self is central to the promotion and maintenance of psychological health and successful adaptation. As Epstein (1973) observes, the most fundamental purpose of the individual's self-theory is to optimize the pleasure/pain balance of the individual over the course of a lifetime and to organize the data of experience in a manner that can be coped with effectively. Noam, Kohlberg, and Snarzy (1983) elaborate on this theme, asserting that the self is not merely an entity but a *process* that mediates between the organism and the environment in an effort to respond productively, as well as solicit from the environment adequate "self-nurturance" (see also Blasi, 1988).

Although there is general theoretical consensus that the healthy self should function to optimize the individual's adaptation to reality, less empirical attention has been directed to such a functional perspective. That is, self-esteem has typically been treated as (a) epiphenomenal with no clear function, (b) as a dependent variable rather than a causal influence itself, or (c) as a correlate of some other behavioral system.

In our own work we have sought to examine the functional role of self-esteem, hypothesizing that it mediates the individual's general affective and motivational states. Much of this research has been reported elsewhere (Harter, 1986a, 1987, 1989) and therefore it will merely be summarized here. Utilizing correlational as well as causal modeling techniques, our findings have revealed that global self-esteem has a major impact on an adolescent's mood or general affective state, along a continuum of cheerful to depressed. In fact, the correlations, across several samples (ages 11 to 18) have all fallen between .75 and .82. Thus, the adolescent who likes himself or herself as a person will invariably be quite cheerful, whereas the adolescent with low self-esteem will be affectively depressed. The findings also reveal that affect, in turn, has a critical impact on the adolescent's energy level. Those who report happy or cheerful affect report much greater energy levels than those who appear to be depressed. Thus, this chain of effects reveals that self-esteem does have a functional role, given its impact on affect and subsequent motivation.

Extension to depression and suicidal ideation among adolescents. A growing body of literature reveals that low self-esteem and negative self-attributions are correlates of depression (Beck, 1967; Harter, 1986a; Harter, 1989), and that low self-esteem in conjunction with depression and hopelessness appear to be precursors of suicidal behavior (Cantor, 1987; Kaplan & Pokorny, 1976; Kazdin, French, Unis, Esveldt-Dawson, & Sherich, 1983; Pfeffer, 1986). Much of this literature has reconstructed these relationships through a "psychological autopsy" of suicide victims, or has focused primarily on clinical populations.

One recent effort by Harter and Marold (1989), has looked more directly at a theory-based model of risk factors that impact self-esteem, depressed affect and suicidal ideation among normative samples of adolescents. Several of the factors predictive of self-esteem have already been identified, namely competence in domains deemed important, as well as positive regard from others. Not only is competence in domains of importance to the self quite critical, but competence in domains of importance to parents. Peer support is also critical. Furthermore, not only is the level of support relevant, but the extent to which support is *contingent* upon either meeting high parental expectations or conforming to peer demands. In the model, each of these factors can lead to a specific feeling of hopelessness. These, in turn, determine an adolescent's level on a depression composite defined by low self-esteem, depressed affect, and general hopelessness about the future. Adolescents high on this composite are likely to be engaged in suicidal ideation.

The findings supporting this model suggest one cameo of the suicidal adolescent: he or she is not performing well in areas that are important to the self as well as the parents; he or she is letting down parents in the face of support that is conditional upon meeting high parental expectations. Peer support also appears to be conditional. Hopelessness about ever turning each of these circumstances around leads to low self-esteem, depressed affect, and a feeling of general hopelessness about the future, eventuating in suicidal ideation as the only way out. While there are other paths to suicidal thinking and behavior in adolescents (see Cantor, 1987; Pfeffer, 1986), this particular cameo is instructive because it points to the crucial, functional role played by self-esteem in mediating depressive and suicidal reactions among many adolescents who are distressed about their personal attributes and the availability of social support.

CONTINUITIES AND DISCONTINUITIES IN SELF-DEVELOPMENT

Our developmental perspective on self-concept formation has revealed numerous differences between children and adolescents, many of which appear to be discontinuous in nature. The framework for interpreting these changes relies heavily upon cognitive-developmental change as well as differing societal expectations as one enters adolescence. To the extent that these cognitive processes and societal expectations are discontinuous, qualitative differences in the self should be observed. The very content of self-descriptions differs markedly, given the qualitative changes in the underlying cognitive processes and structures that come to shape the individual's self-definition. Cognitive-developmental changes that usher in the processes of social comparison, perspective-taking, and self-awareness, also dramatically alter the self-concept of the young adolescent. Newfound cognitive abilities and societal pressures also underlie the differentiation of the self into multiple domains and roles, provoking conflict and confusion that is not experienced during childhood. This conflict is exacerbated by the emergence of the ability to construct hypothetical selves that may serve as ideals toward which a person aspires, alternative roles with which he or she can experiment, as well as selves he or she would prefer to shed or abandon. The struggle to integrate diverse self-attributes and multiple selves into a unified self-theory represents another challenge that is not observed in childhood. Moreover, fluctuations or lack of stability within the adolescent self that is caused by both cognitive-developmental and socialization factors become salient in adolescence, as do discontinuities in the self over time as the individual faces the need to construct new identities. All of these qualitative changes provoke intense preoccupation with the self, a phenomenon not observed in childhood. Thus, discontinuity can be observed for numerous features that characterize the construction of the self across the transition to adolescence.

The discussion of those factors determining the adolescent's level of self-esteem, including those systems that self-esteem in turn mediates, placed less emphasis on changes between childhood and adolescence. The particular model of the determinants and mediational role of self-esteem would appear to be quite robust during later childhood as well as in adolescence, although there are some changes in the relative impact that particular significant others have during childhood and adolescence. However, there is continuity with regard to the constructs in the model, as well as the magnitude of general relationships obtained. What differs, we speculate, is an *awareness* of these relationships at different periods of development (see Harter, in press). Thus, while competence in domains deemed important, and social support from significant others appears to have a major impact on the self-esteem of children beginning at age 8, children do not seem to be aware of these causal influences, nor do they appreciate the links between their self-esteem and their mood or energy level. With the capacity for self-reflective thought and the preoccupation with the self that emerges during adolescence, we speculate that one can become much more cognizant of these relationships, an observation that has direct implications for the age at which interventions involving insight may be most effective (see Harter, 1988b; in press).

Thus, not only does the very nature of the self change with the emergence of adolescence, but the individuals' interest in the self changes dramatically as the self becomes a constant object of observation and evaluation. If we fail to appreciate this fact, we will miss much of the phenomenological experience of adolescence. Clearly there are major individual differences in how tortuous an experience this will become for adolescents. Many will engage in a minimum of self-reflection whereas others will agonize to the point of despair, as we suspect with many adolescents at risk for suicide. Our goal, therefore, will be to respect the multiple paths that self-development may pursue, while at the same time appreciating the fundamental integrity of the period of adolescence that brings about profound changes in the content, structure, and function of the self.

REFERENCES

Adams, G. (1977). Physical attractiveness research. *Human Development. 20,* 217-239.

Allport, G. W. (1955). *Becoming: Basic considerations for a psychology of personality.* New Haven: Yale University Press.

Allport, G. W. (1961). *Pattern and growth in personality.* New York: Holt, Rinehart, & Winston.

Baumeister, R., & Tice, D. (1986). How adolescence became the struggle for self: A historical transformation of psychological development. In J. Suls & A. Greenwald (Eds.), *Psychological perspectives on the self.* Vol. 3 (183-201) Hillsdale, NJ: Erlbaum.

Beck, A. (1967). *Depression: Causes and treatment.* Philadelphia: University of Philadelphia Press.

Blasi, A. (1988). Identity and the development of self. In D. K. Lapsley & F. C. Power (Eds.), *Self, ego, and identity: Integrative approaches.* New York: Springer-Verlag.

Bleiberg, E. (1984). Narcissistic disorders in children. *Bulletin of the Menninger Clinic, 48,* 501-517.

Blos, P. (1962). *On adolescence.* New York: Free Press.

Boggiano, A. K., & Ruble, D. N. (1979). Competence and the overjustification effect: A developmental study. *Journal of Personality and Social Psychology, 37,* 1462-1468.

Brim, O. G. (1976). Life span development of the theory of oneself: Implications for child development. In H. W. Reese (Ed.), *Advances in child development and behavior* Vol. II. New York: Academic Press.

Brooks-Gunn, J. and Peterson, A. (1983). *Girls at puberty: Biological and psychosocial perspectives.* New York: Plenum Press.

Broughton, J. (1978). The development of the concepts of self, mind, reality, and knowledge. In W. Damon (Ed.), *Social Cognition.* San Francisco: Jossey-Bass.

Broughton, J. (1981). The divided self in adolescence. *Human Development, 24,* 13-32.

Cantor, P. (1987). "Young people in crisis: How you can help." A film presentation of the National Committee on Youth Suicide Prevention and American Association of Suicidology, in consultation with Harvard Medical School, Department of Psychiatry, Cambridge Hospital.

Cooley, C. H. (1902). *Human nature and the social order.* New York: Charles Scribner & Sons.

Coopersmith, S. (1967). *The antecedents of self-esteem.* San Francisco: W. H. Freeman.

Damon, W., & Hart, D. (1982). The development of self-understanding from infancy through adolescence. *Child Development, 53,* 841-864.

Damon, W. and Hart, D. (1988). *Self understanding in childhood and adolescence.* New York: Cambridge University Press.

Elkind, D. (1967). Egocentrism in adolescence. *Child Development, 38,* 1025-1034.

Elkind, D. (1984). Growing up faster. *Psychology Today, 12,* 38-45.

Engel, M. (1959). The stability of the self-concept in adolescence. *Journal of Abnormal and Social Psychology, 58,* 211-217.

Epstein, S. (1973). The self-concept revisited or a theory of a theory. *American Psychologist, 28,* 405-416.

Erikson, E. (1959). Identity and the life cycle. *Psychological Issues, 1,* 18-164.

Erikson, E. (1968). *Identity, youth and crisis.* New York: Norton.

Fischer, K. W. (1980). A theory of cognitive development: The control and construction of hierarchies of skills. *Psychological Review, 87,* 477-531.

Freud, A. (1965). *Normality and pathology in childhood.* New York: International Universities Press.

Gecas, V. (1972). Parental behavior and contextual variations in adolescent self-esteem. *Sociometry, 35,* 332-345.

Gergen, K. J. (1968). Personal consistency and the presentation of self. In C. Gordon, & K. J. Gergen (Eds.), *The self in social interaction.* New York: John Wiley.

Glick, M., & Zigler, E. (1985). Self-image: A cognitive-developmental approach. In R. L. Leahy (Ed.), *The development of self.* New York: Academic Press.

Griffin, N., Chassin, L., & Young, R. D. (1981). Measurement of global self-concept versus multiple role-specific self-concepts in adolescents. *Adolescence, 16,* 49-56.

Grotevant, H. D., & Cooper, C. R. (1983). *Adolescent development in the family.* New Directions for Child Development: San Francisco: Jossey-Bass.

Hare, B. R., & Lastenell, L. A. Jr., (1985). No place to run, no place to hide: Comparative status and future prospects of Black boys. In M. B. Spender, G. K. Brookins and W. R. Allen (Eds.), *Beginnings: The social and affective development of Black children.* New Jersey, Hillsdale.

Hart, D. (1988). The adolescent self-concept in social context. In D. K. Lapsley & F. C. Power (Eds.), Self, ego, and identity (pp. 71-90). New York: Springer-Verlag.

Harter, S. (1982). The perceived competence scale for children. *Child Development, 53,* 87-97.

Harter, S. (1983). Developmental perspectives on the self-system. In M. Hetherington (Ed.), *Handbook of Child Psychology,* Vol. 4, Socialization, personality, and social development. New York: John Wiley.

Harter, S. (1986a). Processes underlying the construction, maintenance and enhancement of the self-concept in children. In J. Suls & A. Greenwald (Eds.), *Psychological perspective on the self,* Vol. 3. Hillsdale, NJ: Lawrence Erlbaum.

Harter, S. (1986b). Cognitive-developmental processes in the integration of concepts about emotion and the self. *Social Cognition, 4*, 119-151.

Harter, S. (1987). The determinants and mediational role of global self-worth in children. In N. Eisenberg (Ed.), *Contemporary issues in developmental psychology.* New York: John Wiley.

Harter, S. (1988a). The construction and conservation of the self: James and Cooley revisited. In D. K. Lapsley & F. C. Power (Eds.), *Self, ego and identity: Integrative approaches.* New York: Springer-Verlag.

Harter, S. (1988b). Developmental and dynamic changes in the nature of the self concept: Implications for child psychotherapy. In S. Shirk (Ed.), *Cognitive development and child psychotherapy.* New York: Plenum.

Harter, S. (1988c). *The self-perception profile for adolescents.* Unpublished manuscript. University of Denver.

Harter, S. (1989). Causes, correlates and the functional role of global self-worth: A life-span perspective. In J. Kolligian & R. Sternberg (Eds.). *Perceptions of competence and incompetence across the life-span.* New Haven, CT: Yale University Press.

Harter, S. (in press). Developmental differences in the nature of self-representations, *Cognitive therapy and research.*

Harter, S., & Bresnick, S. (1989). *Developmental and gender differences in the conflict caused by opposing attributes within the adolescent self.* Unpublished manuscript, University of Denver.

Harter, S., & Lee, L. (1989). *Manifestations of true and false selves in early adolescence.* S.R.C.D. presentation, Kansas City, MO.

Harter, S., & Marold, D. (1989). *A model of risk factors in adolescent suicide.* Presentation at S.R.C.D., Kansas City, Missouri.

Harter, S., & Pike, R. (1984). The pictorial scale of perceived competence and social acceptance for young children. *Child Development, 55*, 1969-1982.

Harter, S., & Robinson, N. (1989). *The function and source of different types of social support and their impact on global self-worth.* University of Denver. Unpublished manuscript.

Hatfield, E., & Sprechner (1986). *Mirror, mirror - The importance of looks in everyday life.* Albany: State University of New York Press.

Hauser, S. T., & Follansbee, D. J. (1984). Developing identity: Ego growth and change during adolescence. In H. E. Fitzgerald, B. M. Laster, & M. W. Yogman (Eds.), *Theory and research in behavioral pediatrics,* Vol. 2. New York: Plenum Press.

Higgins, E. T. (1987). Self-discrepancy: A theory relating self and affect. *Psychological Review, 94*, 319-340.

Horney, K. (1950). *Neurosis and human growth.* New York: Norton.

James, W. (1892). *Psychology: The briefer course.* New York: Holt, Rinehart & Winston.

Josselson, R. (1980). Ego development in adolescence. In J. Adelson (Ed.), *Handbook of adolescent psychology,* (pp. 188-210). New York: John Wiley.

Jung, C. G. (1928). *Two essays on analytical psychology.* New York: Dodd, Mead.

Kaplan, H. B., & Pokorny, A. D. (1976). Self-attitudes and suicidal behavior. *Suicide and Life-Threatening Behavior, 6*, 23-35.

Kazdin, A. E., French, N. H., Unis, A. S., Esveldt-Dawson, K., & Sherrich, R. B. (1983). Hopelessness, depression, and suicidal intent among psychiatrically disturbed in-patient children. *Journal of Consulting and Clinical Psychology, 51*, 504-510.

Kelly, G. A. (1955). *The psychology of personal constructs.* New York: Norton.

Langlois, J. H. (1981). Beauty and the beast: The role of physical attractiveness in the development of peer relations and social behavior. In S. S. Brehn, S. M. Kassin & F. X.

Gibbons (Eds.), *Developmental social psychology: Theory and research*. New York: Oxford University Press.

Lapsley, D. K., & Rice, K. (1988). The "New Look" at the imaginary audience and personal fable: Toward a general model of adolescent ego development. In D. K. Lapsley & F. C. Power (Eds.), *Self, ego, and identity: Integrative approaches*. New York: Springer-Verlag.

Leahy, R. L. (1985). The costs of development: Clinical implications. In R. L. Leahy (Ed.), *The development of the self*. New York: Academic Press.

Leahy, R. L., & Shirk, S. R. (1985). Social cognition and the development of the self. In R. L. Leahy (Ed.), *The development of the self*. Orlando, FL: Academic Press.

Lecky, P. (1945). *Self-consistency: A theory of personality*. New York: Island Press.

Lerner, R. M., & Brackney, B. E. (1978). The importance of inner and outer body parts attitudes in the self-concept of late adolescents. *Sex Roles, 4*, 225-237.

Lerner, R. M., Orlos, J. B., & Knapp, J. (1976). Physical attractiveness, physical effectiveness, and self-concept of late adolescents. *Adolescence, 11*, 313-326.

Lewis, M., & Brooks-Gunn, J. (1979). *Social cognition and the acquisition of self*. New York: Plenum Press.

Lively, W. J., & Bromley, D. B. (1973). *Person perception in childhood and adolescence*. London: John Wiley.

Maccoby, E. E. (1983). Socio-emotional development and response to stressors. In N. Garmazy & M. Rutter (Eds.). *Stress, coping and development in children*. New York: McGraw Hill.

Maccoby, E. E., & Martin, J. A. (1983). Socialization in the context of the family: Parent-child interaction. In E. M. Hetherington (Ed.), P. H. Mussen (Series Ed.), *Handbook of child psychology. Vol. 4: Socialization, personality and social development*. New York: John Wiley.

Marcia, J. E. (1966). Development and validation of ego-identity status. *Journal of Personality and Social Psychology, 3*, 551-558.

Marcia, J. E. (1980). Identity in adolescence. In J. Adelson (Ed.), *Handbook of adolescent psychology*. New York: John Wiley.

Marcia, J. E. (1988). Common processes underlying ego identity, cognitive/normal development, and individuation. In D. K. Lapsley & F. C. Power (Eds.), *Self, ego and identity*. New York: Springer-Verlag.

Markus, H., & Nurius, P. (1986). Possible selves. *American Psychologist, 41*, 954-969.

Marsh, H. W. (1986). Global self-esteem: Its relation to specific facets of self-concept and their importance. *Journal of Personality and Social Psychology, 51*, 1224-1236.

Maslow, A. H. (1961). Peak-experience as acute identity-experiences. *American Journal of Psychoanalysis, 21*, 254-260.

Masters, J. E. (1971). Social comparison by young children. *Young Children, 27*, 37-60.

McCarthy, J., & Hoge, D. (1982). Analysis of age effects in longitudinal studies of adolescent self-esteem. *Developmental Psychology, 18*, 372-379.

Mead, G. H. (1934). *Mind, self, and society*. Chicago: University of Chicago Press.

Monsour, A. (1985). *The structure and dynamics of the adolescent self-concept*. Doctoral dissertation, University of Denver.

Montemayor, R., & Eisen, M. (1977). The development of self-conceptions from childhood to adolescence. *Developmental Psychology, 13*, 314-319.

Mullener, N., & Laird, J. D. (1971). Some developmental changes in the organization of self-evaluations. *Developmental Psychology, 5*, 233-236.

Nicholls, J. G. (1978). The development of the concepts of effort and ability, perception of academic attainment, and the understanding that difficult tasks require more ability. *Child Development*, 800-814.

Noam, G. G., Kohlberg, L., & Snarey, J. (1983). Steps toward a model of the self. In B. Lee & G. G. Noam (Eds.). *Developmental approaches to the self*. New York: Plenum Press.

Offer, D., Ostrow, E., & Howard, K. (1981). *The adolescent: A psychological self-portrait*. New York: Basic Books.

O'Malley, P., & Bachman, J. (1983). Self-esteem: Change and stability between ages 13 and 23. *Developmental Psychology, 19*, 257-268.

Peterson, A. C., & Taylor, B. (1980). Puberty: Biological change and psychological adaptation. In J. Adelson (Ed.), *Handbook of adolescent psychology* (pp. 117-158). Hew York: John Wiley.

Pfeffer, C. (1986). *The suicidal child*. New York: Guilford Press.

Piaget, J. (1960). The psychology of intelligence. Paterson, NJ: Littlefield, Adams.

Piaget, J. (1963). *The origins of intelligence in children*. New York: Norton.

Rogers, C. R. (1950). The significance of the self-regarding attitudes and perceptions. In M. L. Reymart (Ed.). *Feelings and emotions: The Mooseheart symposium*. New York: McGraw-Hill.

Rogers, C., & Dymond, R. (1954). *Psychotherapy and personality change*. Chicago: University of Chicago Press.

Rosenberg, M. (1979). *Conceiving the self*. New York: Basic Books.

Rosenberg, M. (1986). Self-concept from middle childhood through adolescence. In J. Suls & A. G. Greenwald (Eds.), Review, *Psychological perspective on the self*. Hillsdale, NJ: Lawrence Erlbaum Associates.

Ruble, D. N., Parsons, J. E., & Ross, J. (1976). Self-evaluative responses of children in an achievement setting. *Child Development, 47*, 990-997.

Ruble, D. N., Boggiano, A. K., Feldman, N. S., & Loebl, J. H. (1980). Developmental analysis of the role of social comparison in self-evaluation. *Developmental Psychology, 16*, 105-115.

Ruble, D. N., & Rholes, W. (1981). The development of children's perceptions and attributions about their social world. In J. Harvey, W. Ickes, & R. Kidd (Eds.), *New directions in attributions research*. Vol. 3. Hillsdale, NJ: Erlbaum.

Secord, P., & Peevers, B. (1974). The development of person concepts. In T. Mischel (Ed.), *Understanding other persons*. Oxford: Blackwell.

Seligman, M. E. P. (1975). *Helplessness: On depression, development, and death*. San Francisco: Freeman.

Selman, R. (1980) *The growth of interpersonal understanding*. New York: Academic Press.

Simmons, R. G., & Blyth, D. A. (1987). *Moving into adolescence: The impact of pubertal change and school context*. New York: Aldine de Gruyter.

Simmons, R. G., & Rosenberg, F. (1975). Sex, sex-roles, and self-image. *Journal of Youth and Adolescence, 4*(3), 229-258.

Simmons, R. G., Rosenberg, F., & Rosenberg, M. (1973). Disturbance in the self-image at adolescence. *American Sociological Review, 38*, 553-568.

Smollar, J., & Youniss, J. (1985). In R. L. Leahy (Ed.), *The development of self*. New York: Academic Press.

Strachen, A., & Jones, D. (1982). Changes in identification during adolescence: A personal construct theory approach. *Journal of Personality Assessment, 46*.

Suls, J., & Sanders, G. (1982). Self-evaluation via social comparison: A development analysis. In I. Wheeler (Ed.), *Review of personality and social psychology* Vol. 3. Beverly Hills, CA: Sage.

Tesser, A., & Campbell, J. (1980). Self-definition: The impact of the relative performance and similarity of others. *Social Psychology Quarterly.* 43, 341-347.

Tesser, A., & Campbell, J. (1983). Self-definition and self-evaluation maintenance. In J. Suls & A. G. Greenwald (Eds.), *Psychological perspectives on the self,* Vol. 2. Hillsdale, NJ: Erlbaum.

Vallacher, R. R. (1980). An introduction to self theory. In D. M. Wegner & R. R. Vallacher (Eds.), *The self in social psychology.* New York: Oxford University Press.

Waterman, A. S. (1982). Identity development from adolescence to adulthood: An extension of theory and review of research. *Developmental Psychology, 18,* 341-358.

Waterman, A. S. (1985). Identity in the context of adolescent psychology. In A. S. Waterman (Ed.), *Identity in adolescence: Processes and contents.* San Francisco: Jossey-Bass.

Werner, H. (1957). The concept of development from a comparative and organismic view. In D. B. Harris (Ed.), *The concept of development.* Minneapolis: University of Minnesota Press.

Winnicott, D. (1965). *The maturational processes and the facilitating environment.* New York: International Universities Press.

Wylie, R. (1979). *The self concept,* Volume II. *Theory and research on selected topics.* Lincoln, NE: University of Nebraska Press.

10. Prosocial Development in Early and Mid-Adolescence

Nancy Eisenberg
Arizona State University

In the last 25 years, the study of moral development has flourished. Nonetheless, as was noted by Hoffman in 1980, there has been surprising little research on adolescents' moral development. For example, there are relatively few studies concerning adolescents' honesty and resistance to temptation, and only a moderate amount of research concerning aggression and cruelty (especially in nondelinquent samples). Even more striking, however, is the lack of research on adolescents' prosocial development. As was noted by Hill in 1987, the "capability for relatedness, connectedness, communion, and for what Gilligan has termed 'caring morality' have . . . been little studied" (1987, p. 24).

In this chapter, research on adolescents' prosocial behaviors and cognitions about prosocial behavior (i.e., attributions and moral reasoning) is reviewed. *Prosocial behavior* is defined as intentional, voluntary behavior intended to benefit another (Eisenberg, 1986). *Altruism* (voluntary, intentional behavior motivated to benefit another that is not motivated by the expectation of external rewards or avoiding externally produced punishments or aversive stimuli) is considered to be a morally advanced form of prosocial behavior. Consistent with the focus of this volume on transition into and during adolescence, research conducted with children in late elementary school (e.g., sixth grade) and high school is reviewed in this chapter. Although young college students could be considered to be adolescents, research involving college students is not included because many college students are in their twenties or older and college students are a select group of adolescents (for a review of the work on college-aged activists, see Hoffman, 1980).

AUTHOR'S NOTE: *Preparation of this manuscript was supported by grants from the National Science Foundation (BNS-8509223 and BNS-8807784) and the National Institute of Child Health and Development (KO4 HD00717). Some of the work reported in this grant was also supported by the Child Development Foundation.*

This chapter is organized into several sections. First, I briefly discuss some of the reasons why one would expect morality to continue to develop in adolescence. Next, data on adolescents' prosocial *behaviors* are reviewed, and issues such as change with age and socialization and sociocognitive correlates of prosocial development are considered. Then the research on adolescents' prosocial cognitions (attributions regarding motives for prosocial behavior and prosocial moral reasoning) is examined, followed by a brief discussion of correlates of level of prosocial cognitions during adolescence. Finally, possible future directions for research concerning change in prosocial development during adolescence are discussed.

THE FOUNDATIONS FOR PROSOCIAL MORAL DEVELOPMENT IN ADOLESCENCE

There is a large body of literature documenting the many and large changes in moral functioning during childhood. During the preschool and elementary school years, major advances are evident in moral judgment (e.g., Damon, 1977; Eisenberg, 1986; Rest, 1979) and in regard to the frequency of some types of morally relevant behaviors (e.g., some positive behaviors, not honesty; Burton, 1976; Radke-Yarrow, Zahn-Waxler, & Chapman, 1983; Underwood & Moore, 1982b). Given the magnitude of these changes in childhood, one might reasonably ask if there is a basis to expect further moral development—in particular, prosocial development—in adolescence.

The answer is yes. This is for several reasons. First, prosocial behaviors such as helping, sharing, and comforting have been linked both conceptually and empirically with perspective-taking skills (Eisenberg, 1986; Underwood & Moore, 1982b), empathic and sympathetic responding (i.e., the tendency to experience vicariously another's state and to sympathize; Batson, 1987; Hoffman, 1984; Eisenberg & Miller, 1987), problem-solving skills (Eisenberg, 1986; Shure, 1980), and level of moral reasoning (Eisenberg, 1986; Blasi, 1980; Underwood & Moore, 1982b). All of these skills appear to develop into adolescence (Hill & Palmquist, 1978). Consider, for example, perspective taking. It is not until preadolescence (age 10 to 12) that individuals are "aware of the infinite regress (I know that you know that I know that you know, etc.) characteristic of dyadic relations; that each person is simultaneously aware of his own and others' subjective abilities . . . (and begin) to view his own interactions with and subjective perspectives of others from a third person perspective" (Selman, 1975, p. 40). Moreover, later in adolescence, the individual may become aware that in taking another's perspective, "the mutuality of perspectives includes a view of both self and other as complex psychological systems of values, beliefs, attitudes, etc. [and the] . . . further awareness that the mutuality of understanding of each other's point of view can take place at different qualitative levels—for example, persons can 'know' each other as acquaintances, friends, closest friends, lovers, etc." (1975, p. 40). Indeed, Selman (1980) has reported a linear pattern of change in social perspective taking from childhood to adulthood, including advances for many persons from adolescence to adulthood (Selman, 1975; 1980). Given the importance of understanding another's perspective for altruistic behavior and higher level moral reasoning (Kohlberg, 1976; Underwood & Moore, 1982b), advances in perspective-taking skills in adolescence would be expected to be associated with enhanced prosocial development.

Similarly, there is a large data base indicating that reasoning about justice-oriented moral dilemmas becomes more sophisticated during adolescence (see, for example, Colby, Kohlberg, Gibbs, & Lieberman, 1983; Rest, 1979, 1983). Thus, moral reasoning about moral dilemmas concerning the conflict between two people's needs in a context in which the role of prohibitions and other formal justice-related criteria are irrelevant or minimal (prosocial dilemmas; Eisenberg-Berg, 1979a)—which is similar in many aspects to reasoning about justice dilemmas (Eisenberg, 1986; Higgins, Power, & Kohlberg, 1984)—could be expected to change during adolescence. Moreover, because higher level moral reasoning (including justice-oriented moral reasoning) tends to be positively related to quantity and quality of individuals' prosocial behaviors (i.e., amount of the behavior and the motivational basis for the behavior; Bar-Tal, Korenfeld, & Raviv, 1985; Blasi, 1980), a trend towards more altruistic, other-oriented behavior can be expected during adolescence.

Analogously, the advances in social problem-solving skills and interpersonal negotiation skills noted during childhood and adolescence (Brion-Meisels & Selman, 1984; Marsh, 1982; Selman & Demorest, 1984) would be expected to contribute to the development of prosocial styles of interaction, as would advances in conceptions of friendship (Berndt, 1986; Eisenberg & Harris, 1984; Selman, 1980) and in the ability to make accurate attributions about others' motives

(Dodge, 1986; Eisenberg, 1986). Also relevant to adolescent moral development are the changes in conceptions of self from childhood into adolescence. In childhood, the self is defined primarily in terms of bodily properties, material possessions, or typical behavior, none of which is moral in essence. In contrast, in adolescence, conceptions of the self and morality seem to be inextricably linked. This is because the self is defined in terms of social and psychological aspects of the self, and morality is a major regulator of social interactions, whereas belief systems are central to characterizing the psychological self (see Damon, 1984; Damon & Hart, 1982). Given the nature of the aforementioned changes in conceptions of the self, it is reasonable to expect children and adolescents to differ in their conceptions of positive morality and in their motives for morally relevant behaviors (including altruism).

Finally, empathic and sympathetic responses (at least as measured with age-appropriate questionnaires) tend to increase with age into and during adolescence (e.g., Francis & Pearson, 1987; Davis & Franzoi, 1987; Lennon & Eisenberg, 1987) and, as was noted previously, are associated with preadolescents' and adolescents' prosocial behavior and level of prosocial moral reasoning (e.g., Eisenberg, Shell, Pasternack, Lennon, Beller, & Mathy, 1987; Eisenberg-Berg & Mussen, 1978; Estrada, 1987). In this regard, Hoffman (1984) has argued that the ability to sympathize with the distresses of others who are abstract (i.e., are not in the immediate situation) and with the chronic distress of others (including disadvantaged social groups) develops in late childhood or early adolescence. This capability is believed to be based upon the individual's newfound ability to view others as having personal identities and life experience beyond the immediate situation. If Hoffman is correct, we would expect adolescents, in comparison to children, to be more sympathetic (and therefore more prosocial) toward members of disadvantaged groups and other individuals whose distress is chronic and/or not immediately observable.

In brief, during late childhood and adolescence there are significant changes in sociocognitive skills and affective responses—changes that conceptually and empirically have been linked to the development of prosocial skills and cognitions. Therefore, adolescence would be expected to be a period of growth for prosocial tendencies. The literature pertaining to this issue is now reviewed. As will become evident, the empirical data are not always consistent with expectations.

PROSOCIAL BEHAVIOR IN ADOLESCENCE

When studying prosocial development, the most obvious focal point is on actual behavior and quantitative changes in such behavior. Thus, it is not surprising that much of the existing work on prosocial development in adolescence concerns the presence, absence, or quantity of various prosocial behaviors such as sharing and helping. Unfortunately, in much (although not all) of this research, the motive for a given prosocial action was not assessed or considered; therefore, it is not possible to assess the quality of the focal prosocial behaviors. For this reason, it is impossible to draw firm conclusions about qualitative change (i.e., change in the motivational bases) in prosocial behaviors during adolescence from most of the research on adolescents' prosocial behavior.

Age Changes

There is relatively little research available concerning changes with age in the frequency and quality of prosocial behaviors during the preadolescent and adolescent years. Moreover, the results of the limited extant work sometimes are inconsistent across studies.

Helping. For example, with regard to helping behaviors, Berndt (1985) and Collins and Getz (1976) found that helping a peer with a task increased from fourth to eighth or tenth grade, respectively (helping for sixth or seventh graders was at an intermediate level). In contrast, in a study of elementary-school children and 13- to 14-year-olds, helping to pick up pencils did not increase from age 9-10 to 13-14 years (perhaps because virtually all children were helping by age 9-10 years) and older children were no more likely than younger children to volunteer to work for needy children (Green & Schneider, 1974). Similarly, Lowe and Ritchey (1973) found no differences in the frequency with which junior high and senior high school students mailed unstamped letters dropped in their schools, although helping was higher among college students and adults than adolescents; nor did Midlarsky and Hannah (1985) find that helping in an emergency increased linearly with age (helping an injured peer or toddler was higher among fourth and tenth graders than among first and seventh graders). Finally, in studies of preadolescents, researchers have obtained mixed results: no increase from fourth to sixth grader in public helping done to benefit a stranger (Payne, 1980); no difference between sixth graders' and younger children's helping of an adult if the children had training in how to assist (however, older children helped more than younger children on tasks requiring age-related experience; Peterson, 1983a); an increase with age in helping in an emergency in a sample of first, fourth and sixth graders (Peterson, 1983b); and a decrease in helping in an emergency with age when children were with a peer (Staub, 1970).

Obviously adolescents are not necessarily more helpful than are younger children. Nonetheless, they do help more on tasks that involve certain age-related knowledge and skills (Midlarsky & Hannah, 1985; Peterson, 1983a). It is also likely that adolescents help more than younger children if higher levels of role taking are required to discern another's need; however, in most of the existing research, the other's distress or need was fairly obvious, and even the younger children had the prerequisite skills for helping.

Other issues to be considered when examining age trends in helping are the type of helping and the motive for helping. For example, Bar-Tal and Nissim (1984) found that 16- to 17-year-old Israeli students were *less* likely than 12-13 and 14-15 year-olds to agree to help bind and repair books for old people. Among those who agreed to assist, there were no age differences in number who appeared to help. Interestingly, the seventh graders (12-13 year olds) were more likely to assist when offered a reward or social recognition than when neither was offered and the eleventh graders (16-17 year olds) helped most when there would be social recognition (there was no difference in helping in the various contexts for ninth graders). Moreover, among those who agreed to assist, self-reported altruistic motives were much higher for the eleventh graders (82%) than for the ninth (44%) or seventh (34.5%) graders. This pattern of results suggests that even though the younger adolescents helped more than the oldest ones, they were more likely to assist for nonaltruistic motives such as obtaining a concrete reward. In addition, it is likely that the older adolescents had more conflicting extracurricular activities than did the younger ones.

Indeed, adolescents' failures to help often may be due to different factors than are those of younger children. In a study of emergency helping, adolescents reported being more hesitant to help than were younger children because of fear of disapproval from the recipient and fear that the recipient of help would be embarrassed or feel that the help was condescending (Midlarsky & Hannah, 1985). Younger children reported not helping because of perceptions of incompetence. Similarly, when asked about times when they failed to help others, adolescents frequently cited the desire not to interfere in another's personal situation or/and the desire not to violate internalized values, laws, or rules. In contrast, elementary school children were more likely to cite perceived incompetence (Barnett, Thompson, & Schroff, 1987).

In summary, although there is little evidence of change in the quantity of helping during the transition into adolescence or during adolescence, it is likely that adolescents are more proficient at effective helping than are younger children, and that adolescents' motives for helping or not helping are more other-oriented or value-based than are those of younger persons. However, the data are too scarce to draw firm conclusions with regard to such qualitative changes in actual helping behaviors.

Donating and sharing. The findings with regard to sharing and donating behaviors are somewhat more consistent than are those pertaining to helping. Donating and sharing have been found to increase with age into preadolescence (i.e., sixth grade) or early adolescence in several, although not all, studies (Dreman, 1976; Emler & Rushton, 1974; Green & Schneider, 1974; Grunberg, Maycock, & Anthony, 1985; Levin & Bekerman-Greenberg, 1980; Payne, 1980; Ugurel-Semin, 1952; not Berndt, 1985; Dlugokinski & Firestone, 1973). In only one of these studies (Ugurel-Semin, 1952) were any high-school-aged subjects included, so it is impossible to determine change from early to middle adolescence in donating or sharing. In studies such as these, children usually have been provided with the commodity to be donated (e.g., money); therefore differences across age groups were not attributable to availability of the commodity. Whether the pattern of findings is due to differences in the value of the commodity across ages or in willingness to deny oneself of a desirable commodity has not been tested adequately.

Comforting. There are few available studies regarding age differences in comforting behavior. Berndt and Perry (1986) interviewed second, fourth, sixth, and eighth graders about their perceptions of social support provided by friends. Reports that friends and acquaintances provided emotional support increased markedly from second to fourth grade but not thereafter. Reports of emotional support from acquaintances increased nonsignificantly from second to eighth grade.

In another relevant study, Burleson (1982) found that comforting communication skills (language used in a hypothetical situation to comfort a friend) increased substantially from childhood through adolescence (i.e., from first to twelfth grade). Although statistical tests were used to examine age trends rather than differences among age groups, it appeared that development of higher level comforting skills was not complete by ninth grade. Thus, the limited data on comforting suggest that adolescents sometimes are more able (or at least more likely) to comfort others in optimal ways, but may not be more likely than younger children to provide emotional support.

Summary. A simple pattern does not emerge from the research concerning age-related changes in prosocial behaviors. In general, helping behavior does not appear to increase into or in adolescence, although motives for helping (when helping occurs) may become more altruistic with age. In contrast, adolescents donate more than do younger individuals and may exhibit more appropriate comforting behaviors. Overall, then, it does not appear that there are marked quantitative changes in most kinds of prosocial behavior during adolescence, although the motivational bases of prosocial actions may change during the transition into adolescence. At this time, little is known about changes in prosocial behavior *during* adolescence, or the reasons why some types of prosocial behaviors and not others seem to increase from childhood into adolescence.

Consistency in Prosocial Responding

The issue of consistency in personality—a topic of much debate among personality psychologists—has also received considerable attention in the prosocial literature. Specifically, researchers have sought to determine whether there is an altruistic personality, that is, whether there is consistency across situations in level of prosocial responding.

Two kinds of consistency are frequently examined—consistency across situations and across time. If adolescents were found to be more consistent across situations or time than were younger children, the data would support the view that morality, with age, becomes increasingly based on internalized values or orientations (such as an other-orientation) rather than on situational factors. This is because moral behavior seems to be more consistent if it is engendered by higher level moral values and orientations (Rholes & Lane, 1985). Such an inference would be indirect because in the relevant prosocial research, quantity, not quality, of prosocial behavior is assessed. Moreover, a finding of greater consistency during adolescence than prior to adolescence could be interpreted as indicating that individual differences in prosocial orientations are consolidated during adolescence.

Unfortunately, the available data are not very informative because researchers seldom have studied consistency in more than one age group; thus, change in consistency across situations during the transition into adolescence or during adolescence cannot be examined. Nor has consistency over an extended time period during adolescence been examined with longitudinal data. Therefore, although individual differences in level of prosocial responding are somewhat stable across situations for preadolescents and adolescents (e.g., Bar-Tal & Raviv, 1979; Dlugokinski & Firestone, 1973; Eisenberg, Cialdini, McCreath, & Shell, 1987; Hampson, 1981; Savin-Williams, Small, & Zeldin, 1981; Small, Zeldin, & Savin-Williams, 1983; Zeldin, Small, & Savin-Williams, 1982; Zeldin, Savin-Williams, & Small, 1984; cf. Payne. 1980), we know relatively little about *changes* in the consistency of prosocial behavior during adolescence or consistency across the period of adolescence.

Sociocognitive and Affective Correlates of Prosocial Behavior

Prosocial behavior and reported willingness to assist others have been positively associated with adolescents' scores on tests of empathy and sympathy (e.g., Barnett, Howard, King, & Dino, 1981; Eisenberg-Berg & Mussen, 1978; Estrada, 1987), as is true for other age-groups (see Eisenberg & Miller, 1987). Moreover, as was mentioned previously, level of moral reasoning has been positively correlated with preadolescents' or adolescents' prosocial behavior (Dreman, 1976; Eisenberg-Berg, 1979b; Emler & Rushton, 1974; O'Connor & Cuevas, 1982; see Blasi, 1980, and Eisenberg, 1986, for general reviews). Thus, it is reasonable to assume that the changes in moral reasoning and sympathetic responsiveness that appear to occur in early and mid adolescence affect the motivational bases of adolescents' prosocial behavior, although firm conclusions cannot be drawn because of the limited relevant data.

Findings concerning the relation of prosocial behavior to adolescents' perspective-taking abilities have not been consistent across studies, although few relevant studies are available (Emler & Rushton, 1974; Karpf, 1977). Thus, the perspective taking data do not strongly support the prediction that changes in perspective taking result in changes in quantity or quality of prosocial behavior. However, it is possible that prosocial behavior would be positively related to those indices of perspective taking that optimally assess change in role taking in adolescence; to my knowledge, no one has examined the relation of Selman's (1980) or other more sophisticated measures of perspective taking to adolescents' actual prosocial behavior. In addition, if one considers measures of moral reasoning to reflect level of perspective taking—a common assumption of prominent researchers (e.g., Kohlberg, 1976; Underwood & Moore, 1982b)—then there is considerable evidence that changes in perspective taking are reflected in quantity of prosocial behavior (Blasi, 1980; Eisenberg, 1986; Underwood & Moore, 1982b).

Socialization Correlates

There is a relatively large body of literature concerning the association between childrearing practices and children's prosocial behavior (see Eisenberg & Mussen, 1989; Moore & Eisenberg, 1984; Radke-Yarrow et al., 1983). The general pattern of findings emerging from this body of literature is that high levels of prosocial behavior are associated with supportive parenting accompanied by the use of reasoning (i.e., inductions), but not overly punitive techniques, in disciplinary contexts. Moreover, prosocial behavior in childhood is associated with socializers' modeling of prosocial behaviors, provision of opportunities for children to engage in prosocial actions, exposure to preachings about prosocial behavior, and the setting of high standards for children.

The data from the few relevant studies involving adolescents are, in general, consistent with the pattern obtained for children. The use of inductions has been positively correlated with prosocial behavior in preadolescent and early adolescent samples (Bar-Tal, Nadler, & Blechman, 1980, for boys but not girls; Dlugokinski & Firestone, 1974; Hoffman & Saltzstein, 1967, for girls but not boys; Karylowski, 1982, for a sample of females only; also see Hoffman, 1970), particularly for individuals with a history of inductive discipline (Dlugokinski & Firestone, 1974). Parental emphasis on autonomy (Bar-Tal et al., 1980; Karylowski, 1982) and supportive parenting (Bar-Tal et al., 1980, especially for females) also appear to be positively correlated with prosocial responding. This latter finding is consistent with Baumrind's (1987) findings indicating a positive association between authoritative childrearing and adolescents' social responsibility. In contrast, parental use of physical punishment and isolation as punishment tends to be negatively correlated with sixth graders' sociometric ratings of prosocial behavior (Bar-Tal et al., 1980; Hoffman & Saltzstein, 1967, for females only). In addition, because junior high students report feeling that their family and school should assist in the development of moral values (Zern, 1985) and share many values with their parents (see Hill, 1987), it is likely that adolescents pay attention to authorities' views on altruistic values.

In summary, for adolescents as well as for younger children, prosocial behavior is enhanced by supportive parenting combined with procedures that focus the individual's attention on others rather than on themselves and implicitly provide positive modeling (e.g., supportive parents are themselves models of caring behavior). Whether these relations are due solely to patterns established before adolescence or to a continuing relation between socializers' practices and offsprings' prosocial behaviors (during childhood and adolescence) is unknown, although it is likely that there is a continuing relation. In any case, there is no evidence that the relation between parental socialization practices and the quantity of prosocial behavior changes during adolescence.

Other aspects of adolescents' socialization may also shape their prosocial proclivities. For example, encouragement to engage in extracurricular helping activities by peers or teachers may be associated with enhanced prosocial behavior because such participation is positively correlated with helping behavior (Cox, 1974; also see Eisenberg, Cialdini, McCreath, & Shell, 1987, and Staub, 1979, for discussion of socializers' encouragement of participation in prosocial activities). In contrast, adolescents' participation in the working world seems to have relatively little effect on their feelings of social responsibility (Steinberg, Greenberger, Garduque, Ruggiero, & Vaux, 1982). Unfortunately, we know little about the ways in which exposure to new socializers and socializing contexts during adolescence affects prosocial behavior.

Summary

Although it is possible to draw some tentative conclusions about the development and correlates of prosocial behavior in adolescence, it is clear that we know much less about adolescents' helping, sharing, and comforting behaviors than about those of children and adults. In general, the age trends for, and correlates of, prosocial behavior that have been found for children hold as well for adolescents, although the data often are too scarce to draw firm conclusions. Thus, there is little evidence that the *processes* that influence the quantity of prosocial behavior differ between childhood and adolescence. Moreover, with the exception of donating behavior, there is little evidence that the quantity of prosocial behavior changes in adolescence or during the transition to adolescence. Nonetheless, it is likely that adolescents' and children's prosocial behaviors differ both in their effectiveness and in their motivational bases, and that age-related changes in capabilities such as perspective taking and moral reasoning are reflected in the reasons that adolescents act in prosocial ways towards others. Thus, quantitative changes between children's and adolescents' prosocial behaviors might be evident if researchers differentiated among qualitatively different modes of prosocial behavior. For example, it might be useful to distinguish between altruistic and nonaltruistic behaviors, and between behaviors involving a needy or distressed person and behaviors that are considerate or nice but not directed at a needy other (perspective taking and empathic capabilities might be relevant primarily for altruistic behaviors and those involving needy or distressed others).

If most of the differences between children's and adolescents' prosocial behaviors are in the motivational bases of the behaviors rather than in regard to mere quantity, it is important to examine carefully changes in those prosocial cognitions that play a role in prosocial action. Thus, in much of the remainder of the chapter, I review the literature on attributions about prosocial behavior and prosocial moral reasoning.

ADOLESCENTS' COGNITIONS ABOUT PROSOCIAL BEHAVIORS

Given the previously discussed evidence of sociocognitive changes during preadolescence and adolescence, it is reasonable to expect changes in the quality of prosocial cognitions during the transition into adolescence and throughout adolescence. Specifically, advances in perspective taking abilities and conceptions of the self, as well as in related capabilities (e.g., sympathy and empathy), may be expected to affect the ways in which adolescents think about prosocial opportunities and actions.

Attributions About the Value of Others' Positive Behaviors

People often draw inferences or attributions about the causes of others' and their own behaviors, including prosocial behaviors. Such attributions are an important window into the attributor's mind; they provide information about how people conceptualize the motivational bases of prosocial behavior. For example, it is possible to determine from examining attributions the criteria people use to evaluate the merit (e.g., kindness) of others' prosocial behaviors. Moreover, the attributions people make can affect if they assist others (Weiner, 1986) or reciprocate help, how they view themselves (e.g., whether they view themselves as an altruistic person; see Grusec, 1983), and the manner in which they respond to another's attempts to assist (Eisenberg, 1983).

By preadolescence, children are fairly adept at using intentionality to evaluate prosocial behaviors. They, like adults, do not view behaviors that unintentionally result in positive consequences for others as particularly meritorious or kind (e.g., Baldwin & Baldwin, 1970; Baldwin, Baldwin, Castillo-Vales, & Seegmiller, 1971; see Eisenberg, 1986). Moreover, elementary-school children, like adults, view prosocial acts that are not voluntary, are based on obedience to authority, involve an obligation to a guest, or are performed to promote a trade, obtain an reward, or avoid punishment as less kind and altruistic than are prosocial acts not based on these motivations (Baldwin & Baldwin, 1970; Cohen, Gelfand, & Hartmann, 1981; Leahy, 1979). In attributional terms, school children discount the internal motivation (i.e., altruism) of many acts that appear to have been performed due to external rewards, punishments, or pressures (see Eisenberg, 1986, for a review of this work). Further, prosocial behaviors enacted despite valid reasons not to do so (e.g., despite the potential beneficiary's previously refusing to do a favor or in spite of a cost to the self) are judged as relatively kind (this pattern is consistent with the augmentation principal; see Leahy, 1979; Suls, Witenberg, & Gutkin, 1981).

Changes in attributional tendencies continue into adolescence. Between sixth grade and college age, students appear to increase in the degree to which they devalue or discount prosocial actions done for tangible rewards and praise or to avoid criticism or physical punishment (Peterson & Gelfand, 1984). Similarly, eighth graders (Baldwin & Baldwin, 1970) and adults (Baldwin & Baldwin, 1970; Peterson & Gelfand, 1984; Suls, Witenberg, & Gutkin, 1981) value prosocial acts that involve returning a favor less than do sixth graders. Finally, helping based on norms concerning helping (i.e., helping because the actor felt he or she should help and that others in the situation would help) is viewed less positively by college students than is helping due to empathy or performed for no specific reason whereas this is not true for sixth graders (Peterson & Gelfand, 1984). Indeed, high school students rate empathically motivated helpers as friendlier and more kind and sensitive than helpers who assisted for nonempathic (basically normative) reasons (Barnett, McMinimy, Flouer, & Masbad, 1987).

In summary, attributions regarding the altruistic (e.g., intrinsically motivated) bases of prosocial acts become somewhat more refined and differentiated during adolescence. Consequently, adolescents would be expected to be more likely than school-aged children to react to nuances indicative of extrinsic motives in their own and others' prosocial actions. Thus, they frequently may devalue others' attempts to assist them (see Peterson & Gelfand, 1984), a tendency that would be expected to be associated with negative reactions to aid (Fisher, Nadler, & Whitcher-Alagna, 1982). In addition, adolescents may be relatively cynical about their own motives for positive behaviors.

In the aforementioned attributional studies, study participants merely rated or ranked others or their prosocial behaviors on dimensions such as goodness or kindness; they did not indicate whether the actor's prosocial behaviors were due to factors such as desire for rewards, empathy, or adherence to internalized values. In other research, individuals have been asked to identify their own or others' motives for hypothetical or real prosocial behaviors. Strictly speaking, identifying one's own or others' motivations for previous actions can be viewed as an attributional process; however, much of this work has been considered to be part of the literature on moral judgment (e.g., Gilligan, 1982). This is because some investigators assume that explanations for past behaviors are analogous to reasoning about why one should or should not behave in a given manner (i.e., moral reasoning). But attributions about one's own past behaviors also may reflect conscious or unconscious self-justifications or changes in self-perceptions as a consequence of reflection on the previous behavior (Bem, 1972; Eisenberg & Silbereisen, 1984). Moreover, attitudes about others' behaviors may reflect the attributions and assumptions about how the average person (rather than oneself) operates. Nonetheless, because attributions or judgments about one's own or others' specific motives for prosocial behaviors frequently are viewed as an index of moral reasoning, research on this topic is reviewed along with that on moral judgment.

Moral Reasoning About Prosocial Dilemmas

Although there are myriad studies on moral judgment, most of this work concerns prohibition- or justice-oriented moral reasoning. In research of this sort, people are asked to discuss moral dilemmas in which the roles of rules, laws, punishment, authorities and their dictates, and formal obligations are central (e.g., one must choose between stealing or killing someone and breaking a law, or between breaking a promise and disobeying an authority figure). Only in the last decade has there been much work on prosocial moral dilemmas, dilemmas in which the needs of one person conflict with those of another or others in a context in which the role of rules, laws, authorities, punishment, and formal obligations is minimal. These types of moral dilemmas have been called prosocial moral reasoning dilemmas (Eisenberg-Berg, 1979a), and dilemmas about caring and responsibility (Gilligan, 1977; Higgins, Power, & Kohlberg, 1984). In addition, investigators have studied cognitions about prosocial moral conflicts by asking subjects to discuss their motives for their own prior prosocial behaviors (e.g., Bar-Tal, 1982; Eisenberg, 1986) or for a hypothetical other's prior behavior rather than asking the subject to *resolve* moral dilemmas (e.g., O'Connor, Cuevas, & Dollinger, 1981; Boehnke, Silbereisen, Eisenberg, Reykowski, & Palmonari, 1989).

It is reasonable to expect substantial changes in prosocial moral reasoning in adolescence. Kohlberg and his colleagues have found systematic changes in moral reasoning from childhood into adolescence (e.g., Colby et al., 1983). In elementary school, most students reason primarily at Stage 2, which is the stage of instrumental purpose and exchange. At this stage, right is fair exchange, following rules only when it is in someone's immediate interest, and acting to meet one's own self interest and allowing others to do the same. Moreover, actions are chosen to serve one's own self-interest. By age 14, most students reason at Kohlberg's conventional level (especially Stage 3). At this level, what is right is living up to what is expected by people close to you or what people generally expect of people in your role. Being good is quite important, and this means having good motives, showing concern for others, and maintaining trust, loyalty, respect, and gratitude. Thus, the focus in moral reasoning shifts from self-interest to fulfilling others' expectations and concern with one's position in others' eyes (one's reputation; see Damon, 1984), as well as maintaining positive interpersonal relations with others.

The expression of some Stage 4 reasoning also is common in adolescence, especially late adolescence. At Stage 4, the focus is on fulfilling actual duties to which one has agreed, upholding the law, and contributing to the society, group, or institution. Thus, with age, the adolescent's moral thinking becomes more abstract (e.g., is focused on concepts like laws and society) and more ideological in flavor (see Damon, 1984). It is reasonable to expect some of the same changes that occur in justice-oriented moral reasoning (Kohlberg's schema of moral judgment) to occur in adolescents' moral reasoning about prosocial moral dilemmas.

In fact, it appears that cognitions about prosocial dilemmas and behaviors do change during preadolescence and adolescence, and that there are modest gender differences in these cognitions. For example, in a longitudinal study on prosocial moral reasoning, we have found that there are increases during the elementary school years in reasoning reflecting concern about others' approval and the quality of interactions with others. In addition, in the later elementary-school years, stereotypic conceptions of good and bad behavior were verbalized with increasing frequency, as was concern for direct reciprocity. For girls only, increases in reasoning reflecting role-taking and a sympathetic orientation were also found from age 9-10 to 11-12 (Eisenberg, Shell, Pasternack, Lennon, Beller, & Mathy, 1987).

According to cross-sectional and longitudinal data, additional changes in prosocial moral reasoning seem to occur during the transition from grade school into adolescence (Eisenberg, 1989; Eisenberg-Berg, 1979a). Specifically, high school students, in comparison to grade school children, use more reasoning reflecting internalized norms and values, positive and negative affect related to the consequences of one's behavior for others or self-respect for living up to one's own values, and concern for the rights of others and the condition of society (Eisenberg, 1977; Eisenberg-Berg, 1979a). Approval/interpersonally oriented and stereotypic reasoning appear to peak in or prior to ninth grade, and then to decrease in usage. In addition, consistent with the longitudinal trends in late elementary school, high school females and males may verbalize somewhat different reasoning (and may differ more than do younger children), with males focusing more on issues related to self gain and females verbalizing more other-oriented modes of reasoning (Eisenberg, 1977). The gender differences in prosocial moral reasoning during adolescence are very modest, however, and may decrease with age (Eisenberg, 1989).

Similar (although not identical) findings have been obtained by other researchers using a variety of methods. For example, Battistich, Watson, and Solomon (1983) presented elementary-school children with hypothetical vignettes about helping and asked the children why the story protagonists assisted. The largest changes in response between fourth and sixth grade were in attributions about role obligations and the expression of caring in a relationship (whether this change in late childhood was significant or not is unclear). Using a similar vignette procedure and children in grades 3, 5, and 7, O'Connor et al. (1981) found increases in conceptual/normative reasoning (which appeared to be similar to our stereotypic reasoning), and this increase was substantial (although significance was not tested) between grades 5 and 7 (unpublished data). Similarly, in a study of Israeli 12- to 13-, 14- to 15-, and 16- to 17-year-olds' self-reported motives for volunteering to help, self-attributions of altruistic motives (i.e., personal willingness to assist without any expectation of reward or approval, and without reference to compliance) increased with age (Bar-Tal & Nissim, 1984). In other studies in which children were asked about their own motives for sharing, references to altruism, justice, cooperation and enlarged reciprocity were more frequent in preadolescence than at a younger age (Levin & Bekerman-Greenberg, 1980; Ugurel-Semin, 1952), as was stereotypic reasoning about "good" behavior (Furby, 1978). However, when asked about why and with whom they share, 40- to 50-year-olds were more likely than 16- to 17-year-olds to mention that they shared merely because it made them happy to do so (Furby, 1978).

In a cross-cultural study, Boehnke et al. (1989) examined German, Polish, Italian, and American elementary, junior, and/or high school students' attributions for hypothetical story characters' prosocial actions. Interest in others was a relatively favored type of motive at all ages, whereas self-focused motives were chosen infrequently by the preadolescents and junior and senior high school students. The choice of conformity-related reasons decreased with age in the sample of Italian, German, and Polish students in grades 6, 9, 10, and 12 whereas task-oriented reasons (i.e., pragmatic concerns related to the completion of a task) increased with age. In another sample of German students in grades 5-6 or 7-9, preference for hedonistic motives (i.e., motives related to an individual's feelings of physical well being) decreased with age whereas preference for task-oriented motives increased. For American children in grades 2-3, 5-6, and 7-8, selection of hedonistic motives decreased with age; other self-interested motives (e.g., concern with concrete material gain) were chosen more with age but did not increase from grade 5-6 to 7-8. Thus, in general, adolescents preferred other-oriented or task-oriented motives for assisting, and there was some evidence that conformity and hedonistic motives were less preferred with age.

In addition, in Poland only, high school females preferred other-oriented motives more than did high school males. In the samples of Europeans, females preferred task-oriented motives more than did males. Moreover, for two of the three gender differences in preference for low level, self-oriented, hedonistic motives, males preferred the self-related motives more. Thus, when there were gender differences, they were consistent with the pattern of females favoring other-oriented reasoning and motives and males favoring self-related cognitions.

A Caring Moral Orientation (Gilligan's Model)

Gilligan and her colleagues (e.g., Gilligan, 1977, 1982; Gilligan & Attanucci, 1988; Lyons, 1983) also have studied adolescents' and adults' caring and justice-oriented (i.e., Kohlberg prohibition-oriented) reasoning. Gilligan has argued that there are two different moral orientations, a justice perspective in which the core notion is not to treat others unfairly, and a care orientation, in which the focus is not to turn away from others. Gilligan has suggested that the differentiation between a justice and care orientation is particularly important in adolescence because adolescence is viewed by many as a time of dealing with issues related to autonomy, detachment, and disconnection, rather than these issues in addition to attachment and connection to others.

Gilligan (1982) outlined a sequence for the development of an ethic of caring. At the first level, the individual's focus is on caring for the self, and relationships are conceptualized in self-serving terms. This period is followed by a transitional stage in which such self-oriented concerns are criticized as being selfish. This criticism "signals a new understanding of the connection between self and others which is articulated by the concept of responsibility" (p. 74). At the second level, good is equated with caring for other people, and one's own needs often are subjugated. In the second transitional state, women start to see that a morality of care includes care for the self as well as others. The third level is viewed as developing out of the disequilibrium created by problems in unequal, self-sacrificial relationships. The individual at this level focuses on the dynamics of relationships, and the interconnectedness of self and other. Moral equality between self and other is accomplished by applying an injunction against hurting anyone.

Unfortunately, Gilligan has not systematically studied the emergence of her stages of caring orientation using sizable samples of adolescents. Her initial delineation of levels was based on interviews with 28 adolescents and women regarding their abortion-related decisions (Gilligan, 1977). Based on her anecdotal examples of reasoning, it would appear that adolescents typically reason at Gilligan's first level or transitional stage, although some may be at the second level or higher. However, to my knowledge, Gilligan has not systematically examined change in care-related reasoning during adolescence.

In a recent study involving both males and females in grades 1, 4, 7, and 10 and their parents, Walker (1989) scored care-related concerns in subjects' reasoning about Kohlberg's moral dilemmas and one real-life moral dilemma. He also conducted a two-year follow-up with the same subjects using the same procedures. In general, the group in junior high (who was retested in grade 9) used more care reasoning than did the group in late elementary school (who were initially tested in grade 4 and were retested in grade 6), although this increase was not significant (Walker, personal communication). Care reasoning did not differ between students in early and late high school, although parents appeared to use the highest levels of care-oriented reasoning in their discussion of the real-life dilemma. There were not significant changes in care-oriented reasoning over the two-year retest period, a finding that suggests that the rate of development of such reasoning is slow (if sequential change occurs at all). Clearly, additional research on adolescents' care-oriented reasoning is needed.

Summary

The available research concerning the development of prosocial cognitions in adolescence is limited. However, it appears that there are rather sizable changes in moral attributions and moral reasoning during the transition to adolescence and during adolescence. These changes may be due in part to age-related changes in sociocognitive capabilities that are positively correlated with moral reasoning (such as perspective-taking abilities), and to the development of higher level logical reasoning skills during adolescence. Whatever the source of the change, it is likely that developments in adolescents' cognitions about prosocial behavior influence the quality of their prosocial actions (Eisenberg-Berg, 1979b; Estrada, 1987).

CONCLUSIONS AND FUTURE DIRECTIONS

Despite the length of this chapter, we know relatively little about the development of prosocial behaviors and reasoning in adolescence or the transition into adolescence. This is because of at least two factors. First, there is relatively little theoretical work on prosocial development during adolescence. Second, investigators generally have not been focused in their empirical work on moral development during adolescence per se. In most studies involving adolescence, adolescents were included because they were a convenient sample to obtain or because the sample ranged in age from children to adults. In many of these studies, the investigators have not specifically examined change for a given index of moral development into or during adolescence. For example, the investigator may report only a significant age-related change in reasoning for a sample of children, adolescents, and adults, thereby rendering it impossible to determine whether the change occurred prior, during, and/or after adolescence. If adolescence per se is not a period of interest to investigators, they are not likely to calculate the statistical tests that would directly address questions related to moral development in adolescence.

If we are to obtain a better understanding of prosocial development in adolescence, it would seem worthwhile to examine the relation of prosocial behavior to some of variables of particular conceptual importance in current work concerning adolescence. For example, it is clear from the research with children that parental childrearing practices and the quality of the relationship between mothers and their children correlate with children's prosocial development (Eisenberg & Mussen, 1989; Radke-Yarrow et al., 1983). In current work on adolescents, it appears that family processes related to the degree of individuality and connectedness in family relationships (i.e., individuation) are correlated with adolescents' ego development and role-taking skills (Grotevant & Cooper, 1986). Given the conceptual and empirical relations between role taking and moral development, including altruism (Underwood & Moore, 1982b), it may be fruitful for investigators to examine the role of family interaction in prosocial development during adolescence. In particular, Cooper, Grotevant, and Condon's work (1983) suggests that aspects of familial interactions that affect separateness (the ability to express distinctiveness of self from others), permeability (the responsiveness or openness of an individual to the ideas of others), and mutuality (the demonstration of sensitivity to and respect for the beliefs, feelings, and ideas of others) may be particularly relevant to the study of role taking, sympathy, and prosocial responding. Familial interactions that promote sensitivity to others' feelings and beliefs and openness to the ideas of others would be expected to foster a realistic other-orientation and positive attitudes towards others in general. This type of orientation, combined with a sense of competence that can arise only if the adolescent has a separate sense of self, might facilitate both the cognitive conflict and searching believed to be associated with higher level moral reasoning (Turiel, 1969) and the positive orientation toward others underlying much altruistic behavior (Batson, 1987; Staub, 1978).

Ego development (Loevinger & Wessler, 1970), conceptions of the self (Damon & Hart, 1982), and identity status (Waterman, 1982) undergo considerable change in adolescence. These changes are likely linked to prosocial development because they seem to be associated with changes in moral reasoning (Damon, 1984; Podd, 1972; Rowe & Marcia, 1980; Rest, 1979). For example, in Loevinger and Wessler's (1970) conformist stage (which is found in adolescence), the individual is concerned with conformity to external rules; his or her interpersonal style is characterized by belonging, helping, and superficial niceness; the individual is consciously preoccupied with appearance, social acceptability, his or her behavior; and one's cognitive style is conceptually simple and stereotypic. Individuals at this level would be likely to use stereotypic and approval-oriented prosocial moral reasoning, and to assist others when their behavior will be appreciated and recognized, when the social norms indicating helping is desirable are clear, or when their reputation is at stake (also see Damon, 1984). In contrast, during Loevinger's next stage of ego development—the conscientious stage—the individual is characterized by self-evaluated standards, self-criticism, and guilt for consequences; he or she tends to be responsible and concerned about communication; the individual is consciously preoccupied with issues related to motives for behavior, differentiated feelings, and self-respect; and one's cognitive style is relatively conceptually complex. The person at this stage is more concerned about hurting others than breaking rules. Thus, adolescents and young adults at this stage might be expected to use prosocial moral reasoning reflecting self-evaluated values, positive or negative affect related to self-respect and living up to one's own values, and reasoning reflecting role taking and a sympathetic orientation. Moreover, their prosocial behaviors are likely to be motivated by internalized values or concern for others rather than the desire to behave in stereotypically good ways. As a consequence, they are likely to behave prosocially in situations in which others' distresses are obvious and are less likely than people at the conformist stage to vary their prosocial responding as a function of the possibility of evaluation or recognition by others. Similarly, because identity achievement (which is correlated with ego development; see Waterman, 1982) is associated with good adaptive capabilities (Marcia, 1980), one might expect adolescents who have attained identity achievement to be more effective in their attempts to help or comfort others.

To my knowledge, virtually no one has examined the associations between adolescents' prosocial responding and ego development or identity status (Cox, 1974, is an exception). Different needs or orientations such as the need for approval or a sympathetic orientation do seem to be associated with modes of prosocial behavior reflecting these needs (see Eisenberg, 1986; Eisenberg et al., 1987); thus, it is reasonable to expect the preoccupations, needs, values, and motives associated with different stages of ego development or identity attainment to influence prosocial behavior. In addition, the types of parenting practices associated with higher stage ego development and identity achievement in adolescence (e.g., a climate of individuality and connectedness between parent and child [Grotevant & Cooper, 1986] and some conflict [Marcia, 1980]) might be expected to facilitate high level prosocial moral reasoning and intrinsically motivated (i.e., altruistic) behavior.

Peer influence is another topic of much interest to researchers and practitioners dealing with adolescents. Adolescents' values and behaviors are influenced by peers as well as adults (e.g., Brody & Shaffer, 1982; Youniss & Smollar, 1985), yet there is relatively little research concerning the role of peers in the socialization of prosocial behavior, especially in adolescence (see Brody & Shaffer, 1982; Eisenberg & Mussen, 1989). The differences in the structure of adult versus peer interaction seem to influence children's and adolescents' conceptions of kindness (with adult-directed acts of kindness being characterized by obedience and compliance and peer-directed acts involving more equalitarian and prosocial elements; Eisenberg, Lundy, Shell, & Roth, 1985; Youniss, 1980); however, the gap in perceptions about peer- and adult-directed kindness seems to narrow considerably in adolescence (Youniss, 1980). Nonetheless, it is likely that adolescents are not only differentially affected by peers' and adults' values and modeling, but that they also learn about and engage in somewhat different types of prosocial acts with peers and adults.

In summary, there is an obvious need for additional research and theory concerning prosocial development in preadolescence and adolescence. Adolescents' positive development has been examined much less frequently than have negative outcomes (e.g., delinquency and aggression), and an understanding of prosocial development can complement the work on undesirable outcomes in adolescence. One potentially productive approach to the study of altruistic responding in adolescence would be to select variables that change in meaningful ways in adolescence and examine the role of these variables (and their antecedents) in prosocial development.

REFERENCES

Baldwin, A. L., Baldwin, C. P., Castillo-Vales, V., & Seegmiller, B. (1971). Cross-cultural similarities in the development of the concept of kindness. In W. W. Lambert & K. Weisbrod (Eds.), *Comparative perspectives in social psychology* (pp. 151-164). Boston: Little, Brown.

Baldwin, C. P., & Baldwin, A. L. (1970). Children's judgments of kindness. *Child Development, 41,* 29-47.

Barnett, M. A., Howard, J. A., King, L. M., & Dino, G. A. (1981). Helping behavior and the transfer of empathy. *Journal of Social Psychology, 115,* 125-132.

Barnett, M. A., McMinimy, V., Flouer, G., & Masbad, I. (1987). Adolescents' evaluations of peers' motives for helping. *Journal of Youth and Adolescence, 16,* 579-586.

Barnett, M., Thompson, M. A., Schroff, J. (1987). Reasons for not helping. *Journal of Genetic Psychology, 148,* 489-498.

Bar-Tal, D. (1982). Sequential development of helping behavior: A cognitive-learning approach. *Developmental Review, 2,* 101-124.

Bar-Tal, D., Korenfeld, D., & Raviv, A. (1985). Relationships between the development of helping behavior and the development of cognition, social perspective, and moral judgment. *Genetic, Social, and General Psychology Monographs, 11,* 23-40.

Bar-Tal, D., Nadler, A., & Blechman, N. (1980). The relationship between Israeli children's helping behavior and their perception on parents' socialization practices. *Journal of Social Psychology, 111,* 159-167.

Bar-Tal, D., & Nissim, R. (1984). Helping behavior and moral judgment among adolescents. *British Journal of Developmental Psychology, 2,* 329-336.

Bar-Tal, D., & Raviv, A. (1979). Consistency in helping-behavior measures. *Child Development, 50,* 1235-1238.

Batson, C. D. (1987). Prosocial motivation: Is it ever truly altruistic? In L. Berkowitz (Ed.), *Advances in experimental social psychology* (Vol. 20, pp. 65-122). New York: Academic Press.

Battistich, V., Watson, M., & Solomon, D. (1983, August). *Children's cognitions about helping relationships.* Paper presented at the Annual meeting of the American Psychological Association, Anaheim, CA.

Baumrind, D. (1987). Developmental perspective on adolescent risk taking in contemporary America. *New Directions in Child Development, 37,* 93-125.

Bem, D. J. (1972). Self perception theory. In L. Berkowitz (Ed.), *Advances in experimental social psychology* (Vol. 6, pp. 1-62). New York: Academic Press.

Berndt, T. J. (1985). Prosocial behavior between friends and middle childhood and early adolescence. *Journal of Early Adolescence, 5,* 307-317.

Berndt, T. J. (1986). Children's comments about their friendships. In M. Perlmutter (Ed.), Cognitive perspectives on children's social and behavioral development. *The Minnesota symposia on child psychology* (Vol. 18., pp. 189-212). Hillsdale, NJ: Erlbaum.

Berndt, T. J., & Perry, T. B. (1986). Children's perceptions of friendships as supportive relationships. *Developmental Psychology, 22,* 640-648.

Blasi, A. (1980). Bridging moral cognition and moral action: A critical review of the literature. *Psychological Bulletin, 88,* 1-45.

Boehnke, K., Silbereisen, R. K., Eisenberg, N., Reykowski, J., & Palmonari, A. (1989). The development of prosocial motivation: A cross-national study. *Journal of Cross Cultural Psychology, 20,* 219-243.

Brion-Meisels, S., & Selman, R. L. (1984). Early adolescent development of new interpersonal strategies: Understanding and intervention. *School Psychology Review, XIII,* 278-291.

Brody, G. H., & Shaffer, D. R. (1982). Contributions of parents and peers to children's moral socialization. *Developmental Review, 2,* 31-75.

Burleson, B. R. (1982). The development of comforting strategies in childhood and adolescence. *Child Development, 53,* 1578-1588.

Burton, R. V. (1976). Honesty and dishonesty. In T. Lickona (Ed.), Moral development and behavior: *Theory, research, and social issues* (pp. 173-197). New York: Holt, Rinehart, & Winston.

Cohen, E. A., Gelfand, D. M., & Hartmann, D. P. (1981). Causal reasoning as a function of behavioral consequences. *Child Development, 52,* 514-522.

Colby, A., Kohlberg, L., Gibbs, J., & Lieberman, M. (1983). A longitudinal study of moral judgment. *Monographs of the Society for Research in Child Development, 48* (Serial No. 200), 1-124.

Collins, W. A., & Getz, S. K. (1976). Children's social responses following modeled reactions to provocation: Prosocial effects of a television drama. *Journal of Personality, 44,* 488-500.

Cooper, C. R., Grotevant, H. D., & Condon, S. M. (1983). Individuality and connectedness in the family as a context for adolescent identity formation and role-taking skill. In H. D. Grotevant & C. R. Cooper (Eds.), *Adolescent development in the family* (pp. 43-59). San Francisco: Jossey-Bass.

Cox, N. (1974). Prior help, ego development, and helping behavior. *Child Development,* 75, 594-603.

Damon, W. (1977). *The social world of the child.* San Francisco: Jossey-Bass.

Damon, W. (1984). Self-understanding and moral development from childhood to adolescence. In W. M. Kurtines & J. L. Gewirtz (Eds.), *Morality, moral behavior, and moral development* (pp. 109-127). New York: Wiley.

Damon, W., & Hart, D. (1982). The development of self-understanding from infancy through adolescence. *Child Development,* 53, 841-864.

Davis, M. H., & Franzoi, S. L. (1987). *Stability and change in adolescent self-consciousness and empathy.* Unpublished manuscript, Ekerd College, St. Petersburg, FL.

Dlugokinski, E., & Firestone, I. J. (1973). Congruence among four methods of measuring other-centeredness. *Child Development,* 44, 304-308.

Dlugokinski, E., & Firestone, I. J. (1974). Other centeredness and susceptibility to charitable appeals: Effects of perceived discipline. *Developmental Psychology,* 10, 21-28.

Dodge, K. A. (1986). A social information processing model of social competence in children. In M. Perlmutter (Ed.), *Cognitive perspectives on children's social and behavioral development. Minnesota symposia on child psychology* (Vol. 18, pp. 77-125). Hillsdale, NJ: Erlbaum.

Dreman, S. B. (1976). Sharing behavior in Israeli school children: Cognitive and social learning factors. *Child Development,* 47, 186-194.

Eisenberg, N. (1977). The development of prosocial moral judgment and its correlates. (Doctoral Dissertation, University of California, Berkeley). *Dissertation Abstracts International,* 37, 4753B. (University Microfilms No. 77-444).

Eisenberg, N. (1983). Developmental aspects of recipients' reactions to aid. In J. D. Fisher, A. Nadler, & B. M. DePaulo (Eds.), *New directions in helping* (pp. 189-222). New York: Academic Press.

Eisenberg, N. (1986). *Altruistic emotion, cognition and behavior.* Hillsdale, NJ: Erlbaum.

Eisenberg, N. (1989, April). *The development of prosocial moral reasoning in childhood and early adolescence.* Paper presented at the Society for Research in Child Development, Kansas City, MO.

Eisenberg, N., Cialdini, R. B., McCreath, H., & Shell, R. (1987). Consistency-based compliance: When and why do children become vulnerable? *Journal of Personality and Social Psychology,* 52, 1174-1181.

Eisenberg, N., & Harris, J. D. (1984). Social competence: A developmental perspective. *School Psychology Review, XIII,* 267-277.

Eisenberg, N., Lundy, T., Shell, R., & Roth, K. (1985). Children's justifications for their adult and peer-directed compliant (prosocial and non-prosocial) behaviors. *Developmental Psychology,* 21, 325-331.

Eisenberg, N., & Miller, P. (1987). The relation of empathy to prosocial and related behaviors. *Psychological Bulletin,* 101, 91-119.

Eisenberg, N., & Mussen, P. H. (1989). *The roots of prosocial behavior in children.* Cambridge, UK: Cambridge University Press.

Eisenberg, N., & Silbereisen, R. (1984). The development of children's prosocial cognitions: Research, theory, and new perspectives. In H. E. Sypher & J. L. Applegate (Eds.), *Social cognition and communication* (pp. 16-42). Hilldale, NJ: Erlbaum.

Eisenberg, N., Shell, R., Pasternack, J., Lennon, R., Beller, R., & Mathy, R. M. (1987). Prosocial development in middle childhood: A longitudinal study. *Developmental Psychology,* 23, 712-718.

Eisenberg-Berg, N. (1979a). Development of children's prosocial moral judgment. *Developmental Psychology, 15,* 128-137.

Eisenberg-Berg, N. (1979b). The relationship of prosocial moral reasoning to altruism, political liberalism, and intelligence. *Developmental Psychology, 15,* 87-89.

Eisenberg-Berg, N., & Mussen, P. (1978). Empathy and moral development in adolescence. *Developmental Psychology, 14,* 185-186.

Emler, N. P., & Rushton, J. P. (1974). Cognitive-developmental factors in children's generosity. *British Journal of Social and Clinical Psychology, 13,* 277-281.

Estrada, P. (1987, April). *Empathy and prosocial behavior: Discriminating among groups of adolescents.* Paper presented at the annual meeting of the American Education Research Association, Washington, DC.

Fisher, J. D., Nadler, A., & Whitcher-Alagna, S. (1982). Recipient reactions to aid. *Psychological Bulletin, 91,* 27-54.

Francis, L. J., & Pearson, P. R. (1987). Empathic development during adolescence: Religiosity, the missing link? *Personality and Individual Differences, 8,* 145-148.

Furby, L. (1978). Sharing: Decisions and moral judgments about letting others use one's possessions. *Psychological Reports, 43,* 595-609.

Gilligan, C. (1977). In a different voice: Women's conceptions of self and of morality. *Harvard Educational Review, 47,* 481-517.

Gilligan, C. (1982). *In a different voice: Psychological theory and women's development.* Cambridge, MA: Harvard University Press.

Gilligan, C., & Attanucci, J. (1988). Two moral orientations: Gender differences and similarities. *Merrill Palmer Quarterly, 34,* 223-237.

Green, F. P., & Schneider, F. W. (1974). Age differences in the behavior of boys on three measures of altruism. *Child Development, 45,* 248-251.

Grotevant, H. D., & Cooper, C. R. (1986). Individuation in family relationships. *Human Development, 29,* 82-100.

Grunberg, N. E., Maycock, V. A., & Anthony, B. J. (1985). Material altruism in children. *Basic and Applied Social Psychology, 6,* 1-11.

Hampson, R. B. (1981). Helping behavior in children: Addressing the interaction of a person-situation model. *Developmental Review, 1,* 93-112.

Higgins, A., Power, C., & Kohlberg, L. (1984). The relationship of moral atmosphere to judgments of responsibility. In W. M. Kurtines & J. L. Gewirtz (Eds.), *Morality, moral behavioral, and moral development* (pp. 74-106). New York: John Wiley.

Hill, J. P. (1987). Research on adolescents and their families: Past and prospects. *New Directions on Child Development, 37,* 13-31.

Hill, J. P., & Palmquist, W. J. (1978). Social cognition and social relations in early adolescence. *International Journal of Behavioral Development, 1,* 1-38.

Hoffman, M. L. (1970). Conscience, personality, and socialization techniques. *Human Development, 13,* 90-126.

Hoffman, M. L. (1980). Moral development in adolescence. In J. Adelson (Ed.), *Handbook of adolescent psychology* (pp. 295-343). New York: John Wiley.

Hoffman, M. L. (1984). Interaction of affect and cognition on empathy. In C. E. Izard, J. Kagan, & R. B. Zajonc (Eds.), *Emotions, cognition, and behavior* (pp. 103-131). Cambridge, UK: Cambridge University Press.

Hoffman, M. L., & Saltzstein, H. D. (1967). Parent discipline and the child's moral development. *Journal of Personality and Social Psychology, 5,* 45-57.

Karpf, R. (1977). Effects of emotions on altruism and social inference in retarded adolescents. *Psychological Reports, 41,* 135-138.

Karylowski, J. (1982). Doing good to feel good vs. doing good to make others feel good: Some child-rearing antecedents. *School Psychology International, 3,* 149-156.

Kohlberg, L. (1976). Moral stage and moralization: The cognitive-developmental approach. In T. Lickona (Ed.), *Moral development and behavior: Theory research, and social issues* (pp. 84-107). New York: Holt, Rinehart, & Winston.

Leahy, R. L. (1979). Development of conceptions of prosocial behavior: Information affecting rewards given for altruism and kindness. *Developmental Psychology, 15,* 34-37.

Lennon, R., & Eisenberg, N. (1987). Gender and age differences in empathy and sympathy. In N. Eisenberg & J. Strayer (Eds.), *Empathy and its development* (pp. 195-217). Cambridge, UK: Cambridge University Press.

Levin, I., & Bekerman-Greenberg, R. (1980). Moral judgment and moral reasoning in sharing: A developmental analysis. *Genetic Psychological Monographs, 101,* 215-230.

Loevinger, J., & Wessler, R. (1970). *Measuring ego development* (Vol. I). San Francisco: Jossey-Bass.

Lowe, R., & Ritchey, G. (1973). Relation of altruism to age, social class, and ethnic identity. *Psychological Reports, 33,* 567-572.

Lyons, N. P. (1983). Two perspectives: On self, relationships, and morality. *Harvard Educational Review, 53,* 125-145.

Marcia,, J. E. (1980). Identity on adolescence. In J. Adelson (Ed.), *Handbook of adolescent psychology.* New York: John Wiley.

Marsh, D. T. (1982). The development of interpersonal problem solving among elementary school children. *Journal of Genetic Psychology, 140,* 107-118.

Midlarsky, E., & Hannah, M. E. (1985). Competence, reticence, and helping by children and adolescents. *Developmental Psychology, 21,* 534-541.

Moore, B. S., & Eisenberg, N. (1984). The development of altruism. In G. Whitehurst (Ed.), *Annals of child development* (pp. 107-174). Greenwich: JA1 Press.

O'Connor, M. & Cuevas, J. (1982). The relationship of children's prosocial behavior to social responsibility, prosocial reasoning, and personality. *Journal of Genetic Psychology, 140,* 33-45.

O'Connor, M., Cuevas, J. & Dollinger, S. (1981). Understanding motivations behind prosocial acts: A developmental hypothesis. *Journal of Genetic Psychology, 39,* 267-276.

Payne, F. D. (1980). Children's prosocial conduct in structured situations and as viewed by others: Consistency, convergence and relationships with person variables. *Child Development, 51,* 1252-1259.

Peterson, L. (1983a). Influence of age, task competence, and responsibility focus on children's altruism. *Developmental Psychology, 19,* 141-148.

Peterson, L. (1983b). Role of donor competence, donor age, and peer presence on helping on an emergency. *Developmental Psychology, 19,* 873-880.

Peterson, L., & Gelfand, D. M. (1984). Causal attributions of helping as a function of age and incentives. *Child Development, 55,* 504-511.

Podd, M. H. (1972). Ego identity status and morality. The relationship between two developmental constructs. *Developmental Psychology, 6,* 497-507.

Radke-Yarrow, M., Zahn-Waxler, C., & Chapman, M. (1983). Prosocial dispositions and behavior. In P. Mussen (Ed.), *Manual of child psychology* (Vol. 4). *Socialization, personality, and social development* (E. M. Hetherington, Ed.) (pp. 469-545). New York: John Wiley.

Rest, J. R. (1979). Development in judging moral issues. Minneapolis, University of Minnesota Press.

Rholes, W. S., & Lane, J. W. (1985). Consistency between cognitions and behavior: Cause and consequence of cognitive moral development. In J. B. Pryor & J. D. Day (Eds.), *The development of social cognition* (pp. 97-114). New York: Springer-Verlag.

Rowe, I., & Marcia, J. E. (1980). Ego identity status, formal operations, and moral development. *Journal of Youth and Adolescence, 9,* 87-99.

Savin-Williams, R. C., Small, S. A., & Zeldin, R. S. (1981). *Ethology and Sociobiology, 2,* 167-176.

Selman, R. L. (1975). Level of social perspective taking and the development of empathy in children: Speculations from a social-cognitive viewpoint. *Journal of Moral Education, 5,* 35-43.

Selman, R. L. (1980). *The growth of interpersonal understanding: Developmental and clinical analyses.* New York: Academic Press.

Selman, R. L., & Demorest, A. P. (1984). Observing troubled children's interpersonal negotiation strategies: Implications of and for a developmental model. *Child Development, 55,* 288-304.

Shure, M. B. (1980). Interpersonal problem solving in ten-year-olds. Final grant report to the National Institute of Mental Health (grant #R01 MH27741).

Small, S. A., Zeldin, R. S., & Savin-Williams, R. C. (1983). In search of personality traits: A multimethod analysis of naturally occurring prosocial and dominance behavior. *Journal of Personality, 51,* 1-16.

Staub, E. (1970). A child in distress: The influence of age and number of witnesses on children's attempts to help. *Journal of Personality and Social Psychology, 14,* 130-140.

Staub, E. (1978). *Positive social behavior and morality.* Vol. 1. *Social and personal influences.* New York: Academic Press.

Staub, E. (1979). *Positive social behavior and morality.* Vol. 2. *Socialization and development.* New York: Academic Press.

Steinberg, L. D., Greenberger, E., Garduque, L., Ruggiero, M., & Vaux, A. (1982). Effects of working on adolescent development. *Developmental Psychology, 18,* 385-395.

Suls, J., Witenberg, S., & Gutkin, D. (1981). Evaluating reciprocal and nonreciprocal prosocial behavior: Developmental changes. *Personality and Social Psychology Bulletin, 7,* 25-31.

Turiel, E. (1969). Developmental processes in the child's moral thinking. In P. Mussen, J. Langer, & M. Covington (Eds.), *Trends and issues in developmental psychology* (pp. 92-133). New York: Holt, Rinehart, & Winston.

Ugurel-Semin, R. (1952). Moral behavior and moral judgment of children. *Journal of Abnormal and Social Psychology, 47,* 463-474.

Underwood, B., & Moore, B. S. (1982a). The generality of altruism in children. In N. Eisenberg (Ed.), *The development of prosocial behavior.* (pp. 25-52). New York: Academic Press.

Underwood, B., & Moore, B. S. (1982b). Perspective-taking and altruism. *Psychological Bulletin, 91,* 143-173.

Walker, L. J. (1989). A longitudinal study of moral orientation. *Child Development, 60,* 157-166.

Waterman, A. S. (1982). Identity development from adolescence to adulthood: An extension of theory and a review of research. *Developmental Psychology, 18,* 341-358.

Weiner, B. (1986). *An attributional theory of motivation and emotion.* New York: Springer-Verlag.

Youniss, J. (1980). *Parents and peers in social development: A Sullivan-Piaget perspective.* Chicago: University of Chicago Press.

Youniss, J., & Smollar, J. (1985). *Adolescent relations with mothers, fathers, and friends.* Chicago: University of Chicago Press.

Zeldin, R. S., Savin-Williams, R. C., & Small, S. A. (1984). Adolescent prosocial behavior in a naturalistic context. *Journal of Social Psychology.*

Zeldin, R. S., Small, S. A., & Savin-Williams, R. C. (1982). Prosocial interactions in two mixed-sex adolescent groups. *Child Development, 53,* 1492-1498.

Zern, D. S. (1985). The expressed preference of different ages of adolescents for assistance in the development of moral issues. *Adolescence, XX,* 405-423.

11. Distinctive Features and Effects of Early Adolescent Friendships

Thomas J. Berndt
Purdue University

T. Bridgett Perry
Framingham State University

When early adolescents talk about their closest friendships, the importance they attach to these relationships is abundantly clear. We asked the eighth graders in one study (Berndt, Hawkins, & Hoyle, 1986) to describe one particularly close friendship. One eighth-grade girl replied by saying, "I can tell Karen (her friend) things and she helps me talk. If we have problems in school, we work them out together. And she doesn't laugh at me if I do something weird—she accepts me for who I am." In short, this girl perceived her friendship as a valuable and supportive relationship.

Interactions between friends are not always supportive. Adolescents have conflicts with friends as well. When we asked the same eighth grader about problems in her friendship with Karen, she replied, "When she's in a bad mood, she ignores you and yells at you and sulks—I hate it when people sulk. And she likes to be everybody's boss—she puts herself above other people that aren't as good as she is." These comments show that adolescents attach considerable emotional energy both to the problems and to the joys of their friendships.

Despite the evident significance of friendships to adolescents themselves, psychologists and other social scientists virtually ignored these relationships until the 1970s. In the early 1930s, Piaget (1932/1965) discussed the impact of peer relationships on the development of morality in later childhood and early adolescence, but he did not distinguish between friendships and less intense relationships between peers. Two decades later, Harry Stack Sullivan (1953), a neo-Freudian psychiatrist, extolled the benefits of friendships in later childhood and early adolescence. His comments on friendship were brief, however, and not linked to any explicit theory of developmental processes. Even so, many researchers took Sullivan's ideas as a theoretical basis for their studies of friendship. For this reason, we discuss Sullivan's views in more detail later in the chapter.

Perhaps the most important reason for the surge in research on adolescent friendships during the 1970s was simply the desire of researchers to understand more of an adolescent's social world. That is, researchers aimed less at testing specific theories than at learning about the nature of friendship. Moreover, researchers assumed that friendships significant *to* adolescents were likely to be significant *for* their development. As information about the nature of friendships increased, researchers began to formulate more explicit hypotheses about the effects of friendships on adolescents' development.

Our main goal in this chapter is to review current knowledge about friendships in early adolescence. In the first section of the chapter, we consider the findings of research on the features of early adolescent friendships. We begin with a brief description of the similarities between early adolescents' friendships and those of younger children. Then we examine the distinctive features of early adolescent friendships, that is, ways in which early adolescent friendships are different from those found at other ages.

In the next two sections of the chapter, we focus on the effects of friendship. We first consider the research on friends' influence. That is, we review research designed to investigate how adolescents are influenced by the attitudes and behavior of their friends. If friendships have distinctive features in early adolescence, friends' influence might be distinctive in its strength or its patterning during this age period. We give special attention to evidence on this hypothesis.

In the third section, we examine a radically different perspective on the effects of friendship. Many theorists and researchers have suggested that children and adolescents are affected by the degree of support or the amount of conflict in their relationships, independent of the friends' own characteristics (Berndt, 1989; Berndt & Ladd, 1989; Youniss & Smollar, 1985). We examine this perspective on the effects of friendship in the third section of the chapter. Once again, we give special attention to questions about the importance of friendship features in early adolescence versus other age periods.

In a brief fourth section of the chapter, we identify promising new directions for research on friendship. We focus particularly on the need for research that explores the connections between adolescents' friendships and their status in the larger peer group of a classroom or school.

FRIENDSHIPS IN CHILDHOOD AND ADOLESCENCE

Common Features of Children's and Adolescents' Friendships

Before we consider the distinctive features of early adolescent friendships, we should mention important features of friendships that hold across a wide age range. Friendship refers to a relationship between two (or more) individuals who like each other. Even preschool children understand that mutual liking is part of the definition of friendship (see Berndt, 1988). In addition, children and adolescents agree that friends are helpful to each other. This feature of friendship is expressed in the old adage, "A friend in need is a friend in deed." Friends also spend large amounts of time interacting with each other: friends are companions for each other.

In one study (Berndt et al., 1986), fourth graders made as many comments as eighth graders about their liking for their friends and the frequency of sharing, helping, and other types of prosocial behavior by friends. In a second study (Berndt & Perry, 1986), children and adolescents from the second through the eighth grade made roughly as many comments about friends' prosocial behavior and their frequency of interactions with friends. These results suggest that the core definition of friendship as a relationship of mutual liking, mutual assistance, and frequent interactions applies equally well to friendships in middle childhood and in early adolescence.

There are also similarities in the actual behavior of children and adolescents with their friends. For example, Newcomb and Brady (1982) found that pairs of second-grade boys who were close friends showed as much talking, laughing, and smiling with each other as did sixth-grade boys who were close friends. In several other studies (see Berndt, 1987), the frequency of talking, smiling, joking, and other kinds of positive interactions between friends did not change consistently between middle childhood and early adolescence. Thus several positive aspects of friends' interactions are as apparent during middle childhood as during early adolescence.

Worth noting, briefly, is limited evidence on the negative features or conflicts in friendships. The available data suggest that conflicts or problems in friendships are equally common in childhood and adolescence. In one study (Berndt et al., 1986), eighth graders made approximately as many negative comments about the friendships as did fourth graders. In another study (Berndt & Perry, 1986), ratings of conflicts with friends changed little between second and eighth grade. In friends' interactions, disagreements, criticism, and other indicators of conflict occur as often in childhood as in early adolescence (see Berndt, 1987).

Finally, the stability of friendships does not change dramatically between childhood and adolescence (Berndt and Hoyle, 1985). Most friendships among elementary-school children and adolescents last for several months at least. By contrast, Epstein (1986) suggested friendship stability increases with age but is low even in adolescence. She based this conclusion on several studies done a few decades ago, however, that seem to have methodological flaws (see Berndt & Hoyle, 1985).

Distinctive Features of Early Adolescent Friendships

The research reviewed in the preceding section illustrates that the core meaning of friendship changes little between childhood and adolescence. Other aspects of friendship, such as the frequency of positive interactions between friends and the stability of friendship itself, show substantial continuity between childhood and adulthood. What, then, are the distinctive features of early adolescent friendships? How much do friendships change in the transition to adolescence? Researchers have identified several differences between early adolescents' friendships and those of younger children. Three of these differences seem especially significant. The following statements summarize the evidence on these developments in friendship.

1. *Early adolescents view their friendships as intimate and supportive relationships more often than do younger children.* When early adolescents are asked how they can tell that someone is their best friend, they often say that the friend shares problems with them, understands them, and will listen when they talk about their feelings (e.g., Berndt, 1981; Youniss & Smollar, 1985). In addition, early adolescents mention the intimate sharing of confidences when describing their own friendships. The eighth-grade girl quoted at the beginning of the chapter illustrated this feature of friendship when she said, "I can tell Karen (her friend) things and she helps me talk." When younger children describe their friendships, they rarely refer to intimate self-disclosure or mutual understanding.

Sullivan (1953) proposed that friendships increase in their intimacy during the preadolescent years, most often between the ages of 8 and 10. Recent studies, however, have confirmed the early results of

Douvan and Adelson (1966) in showing that intimacy first becomes important in friendships in early adolescence. The age change is evident not only in children's and adolescents' responses to open-ended questions about friendship (e.g., Berndt et al., 1986), but also in their ratings of statements about intimacy (e.g., Berndt & Perry, 1986; Furman & Bierman, 1984; but see Bukowski, Newcomb, & Hoza, 1987). Moreover, one study (Gottman & Mettetal, 1986) showed a significant increase with age in the intimacy of actual conversations between friends.

Douvan and Adelson (1966) found that intimacy was more central to the friendships of girls than boys. This finding has been replicated in many but not all studies of friendship (e.g., Buhrmester & Furman, 1987; Bukowski et al., 1987). Whether boys lag behind girls in developing intimate friendships, or never develop friendships that on the average are as intimate as girls' friendships, is not yet clear (see Youniss & Smollar, 1985).

Berndt (1989) pointed out that intimacy is a key element of what Cohen and Wills (1985) and other theorists defined as supportive social relationships. Cohen and Wills reviewed an extensive body of research that has demonstrated the impact of supportive relationships on the physical and psychological health of adults. This research can be linked to the comments of Sullivan (1953) and other writers (e.g., Youniss, 1980) about the positive consequences of intimate friendships among adolescents. The evidence on this issue is reviewed later in the chapter.

2. *Early adolescents regard loyalty or faithfulness as more critical in friendships than do younger children.* Adolescents often say that good friends stand up for them when around other people. For example, they say that a friend would "stick up for you in a fight" and "not talk about you [to other people] behind your back." Most important, a best friend would not "leave you for somebody else." Comments of this kind refer implicitly to the obligations of a friend when in the midst of a larger peer group. These obligations reflect the common sense meanings of loyalty and faithfulness.

Early adolescents talk more about loyalty and faithfulness when describing their ideas about friendships than younger children do (Berndt, 1981). In children's and adolescents' reports on their own friendships, age differences in comments about loyalty are not always significant (Berndt et al., 1986; Berndt & Perry, 1986). Especially in adolescence, girls express more concern about the disloyalty or unfaithfulness of friends than do boys (Berndt, 1981; Berndt et al., 1986).

Although the evidence on developmental changes in concerns with loyalty is inconsistent, more research on this feature of friendship is warranted. Concerns with loyalty reflect an awareness of the links between dyadic friendships and the peer group as a whole. These links may assume special importance in early adolescence as cliques become more visible and acquire more distinct identities (Brown, 1989). Thus a better understanding of loyalty in friendship could clarify the place of friendships in the social world of peers.

3. *Under conditions in which competition and sharing are opposed to each other, early adolescents compete less and share more equally with friends than younger children do.* Several researchers have shown that under certain conditions young children compete more and share less with friends than with classmates who are not close friends (see Berndt, 1986). Children are likely to compete rather than to share equally with friends when they believe that they are in a contest that they might lose if they shared equally.

Berndt and his colleagues (1986) found that the tendency of friends to compete rather than to share equally with each other reversed between middle childhood and early adolescence. In their study, fourth graders who were close friends with each other shared less and competed more on an experimental task than did fourth graders who had been close friends a few months before but were no longer close friends. By contrast, eighth graders who were close friends shared more and competed less than eighth graders who were no longer close friends.

Piaget (1932/1965) suggested that peer relationships are based on equality. Berndt (1986) argued that children and adolescents especially like to view themselves as equal to their friends. Problems arise in friendships when this presumption of equality is challenged. The eighth grader quoted at the beginning of the chapter referred to these problems when she said, "she [her friend] likes to be everybody's boss—she puts herself above other people that aren't as good as she is."

When children or adolescents are engaged in a contest with a friend, they face the prospect of losing and so seeming inferior to the friend. According to Berndt et al. (1986), children often respond to this prospect by competing intensely with friends. Early adolescents, by contrast, respond by aiming for equality through equal sharing. The age change in behavior may rest upon a growing sensitivity to a friend's needs and desires (cf. Sullivan, 1953). Alternatively, the change may reflect increasing cognitive sophistication that helps adolescents devise strategies for maintaining equality without risking the conflicts that competition can pose in a relationship. More research is needed on this issue. Research is especially needed in natural settings, because the age change in friends' motives and behavior has so far been demonstrated only in a restricted range of experimental conditions.

In summary, recent studies illustrate three distinctive features of early adolescent friendships. Adolescents have more intimate friendships than do younger children. Adolescents value loyalty or faithfulness in friendships more than do younger children. Adolescents also show a greater preference than younger children for equal sharing over competition with friends. Our next question is whether these distinctive features of early adolescent friendship have implications for the effects of friendships on adolescents' behavior and adjustment.

FRIENDS' SIMILARITY AND FRIENDS' INFLUENCE

Questions about the effects of friendship have a long history. During most of this history, these questions were not phrased in terms of the features of friendship that we have emphasized. Instead, they were phrased in terms of the impact of friends' pressure. This pressure was typically viewed as negative in its direction and effects. Adolescents were regarded, for example, as conforming to peer pressure to engage in delinquent behavior and to limit their effort in academic activities (Bronfenbrenner, 1970; Coleman, 1961).

During the 1970s, theories of friends' influence were refined. Researchers began to focus not on supposedly uniform effects of friends' influence but on the varying influences of specific friends with varying characteristics. Adolescents whose best friends smoked marijuana, for example, were assumed to be influenced by those friends and, therefore, to be more likely to smoke marijuana themselves (e.g., Kandel, 1978b). Adolescents whose best friends received relatively high grades in school, by contrast, were assumed to be influenced by those friends in a positive direction so that they began to receive higher grades themselves (e.g., Ide, Parkerson, Haertel, & Walberg, 1981).

As the examples imply, researchers who emphasize the influence of the attitudes and behaviors of specific friends assume that this influence makes friends more similar to each other. Adolescents may, for example, begin to smoke marijuana just as their friends do. Adolescents may begin to get high grades in school just as their friends do.

For this reason, the similarity between friends on particular characteristics has often been used as an index of their influence on each other (e.g., Ide et al., 1981).

Of course, not all similarities between friends are due to their influence on each other. Adolescents may also select as friends other adolescents whose attitudes and behaviors are similar to their own. To determine how much the similarity between friends on any characteristic is due to selection versus influence, longitudinal studies are required. In a longitudinal study, the selection that makes friends similar initially can be distinguished from the influence that increases friends' similarity over time. Increases over time in friends' similarity on various attitudes and behaviors have been documented in a few longitudinal studies (e.g., Epstein, 1983; Kandel, 1978a).

The crucial question for this chapter is still more specific. We would like to know whether friends' influence is stronger or weaker in early adolescence than in middle childhood. Thus, we need to know if the similarity between friends increases over time to a greater or lesser degree in early adolescence than in other age periods.

Unfortunately, the data necessary to answer this question are unavailable. Moreover, the most relevant data are inconsistent. Berndt, Miller, and Laychak (in preparation) examined the similarity between friends on three measures of school adjustment: involvement in class activities, disruptive behavior in class, and actual report-card grades. To determine whether friends' similarity on these measures varied across adolescence, the study included fifth graders, eighth graders, and eleventh graders. The similarity between friends in report-card grades was equally great at fifth, eighth, and eleventh grade. The friends' similarity in disruptive behavior was greater, however, at eighth grade than at fifth or eleventh grade. The friends' similarity in involvement was also greater at eighth grade than at eleventh grade but was not significantly different at fifth and eighth grade. The results for involvement and disruption imply that friends' influence on school-related activities and behavior is greatest at eighth grade, somewhat weaker at fifth grade, and very weak at eleventh grade. This conclusion must be considered tentative, however, because the study had a strictly correlational design. The measures of friends' similarity thus reflect some combination of selection and influence rather than influence by itself.

Chassin, Presson, Montello, Sherman, and McGrew (1986) argued forcefully that no valid conclusions about friends' influence can be drawn from similarity correlations in cross-sectional studies. They also reported results of a longitudinal study that they interpreted as showing no significant change between sixth and twelfth grade in the influence of friends on adolescents' cigarette smoking. Their findings cannot be treated as definitive because they did not assess the actual similarity in smoking between adolescents and their friends. Instead, they asked adolescents to report on their friends' smoking. Thus, they had data on *perceived* rather than *actual* similarity in smoking. Previous studies have shown there can be little relation between the perceived and actual similarity of adolescents and their friends (Wilcox & Udry, 1986).

Because of the limitations of the existing data on friends' similarity, no firm conclusions can be drawn about the relative influence of friends' characteristics in early adolescence versus other age periods. Data obtained with other methods suggests that friends' influence may peak in early or middle adolescence (Berndt, 1979; Steinberg & Silverberg, 1986), but inconsistencies in those data also exist (cf. Brown, Clasen, & Eicher, 1986). One goal of future research should be to examine friends' influence using more naturalistic methods that shed more light on the processes of influence in adolescents' peer groups. The participant-observation technique of Sherif and Sherif (1964) could be especially illuminating.

EFFECTS OF FRIENDSHIP FEATURES

The effects of friendship cannot be adequately assessed by examining only the influence of having friends with particular characteristics. Attention must also be given to the features of these friendships. In recent years, several theorists have suggested that certain kinds of friendships, those high in intimacy and emotional support, have positive effects on adolescents' social and personality development (e.g., Berndt, 1989; Youniss, 1980). A few theorists have also suggested that friendships marked by frequent conflicts have negative effects on social adjustment and development (see Berndt, 1989; Rook, 1984).

The central question in this chapter is still more specific: Are the effects of friends' support and conflicts with friends greater in early adolescence than at other age periods? As we discuss the findings of recent studies, we will highlight the evidence on this question.

The first step in testing hypotheses about the effects of friendship features is showing that these features are related to important aspects of personality or social adjustment. Sullivan (1953) suggested that early adolescents with intimate friendships should have higher self-esteem than those who do not, and data consistent with this hypothesis have been reported (e.g., McGuire & Weisz, 1982). More recently, Perry (1987) found that eighth graders who described their friendship groups more positively had higher self-esteem. These eighth graders also were less lonely and had more positive impressions of their social, athletic, and academic competence. By contrast, students who reported more conflicts in their friendship groups had lower self-esteem, were more lonely, and described their own conduct and their academic competence less positively.

Miller and Berndt (1987) reported relations between the features of seventh-graders' friendships and their adjustment to school. The seventh graders who described their friendships as having more positive features also said they were more involved in school and valued school more. In addition, they received higher grades. The seventh graders who described their friendships as having more conflicts or negative features reported lower involvement in school, placed a lower value on their schoolwork, and perceived their own competence as lower. The results of this study and the previous studies confirm that students' descriptions of the features of their friendships are related to various aspects of their behavior and adjustment.

The second step in testing hypotheses about the effects of friendship features is to go beyond correlations and see if variations in friendship are causally related to variations in adjustment. Testing hypotheses about causal relationships is best done with experimental designs. Experimental manipulation of the features of actual friendships is difficult, however. A feasible alternative is to use longitudinal designs and assess the relations of friendship features to changes in adjustment over time.

In a longitudinal study of sixth graders moving from elementary school to junior high school (Berndt & Hawkins, 1987), significant relations were found between students' reports on their friendships at one time and changes in their adjustment over time. In particular, students who described their friendships more positively in sixth grade had more positive reputations with peers after the transition to junior high. Students who described their friendships more positively during the fall term of seventh grade increased in their popularity between the fall and the spring. These relations of friendship to changes in adjustment are consistent with the hypothesis that close and supportive friendships have beneficial effects on adolescents' social adjustment in school.

To address the central question in this chapter, we need to take still a third step. In particular, we need to determine if the effects of friendship features on adjustment are especially strong (or especially weak) in early adolescence. Apparently, no researchers have yet taken this step. The most relevant data come from a study discussed earlier in the chapter (Berndt, Miller, & Laychak, in preparation).

Fifth, eighth, and eleventh graders reported both on their friendships and on their attitudes and behavior in school. The measures of friendship and of school-related attitudes and behavior were significantly correlated only at fifth and eighth grade. Students at these grades who described their friendships as having more negative features placed a lower value on doing well in school and said that they were more disruptive in school. The students' reports on the positive features of their friendships were not significantly related to measures of their own attitudes and behavior, but students who described their friendships more positively had friends who were rated by teachers as more involved in school. At eleventh grade, none of the correlations between the measures of friendship and school adjustment was significant. The differences in the correlations across grade levels suggest that the features of adolescents' friendships have stronger effects on their adjustment to school in early or middle adolescence than in late adolescence.

Of course, data from a single study must be interpreted cautiously. Because the study had a correlational rather than a longitudinal design, firm conclusions about the *effects* of friendship on adjustment cannot be drawn. Moreover, the findings may be specific to measures of school adjustment. The effects of friendship features on other aspects of adjustment may be stronger in late adolescence than in early adolescence. More research is needed on the relations, over time, of friendship features to various aspects of adolescents' adjustment. More refined hypotheses are needed about the effects of support from friends and conflicts with friends on specific aspects of adjustment.

FRIENDSHIP AND PEER STATUS: NEW DIRECTIONS IN RESEARCH

The literature on adolescents' friendships overlaps surprisingly little with a vast literature on the nature and consequences of popularity or status in adolescents' peer groups (cf. Berndt, 1988; Brown, 1989; Bukowski & Hoza, 1989; Parker & Asher, 1987). Indeed, some researchers have suggested that there is little relation between the features of adolescents' friendships and their popularity in a larger group (McGuire & Weisz, 1982). Evidence from recent studies indicates that this conclusion must be qualified in two important ways.

First, there is a relation between adolescents' own status in the peer group and the status of their friends. The third and seventh graders in one study (Perry, 1986) who were more popular with their classmates also had more popular friends. Moreover, the similarity in friends' popularity was greater at seventh grade than at third grade. Third and seventh graders who were "socially neglected," or not known by many of their classmates, often had friends who were high in social neglect. Closer analyses showed that friends' similarity in social neglect was strongest for seventh-grade girls. Apparently, adolescent girls who are (or are not) well known by their classmates tend to make friends with other girls in the same situation. Previous research implied that stereotypes about cliquishness among adolescent girls contain a kernel of truth (Eder, 1985), and Perry's findings may reflect part of that truth.

Third and seventh graders who were rejected or disliked by many of their classmates often named friends who were also rejected, but this effect was strongest for seventh-grade boys. The reason for the sex difference is not clear, but the difference between third and seventh graders is consistent with the general trend for greater similarity in friends' social status during adolescence than during middle childhood. In other words, these findings illustrate another distinctive feature of early adolescents' friendships, namely, a stronger connection between friendship selection and peer status than in middle childhood.

Second, recent data indicate that peer status is related to the features of adolescents' friendships. Perry (1987) found that eighth graders who were more popular with their peers viewed their relationships with their friendship groups more positively. They also reported fewer conflicts with friends. Eighth graders who were more rejected by peers viewed their friendship groups as high in conflict but not as lacking in positive features. Eighth graders who were socially neglected viewed their friendship groups as low in positive features but not as high in conflicts. This pattern of relationships is consistent with previous descriptions of the behavioral profiles of popular, rejected, and neglected children (see Bukowski & Hoza, 1989; Parker

& Asher, 1987). The new findings extend previous research by showing that adolescents' status in the peer group is associated not only with their behavior toward classmates but also with the features of their friendships.

Many important questions about the relations of friendships to social status remain to be answered. For example, the relations of popular, rejected, and neglected adolescents' perceptions of their friendships to their actual behavior toward friends have not been examined. In addition, there are reports that some adolescents consciously select friends who are high in status as a tactic for affiliating with the high-status group and becoming more popular themselves (Hirsch & Renders, 1985). The characteristics of adolescents who adopt this strategy are largely unknown. Finally, the means by which demands for loyalty and faithfulness from friends are adjusted in response to changes in friendship or the friends' status have not been explored. Research on these questions could integrate the research on friendship and on peer status. This integration would add immensely to our understanding of the nature and functioning of peer relationships in adolescence.

SUMMARY AND CONCLUSIONS

Early adolescence is the starting point for the transition from childhood to adulthood. Friendships are linked to this transition in two contrasting ways. First, friendships themselves are transformed between childhood and early adolescence into more complex, psychologically richer, and more adultlike relationships. Second, friendships have an influence on the changes in self-perceptions, attitudes, and behavior that accompany the transition from childhood to adulthood. Recent research findings make it possible to sketch in broad outline the complementary roles of friendships as part of, and as contributors to, the transitions associated with early adolescence. The research has important limitations, however, that must be acknowledged. As we consider these limitations, we will also consider new research approaches that would be valuable.

The transformation in friendships at the transition to adolescence is not total. Throughout childhood and adolescence, friendships are defined by mutual liking, mutual assistance or prosocial behavior, and frequent interactions. Friendships are not always harmonious relationships, but early adolescents report conflicts with friends roughly as often as do younger children. When interacting with friends, young children display behaviors that reflect the existence of a mutual positive relationship as often as early adolescents do. Finally, the stability of friendships is not markedly higher or lower in early adolescence than in middle childhood. In all these ways, friendships show continuity across the transition from childhood to adolescence.

Nevertheless, early adolescent friendships have several distinctive features. Most important theoretically is the salience of intimacy in these friendships. Early adolescents describe their friendships as intimate relationships more often than do younger children. In addition, early adolescents regard loyalty or faithfulness as more critical in friendships than do younger children. Under conditions in which younger children compete rather than share equally with friends, early adolescents are likely to choose equal sharing over competition.

Because this chapter is focused on the transition into adolescence, we have most often compared the friendships of early adolescents and younger children. We need to note, however, that the distinctive features of early adolescents' friendships are not unique to that phase of the life span. Intimacy and loyalty remain important in friendships during late adolescence and adulthood (cf. Sharabany, Gershoni, & Hofman, 1981; Youniss & Smollar, 1985). The balance between competition and prosocial behavior not only affects early adolescents' friendships; it also affects friendships and other close personal relationships in adulthood (Tesser, 1984). Thus when early adolescents add these features to their friendships, they begin the transition to adultlike relationships.

The intermediate status of early adolescence was suggested in Sullivan (1953). He argued, in particular, that the development of intimacy in early adolescents' same-sex friendships precedes and sets the stage for intimacy in heterosexual relationships later in adolescence. This developmental progression has not been adequately examined, because most studies of friendships have focused on same-sex friendships (but see Sharabany et al., 1981). To understand fully the transitional status of early adolescent friendships, the connections between early same-sex friendships and later cross-sex friendships or romantic relationships must be explored.

Researchers also need to explore the nature of early adolescent friendships with new research methods. Our current knowledge of the features of friendship rests heavily on adolescents' responses to interviews or questionnaires. Most studies of the age change toward more intimate friendships, for example, assessed intimacy from adolescents' verbal reports on their friendships. Although there have been a few studies of friends' actual behavior toward each other (and these studies have largely confirmed the veracity of adolescents' verbal reports), more detailed information about friends' interactions is needed.

Ethnographic research would be a valuable complement to the previous studies of adolescents' verbal reports and behavior in structured settings. Researchers should attempt to find ways to observe friends' interactions in natural settings over time. A few researchers have observed adolescent peer groups in natural settings (e.g., Eder, 1985; Fine, 1987; Sherif & Sherif, 1964). Adapting their methods and focusing specifically on close friendships could be extremely rewarding.

With greater knowledge of early adolescent friendships, researchers would be better equipped to answer questions about the effects of friendships on adolescents' behavior and development. Until recently, most research on the effects of friendship focused on the influence of a friend's attitudes and behavior. Currently, most theorists and researchers assume that influence between friends is a mutual process that leads over time to an increase in the friends' similarity in attitudes and behavior.

Previous research has shown that adolescents' drug use, delinquency, achievement motivation, and other important attitudes and behaviors are influenced by friends. Yet little is known about age changes in the magnitude of this influence. A few studies suggest that friends' influence peaks in early or middle adolescence; other studies do not show dramatic changes during adolescence in the apparent influence of friends.

Because of the theoretical and practical importance of questions about friends' influence, more research on these questions is needed. The new research should be more firmly based on theories and research regarding the features of adolescent friendships. In retrospect, it is astonishing that researchers have conducted large-scale investigations of friends' influence on adolescents without including any assessments of the relationships between adolescents and their friends. We might assume, for example, that stable friendships are more influential than unstable friendships. In most studies, however, the duration of adolescents' friendships was not assessed (but see Epstein, 1983). Similarly, we might expect adolescents to be particularly influenced by friends with whom they have an intimate relationship based on mutual understanding and support. A direct test of this hypothesis could clarify if the emergence of intimate friendships in early adolescence is associated with an increasing influence of friends' attitudes and behaviors on adolescents.

The features of adolescents' friendships may have a still more direct effect on their behavior and development. The intimate and supportive friendships formed in early adolescence may themselves contribute positively to the social and personality development of children and adolescents. Adolescents who describe their friendships as high in intimacy and other positive features also have higher self-esteem, more positive perceptions of their competence, and a better adjustment to school. Adolescents who describe their friendships as having more conflicts and negative features have lower self-esteem, greater loneliness, and a poorer adjustment to school. Moreover, in one study of adolescents making the transition to junior high school, supportive and harmonious friendships appeared to have a causal influence on improvements in school adjustment.

Do harmonious friendships have more positive effects on adolescents' behavior and adjustment during early adolescence than during middle childhood or later adolescence? Do problems or conflicts in friendships have more damaging effects during early adolescence than during other age periods? The data from one recent study suggest that the answers to these questions are "yes," but additional data are needed. Current evidence is largely correlational and does not provide a firm foundation for conclusions about the influence of specific features of friendship. Moreover, we know little about the processes by which support from friends promotes adjustment or problems with friends impairs adjustment. Once again, these processes may be easiest to identify when researchers use ethnographic methods to study friendships in natural settings.

Researchers must also recognize that an exclusive focus on friendships provides a fragmentary view of adolescents' social world, even the world of peer relationships. Friendships normally exist within a larger social structure of peer relationships. In the larger social structure, each adolescent has a more or less well-defined status. Friendships are not independent of peer status. Friends tend to be similar in their status in the larger group. In addition, the similarity in friends' status increases between middle childhood and early adolescence.

Peer status is related to the features of adolescents' friendships. Adolescents who are more popular with peers typically have more supportive friendships; adolescents who are disliked by many of their peers tend to have conflicts with friends, too. The empirical investigation of the connections between friendships and peer status is just beginning. Investigations of this kind can establish the place of close friendships in larger networks of peer relationships and contribute to a more integrated view of the social world of the early adolescent peer group. If parallel studies are done of younger children, the results will be doubly valuable in enriching our understanding of the changes in peer relationships during the transition to adolescence.

REFERENCES

Berndt, T. J. (1979). Developmental changes in conformity to peers and parents. *Developmental Psychology, 15,* 608-616.

Berndt, T. J. (1981). Relations between social cognition, nonsocial cognition, and social behavior: The case of friendship. In J. H. Flavell and L. D. Ross (Eds.), *Social cognitive development: Frontiers and possible futures* (pp. 176-199). Cambridge, UK: Cambridge University Press.

Berndt, T. J. (1986). Sharing between friends: Contexts and consequences. In E. C. Mueller & C. R. Cooper (Eds.), *Process and outcome in peer relationships* (pp. 105-127). New York: Academic Press.

Berndt, T. J. (1987). The distinctive features of conversations between friends: Theories, research, and implications for sociomoral development. In W. M. Kurtines & J. L. Gewirtz (Eds.), *Moral development through social interaction* (pp. 281-300). New York: John Wiley.

Berndt, T. J. (1988). The nature and significance of children's friendships. In R. Vasta (Ed.), *Annals of child development* (Vol. 5, pp. 155-186). Greenwich, CT: JAI Press.

Berndt, T. J. (1989). Obtaining support from friends in childhood and adolescence. In D. Belle (Ed.), *Children's social networks and social supports* (pp. 308-331). New York: John Wiley.

Berndt, T. J., & Hawkins, J. A. (1987). *The contribution of supportive friendships to adjustment after the transition to junior high school.* Unpublished manuscript, Purdue University.

Berndt, T. J., Hawkins, J. A., & Hoyle, S. G. (1986). Changes in friendship during a school year: Effects on children's and adolescents' impressions of friendship and sharing with friends. *Child Development, 57,* 1284-1297.

Berndt, T. J., & Hoyle, S. G. (1985). Stability and change in childhood and adolescent friendships. *Developmental Psychology, 21,* 1007-1015.

Berndt, T. J., & Ladd, G. W. (Eds.). (1989). *Peer relationships in child development.* New York: John Wiley.

Berndt, T. J., & Perry, T. B. (1986). Children's perceptions of friendships as supportive relationships. *Developmental Psychology, 22,* 640-648.

Bronfenbrenner, U. (1970). *Two worlds of childhood.* New York: Russell Sage.

Brown, B. B. (1989). The role of peer groups in adolescents' adjustment to secondary school. In T. J. Berndt & G. W. Ladd (Eds.), *Peer relationships in child development* (pp. 188-215). New York: John Wiley.

Brown, B. B., Clasen, D. R., & Eicher, S. A. (1986). Perceptions of peer pressure, peer conformity dispositions, and self-reported behavior among adolescents. *Developmental Psychology, 22,* 521-530.

Buhrmester, D., & Furman, W. (1987). The development of companionship and intimacy. *Child Development, 58,* 1101-1113.

Bukowski, W. M., & Hoza, B. (1989). Popularity and friendship: Issues in theory, measurement, and outcome. In T. J. Berndt & G. W. Ladd (Eds.), *Peer relationships in child development* (pp. 15-45). New York: John Wiley.

Bukowski, W. M., Newcomb, A. F. & Hoza, B. (1987). Friendship conceptions among early adolescents: A longitudinal study of stability and change. *Journal of Early Adolescence, 7,* 143-152.

Chassin, L., Presson, C. C., Montello, D., Sherman, S. J., & McGrew, J. (1986). Changes in peer and parent influence during adolescence: Longitudinal versus cross-sectional perspectives on smoking initiation. *Developmental Psychology, 22,* 327-334.

Cohen, S., & Wills, T. W. (1985). Stress, social support, and the buffering hypothesis. *Psychological Bulletin, 98,* 310-357.

Coleman, J. S. (1961). *The adolescent society.* New York: Free Press.

Douvan, E., & Adelson, J. (1966). *The adolescent experience.* New York: John Wiley.

Eder, D. (1985). The cycle of popularity: Interpersonal relations among female adolescents. *Sociology of Education, 58,* 154-165.

Epstein, J. L. (1983). The influence of friends on achievement and affective outcomes. In J. L. Epstein & N. L. Karweit (Eds.), *Friends in school* (pp. 177-200). New York: Academic Press.

Epstein, J. L. (1986). Friendship selection: Developmental and environmental influences. In E. Mueller and C. R. Cooper (Eds.), *Process and outcome in peer relationships* (pp. 129-160). New York: Academic Press.

Fine, G. A. (1987). *With the boys: Little League baseball and preadolescent culture.* Chicago: University of Chicago Press.

Furman, W., & Bierman, K. L. (1984). Children's conceptions of friendship: A multidimensional study of developmental changes. *Developmental Psychology, 20,* 925-931.

Gottman, J. M., & Mettetal, G. (1986). Speculations about social and affective development: Friendship and acquaintanceship through adolescence. In J. M. Gottman & J. G. Parker (Eds.), *Conversations of friends* (pp. 192-237). Cambridge, UK: Cambridge University Press.

Hirsch, B. J., & Renders, R. J. (1985). The challenge of adolescent friendship: A study of Lisa and her friends. In S. E. Hobfoll (Ed.), *Stress, social support, and women* (pp. 17-27). Washington, DC: Hemisphere.

Ide, J. K., Parkerson, J., Haertel, G. D., & Walberg, H. J. (1981). Peer group influences on educational outcomes: A quantitative synthesis. *Journal of Educational Psychology, 73,* 472-484.

Kandel, D. B. (1978a). Homophily, selection, and socialization in adolescent friendships. *American Journal of Sociology, 84,* 427-436.

Kandel, D. B. (1978b). Similarity in real-life adolescent friendship pairs. *Journal of Personality and Social Psychology, 36,* 306-312.

McGuire, K. D., & Weisz, J. R. (1982). Social cognition and behavior correlates of preadolescent chumships. *Child Development, 53,* 1478-1484.

Miller, K. E., & Berndt, T. J. (1987, April). *Adolescent friendships and school orientation.* Paper presented at a conference of the Society for Research in Child Development, Baltimore, MD.

Newcomb, A. F., & Brady, J. E. (1982). Mutuality in boys' friendship relations. *Child Development, 53,* 392-395.

Parker, J., & Asher, S. R. (1987). Peer acceptance and later personal adjustment: Are low-accepted children at risk? *Psychological Bulletin, 102,* 357-389.

Perry, T. B. (1986). *The relation of children's popularity to their friendships.* Unpublished master's thesis, University of Oklahoma, Norman, OK.

Perry, T. B. (1987). *The relation of adolescents' self-perceptions to their social relationships.* Unpublished doctoral dissertation, University of Oklahoma, Norman, OK.

Piaget, J. (1965). *The moral judgment of the child.* New York: Free Press. (Originally published in 1932).

Rook, K. S. (1984). The negative side of social interaction: Impact on psychological well-being. *Journal of Personality and Social Psychology, 46,* 1097-1108.

Sharabany, R., Gershoni, R., & Hofman, J. E. (1981). Girlfriend, boyfriend: Age and sex differences in intimate friendship. *Developmental Psychology, 17,* 800-808.

Sherif, M., & Sherif, C. (1964). *Reference groups: Exploration into conformity and deviance of adolescents.* New York: Harper & Row.

Steinberg, L., & Silverberg, S. B. (1986). The vicissitudes of autonomy in early adolescence. *Child Development, 57,* 841-851.

Sullivan, H. S. (1953). *The interpersonal theory of psychiatry.* New York: Norton.

Tesser, A. (1984). Self-evaluation maintenance processes: Implications for relationships and for development. In J. C. Masters & K. Yarkin-Levin (Eds.), *Boundary areas in social and developmental psychology* (pp. 271-299). New York: Academic Press.

Wilcox, S., & Udry, J. R. (1986). Autism and accuracy in adolescent perceptions of friends' sexual attitudes and behavior. *Journal of Applied Social Psychology, 16,* 361-374.

Youniss, J. (1980). *Parents and peers in social development.* Chicago: University of Chicago Press.

Youniss, J., & Smollar, J. (1985). *Adolescent relations with mothers, fathers, and friends.* Chicago: University of Chicago Press.

PART IV

CONCLUSION

12. Making the Transition from Childhood to Early Adolescence

Raymond Montemayor
Daniel J. Flannery
The Ohio State University

The purpose of this volume is to examine two questions: In what areas are children and adolescents different and in what areas are they similar? and Is the onset of early adolescence a transitional period for those characteristics that are different in childhood and adolescence? The authors of the chapters in this volume separately answer these questions in each of several areas. In this last chapter we look broadly at these diverse areas and draw general conclusions about these questions.

DEVELOPMENTAL CONTINUITY AND DISCONTINUITY BETWEEN CHILDHOOD AND EARLY ADOLESCENCE

In this section we briefly summarize findings about developmental change in the areas of biology, behavior, affect, and social cognition.

Biological Change

Biological change is the hallmark of the transition from childhood to early adolescence and is the one universal aspect of the adolescent experience, found in all primate species, in all cultures, throughout history. Although puberty adds a unique component to growth and physical performance, correlations are positive and high between child and adolescent height, weight, strength, and physical performance, indicating much continuity in physical development. Qualitatively the appearance of primary and secondary sex characteristics in early adolescence differentiates adolescents from children. In addition, sexual dimorphism increases in early adolescence and males become more muscular and agile than females and show increases in strength, motor performance, and aerobic performance relative to girls.

Behavioral Development

The only clear example of behavioral stability is in the area of prosocial behavior, where the evidence now available suggests that adolescents are no more or less prosocial than children. This is a tentative conclusion, however, as we know little about the development of prosocial behavior between childhood and adolescence.

Several authors examine changes in parent-child relations as children enter adolescence. The evidence shows that a gradual physical and psychological separation occurs between parents and children, and that both parents and children contribute to the separation process. In addition, the process of separation begins long before puberty and continues into early adulthood. Puberty accelerates and intensifies the separation process rather than initiates it.

Several generalities about the behavior of friends emerge from studies of child and adolescent friendships: adolescents are more involved with friends than are children and spend more time with them; similarities between friends in behavior and attitudes are greater in adolescence than in childhood; and the impact of friends may be greater in adolescence than in childhood, but more research is needed on this issue and on how friends influence each other.

Interactions between male and female peers are different in childhood and adolescence. Adolescent boys and girls look, touch, smile, and talk more to each other than they do as children (Montemayor & Flannery, 1989). Males and females also become more traditionally sex-typed during early adolescence. Sex differences are generally more pervasive during early adolescence than before. With respect to sexuality, in nonhuman female primates, the onset of regular menstrual cycles initiates adult sexual behavior. While puberty initiates reproductive ability in human females, social factors also influence the timing and type of interactions with opposite-sex peers.

An increase in male aggressiveness during puberty is characteristic of males in most primate species, while female aggressiveness remains low and is largely unaffected by puberty. This increase in male aggressiveness may be partly the result of increases in male hormones during puberty. Even though a general increase in aggression occurs between childhood and early adolescence, the relative ranking of children on aggression remains highly stable.

Some decline is noted in academic motivation and performance during early adolescence. Besides an overall decline in grades, decreases are found for females in math and science courses. These changes are related to the transition from elementary to junior high school.

Emotional Development

Less is known about change in emotional development between childhood and adolescence than in any other area. There is some evidence of increases in negative affect and moodiness during early adolescence, possibly because of pubertal changes, but few studies exist in this area. Self-esteem declines in early adolescence but gradually increases thereafter. This pattern may be the outcome of initial disruptive effects of puberty and school transition and gradual adaptation to these changes. The relative contribution of parents and peers to self-esteem is altered during adolescence, with parents declining in importance and peers increasing in importance. Adolescents remain attached to their parents, and feelings between parents and adolescents stay generally positive between childhood and early adolescence. Some decline in feelings of closeness to parents occurs between childhood and adolescence, however. The major change in emotional development occurs between adolescents and their friends. Young adolescents are closer and more intimate with their friends than they were as children. Also friends become increasingly important sources of social support.

Social Cognitive Development

In virtually every social cognitive ability examined in this volume differences were noted between children and adolescents, who have more complex social cognitive skills than do children. For example, compared to children, adolescents have more differentiated, abstract, and integrated self-concepts; make use of more advanced perspective-taking strategies; and reason about moral issues in a more sophisticated way. In other ways adolescents and children think differently about themselves and other people. Adolescents have a unique form of egocentrism, are more likely to consider the needs of others as a reason for helping, and have somewhat different conceptions of friendship than do children.

EXAMINING THE TRANSITION FROM CHILDHOOD
TO ADOLESCENCE

Is the onset of early adolescence a period when significant developmental change occurs? The data now available suggest that many differences between children and adolescents emerge gradually rather than suddenly. In most cases change begins in childhood and continues throughout adolescence. The graph of development between childhood and adolescence may not be completely smooth, however, and evidence suggests that in some areas the onset of adolescence alters development. Some researchers argue that puberty, changes in socialization pressures, and movement from elementary to junior high school make adolescence discontinuous with childhood and lead to sudden transformations in social cognitive abilities during early adolescence.

Recent advances in the study of puberty indicate that pubertal change begins much earlier than previously thought and is a long-term gradual process (Brooks-Gunn & Warren, 1989). For example, the first signs of breast and pubic hair growth appear in girls at about 10.5 years, while some evidence exists that gonadotropin levels begin to rise at about ages 8 or 9 years. These results indicate that the onset of the transition from childhood to adolescence starts earlier than commonly believed, based on the appearance of secondary sexual characteristics. The implication of these findings is that many individuals classified as children based on age or the absence of observable secondary sexual characteristics, in fact, have already begun the transition into adolescence.

Within the past few years much has been learned about the relationship between puberty and behavior. Studies of the association between observable physical change during puberty and adolescent behavior have been followed more recently by finer-grained research on the impact of hormones on behavior. The accumulation of evidence now available indicates that pubertal change affects a variety of adolescent behaviors such as relations with parents, aggression, and sexuality, and perhaps also mood and peer relations. The evidence also indicates, however, that pubertal effects, by themselves, account for a relatively small proportion of the variance in early adolescent behavior. For example, in a recent study, hormone levels explained 4% of the variance in girls' negative affect while social factors accounted for between 8% and 18% of the variance in depression and anger respectively (Brooks-Gunn & Warren, 1989).

Two conclusions emerge from recent research on puberty: first, the onset of hormonal pubertal change occurs during middle childhood; and second, puberty has some, but not a powerful effect on adolescent behavior. These conclusions indicate that puberty alone, especially observable change, is not an adequate marker of the transition from childhood to adolescence. Within the past few years several research teams have focused on school transition as another event that differentiates childhood from adolescence and alters adolescent behavior. The shift from elementary school to junior high school is accompanied by a decrease in academic motivation and performance, especially for females in regard to math and science, a temporary decline in self-esteem, and general increases in sex-typed behavior. One explanation for these general decreases in adolescent well-being is that a poor fit exists between the developing needs of young adolescents and the academic and social environments of junior high schools. The shift from a familiar school environment to an unfamiliar and more impersonal environment is a major life stressor for most adolescents.

Neither pubertal change nor school transition alone can account for the wide range of behavior change found between childhood and early adolescence. Instead, it is the interplay of pubertal maturation with school transition, and other life changes, which make the transition from childhood to adolescence unique. Authors conceptualize this interaction in two ways. Some view physical change as occurring in a social context, mediated by social factors, and argue for the need to examine the interaction of biological and environmental factors (e.g., Brooks-Gunn & Warren, 1985).

Others focus on the number of transitional events as important determinants of change during early adolescence. This approach is similar to studies of the impact of life events on children and adolescents (e.g., Garmezy, Masten, & Tellegen, 1984; Simmons, Burgeson, & Reef, 1988). For example, adolescents have more adjustment difficulties when pubertal change occurs in conjunction with a school transition than when these transitions occur sequentially (Simmons & Blyth, 1987). Patterson and his colleagues examine puberty as one of several life events. They calculate a "transitional risk score" for adolescents based on the number of transitions occurring within a two-year period. Their results show that children who have experienced many transitions have more coercive interactions with family members than children who have not gone through as many life transitions. Coercive parent-child interactions are related to later child antisocial behavior, indicating that transitional stressors lead to later child deviant behavior.

Puberty and leaving elementary school each uniquely contribute to behavior change and, when they occur close together, have a greater impact on adolescent behavior than when they occur sequentially. Another aspect of transition that affects behavior and psychological change between childhood and adolescence is the timing of transition. Children who experience a transition much earlier or later than their peers are affected differently by the transition than children who go through the transition in-phase. We know most about the impact of the timing of puberty on adolescent behavior. For example, early pubertal maturation in boys leads to increases in mother-son conflict, while late maturation is associated with increases in behavioral autonomy for both genders (Steinberg, 1987). Parents also report more harmonious relations with early maturing sons and late maturing daughters than with late maturing sons and early maturing daughters (Savin-Williams & Small, 1986). Timing of pubertal maturation also affects peer relations (Livson & Peskin, 1980). For example, young adolescent girls whose breasts have begun to develop have more close friends than girls who have not yet begun to develop (Brooks-Gunn, Samelson, Warren, & Fox, 1986), which indicates that early maturing girls are more involved with and integrated into their peer group.

In general the evidence reviewed in this volume shows that the transition from childhood to adolescence is a gradual long-term process. No single transition event demarcates the end of one period and the beginning of another or accounts for much of the alteration of child behavior. Changes in behavior between childhood and adolescence are affected by several transitional factors: hormonal effects, observable physical change, changes in self and other expectations, the number of life transitions that a child experiences, and the timing of those transitions.

EXAMINING PROCESS DURING THE TRANSITION FROM CHILDHOOD TO ADOLESCENCE

Recently researchers have begun to focus their attention on the processes or mechanisms responsible for behavior change. An examination of process is relatively new, as most work in the area of development between childhood and adolescence is concerned with mapping and describing differences between children and adolescents. Process can be examined on two levels. The first focuses on identifying the underlying mechanisms that influence the expression of behavior in either childhood or adolescence. Patterson and his colleagues, for example, have made enormous contributions to our understanding of processes responsible for child aggressive behavior. Accoring to Patterson, child aggressive behavior is first learned and later maintained in interactions between parents and children. Other research indicates that peer relations influence adolescent aggression (Patterson & Dishion, 1985), which suggests that the processes controlling aggression in childhood may be more parent-centered, while in adolescence these processes also include peer interactions.

A second process issue involves identifying processes responsible for change between childhood and adolescence. To continue with the previous example, if one set of processes control aggression in children and another set control it during adolescence, a separate question to ask is What processes lead to change? Little is known about these transitional or "second order" processes. Focusing on processes underlying development leads to an examination of developmental patterns or trajectories rather than individual differences in behavior. For example, for some children the transition from childhood to adolescence is smooth, while for others it is tumultuous. Currently we know little about the processes responsible for different developmental pathways.

THE IMPORTANCE OF SOCIAL CONTEXT IN THE TRANSITION FROM CHILDHOOD TO EARLY ADOLESCENCE

Most researchers interested in the transition from childhood to adolescence examine development in one context. Studies of changes in family relations in white middle-class families are common, as are studies of peer relations among similar types of children. Much is learned about general developmental principles with this approach (i.e., main developmental effects), but what is missing is an examination of the interplay of development embedded in context (interaction effects).

One theme that clearly emerges from the reviews in this volume is the recognition of the importance of context. Numerous studies show that behavior is influenced by characteristics of the physical and social environment. In the past, setting events were often viewed as nuisance background variables from which the real variable of interest needed to be disentangled. Within the past few years researchers have brought these background variables into the foreground and begun to examine the effects of context on behavior. More and more researchers are hypothesizing contextual effects and examining how context affects behavior.

One approach to the study of context effects is to compare the behavior of children growing up in different contexts. There continues to be a dearth of research on development in general and on the transition from childhood to adolescence among non-White and non-middle class children and adolescents. Also, little is known about growing up in non-Western societies. Even among White middle-class families, little is known about the impact of alternative family forms on the transition from childhood to adolescence. With a growing interest in context, perhaps the time is finally right for the appearance of a vigorous research program into the effects of context on development.

A second approach to the study of context is to examine the impact of behavior in one context on behavior in another context. It is clear from the work summarized in this volume that few studies exist of cross-context effects, although it seems clear that variation in development in one context affects development in another context. For example, we know little about the impact of parent-child relations on child-peer relations, although some evidence suggests that changes in relations with parents affect peer involvement (Berndt, 1982). Further, we do not know much about how parent-adolescent relations at home affect adolescent school performance.

A third approach to an examinination of context focuses on the impact of context change on development. The elementary to junior high school transition is a particularly important shift in context. This shift often leads to decreases in adolescent self-esteem and self-efficacy, characteristics that might be expected to increase between childhood and adolescence (Harter, 1983). Further, recent work suggests that large individual differences exist within the same context shift; some children show an increase in self-esteem, while the self-esteem of others decreases during the transition from elementary school to middle school (see Nottelmann, 1987 and Simmons & Blyth, 1987). We do not yet fully understand why some children are adversely affected by transition, while others are not (Petersen & Ebata, 1987).

The transition from childhood to adolescence is embedded in several different educational arrangements: some children attend the same school from grades 1 through 12; some change schools after the eighth grade, some after the sixth grade, and some after the fifth grade. Each of these context shifts may have a characteristic effect on development. Examining the timing of school transition in conjunction with the timing of physical maturation and other normative and non-normative life events and social context changes may substantially increase our ability to understand and predict transitional stress during early adolescence.

Work is another context which becomes increasingly important in early adolescence, and which may affect the transition from childhood to adolescence and adolescent behavior in other contexts. Many young adolescents hold part-time jobs, most of which involve the performance of repetitive menial tasks. Much of this work leads to on-the-job stress for adolescents and may contribute to difficulties in adjustment in other contexts as well. For example, adolescents who work part-time have lower school grades and spend less time with family members and in extracurricular activities than adolescents who do not work (Greenberger & Steinberg, 1986).

Adolescents do not merely react to their environment but also influence it. During the transition from childhood to adolescence a wide array of advanced social and cognitive skills emerge, which make it possible for adolescents to analyze and understand themselves, other people, and their world. These new abilities allow adolescents to exert control over their lives to a degree that was not possible only a few years earlier. One of the important ways they contribute to their own development is by choosing the environments and social contexts they participate in. They make choices about friends, what subjects to take in school, how to spend leisure time, and in a multitude of other areas, all of which affect future developmental pathways. Individuals of all ages influence their environment, but as children grow older and, perhaps especially beginning in early adolescence, this influence increases and significantly influences later development.

CONCLUSIONS

Based on the evidence presented in this volume, both continuity and change characterize the transition from childhood to adolescence. Adolescents are different from children in almost every characteristic that has been examined, but the origins for most of those differences are found in childhood. Differences between children and adolescents emerge gradually rather than suddenly, although puberty and the transition out of elementary school affect adolescent behavior. These conclusions depend upon a variety of factors such as: the particular characteristic under investigation; the number and timing of transitional events; the context in which development occurs; and individual factors, about which we know little. Work in all these areas continues, along with investigations of the important issue of uncovering the processes that influence behavior and behavior change.

REFERENCES

Berndt, T. J. (1982). The features and effects of friendship in early adolescence. *Child Development, 53,* 1447-1460.

Brooks-Gunn, J., Samelson, M., Warren, M. P., & Fox, R. (1986). Physical similarity of and disclosure of menarcheal status to friends: Effects of age and pubertal status. *Journal of Early Adolescence, 6,* 3-14.

Brooks-Gunn, J., & Warren, M. P. (1985). Measuring physical status and timing in early adolescence: A developmental perspective. *Journal of Youth and Adolescence, 14,* 163-189.

Brooks-Gunn, J., & Warren, M. P. (1989). Biological contributions to affective expression in young adolescent girls. *Child Development, 60,* 372-385.

Garmezy, N., Masten, A., & Tellegen, A. (1984). The study of stress and competence in children: A building block for developmental psychopathology. *Child Development, 55,* 97-111.

Greenberger, E., & Steinberg, L. (1986). *When teenagers work.* New York: Basic Books.

Harter, S. (1983). Developmental perspectives on the self-system. In M. Hetherington (Ed.), *Handbook of child psychology: Vol. 4. Socialization, personality, and social development* (pp. 275-386). New York: John Wiley.

Livson, N., & Peskin, H. (1980). Perspectives on adolescence from longitudinal research. In J. Adelson (Ed.), *Handbook of adolescent psychology* (pp. 47-98). New York: John Wiley.

Montemayor, R., & Flannery, D. (1989). A naturalistic study of the involvement of children and adolescents with their mothers and friends. Developmental differences in expressive behavior. *Journal of Adolescent Research, 4,* 3-14.

Nottelmann, E. D. (1987). Competence and self-esteem during the transition from childhood to adolescence. *Developmental Psychology, 23,* 441-450.

Patterson, G. R., & Dishion, T. J. (1985). Contributions of families and peers to delinquency. *Criminology, 23,* 63-79.

Petersen, A. C., & Ebata, A. (1987). Developmental transitions and adolescent problem behavior: Implications for prevention and intervention. In K. Hurrelman, F. Kaufmann, & F. Losel (Eds.). *Social intervention: Potential and constraints* (pp. 167-184). New York: Walter De Gruyter.

Savin-Williams, R. C., & Small, S. A. (1986). The timing of puberty and its relationship to adolescent and parent perceptions of family interactions. *Developmental Psychology, 22,* 342-347.

Simmons, R., & Blyth, D. (1987). *Moving into adolescence: The impact of pubertal change and school context*. New York: Aldine de Gruyter.

Simmons, R., Burgeson, R., & Reef, M. (1988). Cumulative change at entry to adolescence. In M. Gunnar & W. A. Collins (Eds.), *Development during the transition to adolescence* (pp. 123-150). Hillsdale, NJ: Erlbaum.

Steinberg, L. (1987). Impact of puberty on family relations: Effects of pubertal status and pubertal timing. *Developmental Psychology, 23*, 451-460.

Index

About the Authors

Mildred M. Alvarez is a Visiting Fellow in the Department of Human Development and Family Studies at Cornell University. She obtained her B.A. from Florida International University and her M.A. and Ph.D. (developmental psychology) from Boston University. Her interests include the socialization effects of television, parent-child play, and gender differences.

L. Bank is a member of Gerald R. Patterson's research team at the Oregon Social Learning Center, where he has been analyzing data from a 10-year longitudinal study of at-risk youth.

Thomas J. Berndt is a Professor of Psychological Sciences at Purdue University in West Lafayette, Indiana. He did his graduate work at the Institute of Child Development, University of Minnesota. Before coming to Purdue, he taught at Yale University and at the University of Oklahoma. He has done research on several topics in social development, including sibling relationships during the preschool years and developmental changes in sex-role stereotypes. Currently, his primary interests are in the features and effects of friendships in childhood and adolescence. He is especially interested in the effects of friendships on adjustment in the school context.

Jeanne Brooks-Gunn is Senior Research Scientist in the Division of Education Policy Research at Educational Testing Service and a Visiting Scholar at the Russell Sage Foundation. In addition, she is Adjunct Professor at Columbia University, College of Physicians and Surgeons. A developmental psychologist, she received her Master's degree from Harvard University and her Ph.D. from the University of Pennsylvania. Her two major research interests are: (1) the study of girls' academic and psychological adaptation to pubertal events; and (2) policy-oriented research focusing on familial influences upon children's development with a particular emphasis on the long-term consequences of teenage parenting for both parents and children.

W. Andrew Collins is Professor in the Institute of Child Development, University of Minnesota. He received his Ph.D. degree from Stanford University in 1971 with concentrations in communication research and developmental psychology. A specialist in the study of social and cognitive processes in middle childhood and adolescence, he has studied developmental aspects of children's and adolescents' responses to television dramatic fare and is currently conducting research on changes in parent-child and family relationships in middle childhood and adolescence.

Jacquelynne Eccles earned her Ph.D. in developmental psychology from UCLA in 1974 and her bachelor's degree in Psychology from the University of California, Berkeley in 1966. She has taught at Smith College, University of Michigan, and the University of Colorado. She is currently a Professor of Psychology at the University of Colorado and a Research Scientist at The Institute for Social Research at the University of Michigan. Her research and teaching interests include adolescent development, achievement motivation, gender-role socialization, and the impact of families and schools on social development throughout the life span. She is currently directing two large-scale longitudinal studies on these issues focusing on the middle childhood and adolescent periods. The studies reported in this volume come from the early phases of one of these two projects.

Nancy Eisenberg received her Ph.D. in psychology from the University of California, Berkeley. She is presently a professor in the psychology department at Arizona State University. Her interests are in the domain of social development, including the development of altruistic behaviors and cognitions, the development of emotion, and the socialization of gender roles. Recent books include *Altruistic Emotion, Cognition, and Behavior, Empathy and Its Development* (edited with Janet Strayer), and *The Roots of Prosocial Behavior* (written in collaboration with Paul Mussen).

Daniel J. Flannery is a Ph.D. candidate in the Clinical-Child/Developmental Psychology program at the Ohio State University. He obtained his B.A. from the University of Notre Dame in 1984 and his M.A. from Ohio State in 1987. He has published in *Developmental Psychology, Journal of Youth and Adolescence,* and the *Journal of Adolescent Research.* His research interests include the impact of puberty on parent-child relations, and affect and involvement in parent-adolescent relations.

Susan Harter is Professor of Psychology and Director of the Developmental Psychology Program at the University of Denver. Her current research interests include: child and adolescent self-concept and self-esteem; developing models that have implication for depression and suicide; school motivation; and development of emotional understanding in children and adolescents. Her research has resulted in the construction of a battery of self-report instruments that are currently in wide-spread use in this country and abroad. She has published in developmental, educational, and clinical journals, and has written chapters for the *Handbook of Child Psychology* and *At the Threshold: The Developing Adolescent* (Carnegie Foundation).

Aletha C. Huston is Professor of Human Development and Psychology and Co-Director of the Center for Research on the Influences of Television on Children (CRITC) at the University of Kansas. She obtained her B.A. from

Stanford University and her M.A. and Ph.D. (psychology and child development) from the University of Minnesota. Her research interests include the effects of television on children, the development of sex-typing, and children and social policy.

Daniel K. Lapsley received his Ph.D. in the Department of Educational Psychology, University of Wisconsin-Madison, in 1982. Since 1983 he has taught in the Department of Psychology, University of Notre Dame, Notre Dame IN 46556. His research interests are in social cognitive development generally, and in the areas of self, ego, and identity more specifically. He is the editor (with F. Clark Power) of *Self, Ego, Identity: Integrative Approaches* (1988, Springer), and of a forthcoming volume from the University of Notre Dame Press (with Clark Power), entitled *Moral Education in a Pluralist Society*.

Robert M. Malina is a Professor of Kinesiology and of Anthropology at the University of Texas at Austin. He has earned Ph.D. degrees in both physical education (1963, University of Wisconsin, Madison) and anthropology (1968, University of Pennsylvania), and recently was awarded an honorary doctorate from the Catholic University of Leuven in Belgium (1989). Professor Malina's research activities span both kinesiology and physical anthropology/human biology. They include over 200 publications dealing with the growth and performance of American children; the growth, maturation and family background of elite athletes; and the effects of chronic undernutrition on the growth, maturation and performance of school children in Oaxaca, Mexico. He is the co-author of *Manual of Physical Status and Performance in Childhood* (1983), *Adolescent Growth and Motor Performance: A Longitudinal Study of Belgian Boys* (1988), and *La Galgada, Peru: A Preceramic Ceramic Culture in Transition* (1988), co-editor of *Sport and Human Genetics* (1986), and editor of *Young Athletes: Biological, Psychological, and Educational Perspectives* (1988).

Carol Midgley received her Ph.D. in education from the University of Michigan in 1987. She has been involved in several large-scale research studies with Jacquelynne Eccles, including the *Transitions in Early Adolescence Project*, which is described in this volume. She is interested in the influence of teacher beliefs and classroom processes on children's motivation and learning, particularly during the early adolescent years. She is currently a member of the Leadership and Learning Laboratory at the University of Michigan School of Education and is working with Martin Maehr.

Raymond Montemayor received his Ph.D. in developmental psychology from Michigan State University. Currently he is Associate Professor of Psychology at the Ohio State University. Previously he taught at the City University of New York and the University of Utah, and has held visiting appointments in the Department of Psychiatry at Harvard University and the

Oregon Social Learning Center. He is Associate Editor for *Journal of Early Adolescence* and on the editorial board of the *Journal of Adolescent Research*. His research interests include parent-adolescent conflict, transformations in family relations as children enter adolescence, and the impact of parents and peers on adolescent drug use and sexuality.

Roberta L. Paikoff is a Postdoctoral Fellow in the Division of Educational Policy Research at Educational Testing Service. A developmental psychologist, she completed her B.S. degree in Human Development and Family Studies at Cornell University in 1983, and received her Ph.D. from the University of Minnesota in 1987. She also spent a year doing postdoctoral work at The Hebrew University of Jerusalem in Israel. Her major research interests include studying the interplay between biological and social-cognitive processes and family relationships, constructions of the self, and risk-taking behavior.

Gerald R. Patterson has been actively researching aspects of family interactions for the past three decades. His work has encompassed the assessment of children's behavior in school and at home, marital interactions, and the causes of interventions for delinquent behavior. He has authored and coauthored *Families, Living with Children, Coercive Family Process, Families with Aggressive Boys, Parents and Adolescents Living Together* (Volumes 1 and 2), and *Antisocial Boys*. Together with L. Bank and M. Stoolmiller, he has published (and is preparing) a number of articles and papers analyzing data from a 10-year longitudinal study of at-risk youths. He is currently at the Oregon Social Learning Center, Eugene, Oregon.

Bridgett Perry is currently serving as an Assistant Professor of Developmental Psychology at Framingham State College, Framingham, Massachusetts. She completed her undergraduate work at Central State University, Edmond, Oklahoma. Dr. Perry completed her doctoral studies in Experimental Psychology at the University of Oklahoma, Norman, Oklahoma. While at the University of Oklahoma she began a program of research in the area of childhood and adolescent social relationships. Current research projects have extended those interests to include examining adolescent self-perceptions as they relate to both close friendships and larger peer group acceptance.

M. Stoolmiller is a member of Gerald R. Patterson's research team at the Oregon Social Learning Center, where he has been analyzing data from a 10-year longitudinal study of at-risk youth.

NOTES

NOTES

NOTES

NOTES